New Maps for Old

New Maps for Old

Explorations in Science and Religion

Mary Gerhart
and
Allan Melvin Russell

CONTINUUM

New York • London

2001
The Continuum International Publishing Group Inc
370 Lexington Avenue, New York, NY 10017

The Continuum International Publishing Group Ltd
The Tower Building, 11 York Road, London SE1 7NX

Printed in the United States of America

Library of Congress Cataloging-in-Publication Data

Gerhart, Mary.
  New maps for old : explorations in science and religion / Mary Gerhart and Allan Melvin Russell.
      p.   cm
  Includes bibliographical references and index.
  ISBN 0-8264-1310-2 (hardcover) — ISBN 0-8264-1338-2 (pbk.)
  1. Religion and science. I. Russell, Allan Melvin. II. Title.
  BL240.2 G48 2001
  291.1'75—dc21
                                                                                        00-069416

The authors wish to express appreciation to the following periodicals and publishers in whose publications the original versions of many of these essays initially appeared: Peter Lang, *Catholic Theological Society of America Proceedings*, the *Center for Theology and the Natural Sciences Bulletin*, Routledge, *Semeia: An Experimental Journal for Biblical Criticism*, *Listening: Journal of Religion and Culture*, *Zygon: Journal of Religion and Science*. The publication history is given at the bottom of the first page of the respective chapters.

    Credit and thanks for copyright permission received from the following is hereby acknowledged: Patricia S. Churchland and Terrence Sejnowski, *The Computational Brain*, MIT Press; Franz Hundsnurscher and Edda Weigand, eds., *Beiträge zur Dialogforschung: Concepts of Dialogue: Considered from the Perspective of Different Disciplines*, Max Niemeyer Verlag; J. A. Hertz, A. Krogh, and R.G. Palmer's *Introduction to the Theory of Neural Computation*, Addison-Wesley; Herman Feshbach and Victor F. Weisskopf, "Ask a Foolish Question" *Physics Today*; John R. Searle, "The Mystery of Consciousness, Part I," and "The Mystery of Consciousness, Part II," *The New York Review of Books;* and Richard Wilbur, "Mind," from *Things of This World*, copyright © 1956 and renewed 1984 by Richard Wilbur, reprinted by permission of Harcourt, Inc.

Contents

Acknowledgments

This book would not have been completed without the help of many people. Our audiences over the years contributed much with their questions and the ensuing discussions, but they must remain nameless. That is also true of the many men and women in our classes who encouraged us with their interest and enthusiasm. While we do remember many of them as our students, alas we cannot always connect any question or issue with any particular face. We owe them thanks nonetheless.

Among those who have giving us the opportunities to describe our work, we want especially to thank Tomasz Komendzinsky at the Nikolaus Kopernicus University of Torun, Poland. In addition, we thank Phil Hefner at the Lutheran School of Theology, Chicago, Illinois, Robert John Russell at the Center for Theology and the Natural Sciences, Berkeley, California, Kevin Schilbrack at Wesleyan College, Michael Coyle at Colgate University, Joseph Bracken and William Stoeger for inviting us to make presentations at CTSA annual meetings.

We also thank other institutions for giving us the chance to present papers: Wesleyan College in Macon, Georgia, Colgate University in Hamilton, New York, Hamilton College in Clinton, New York, and the John M. Templeton Foundation.

Our friend and sometime colleague, Renée Schoen-René, did the original organizing of the papers and lectures we had given over the fifteen year period since the publication of *Metaphoric Process* in 1984. The archeological work of digging up references, sources, and names was done with graciousness by the staff at The Warren Hunting Smith Library at Hobart and William Smith Colleges.

"The Sublimation of the Goddess in the Deitic Metaphor of Moses" (chapter four) was co-authored with our friend and Hebrew scholar, Joseph P. Healey. Several others read and made helpful comments on this chapter, including William Scott Green, Robert Polzin, Valerie Saiving, David Tracy, Claudia Camp, and Carole Fontaine.

Finally, we wish to thank our editor, Frank Oveis at Continuum International, for having patience beyond all reason.

For faults that remain we have no one to blame but ourselves.

MG and AMR
Geneva, October 2000

Introduction

Mapping Science and Religion Together

> Some see the world through the single eye of theology, others through the single eye of science. These persons experience a flat world of two dimensions. However, when theology and science relinquish the primacy of their individual views, their understandings can reveal a world of meanings that has a full dimensionality, the depth and perspective of stereoscopic visual experience.

THE ESSAYS INCLUDED IN THIS VOLUME WERE WRITTEN AFTER 1984, THE year *Metaphoric Process: The Creation of Scientific and Religious Understanding* (hereafter *MP*) was published. They represent fifteen years of using metaphoric process to survey issues of change in the way human beings understand their world.

Since a map is an abstract description of space human beings can move through and explore, the idea of a map can serve also as an analog for the thinking space available for human investigation. The idea of a map has fascinated not only explorers and treasure hunters but philosophers as well. As an analog for knowledge and understanding, a map can distinguish areas that are well known from those that are only partially known and those that are presumed to exist but are, at the moment, completely unknown. A map also displays relationships (e.g., distances and directions, sizes of regions, cities) between places or, analogously, relationships (e.g., relative proximities, interspersions) between ideas or concepts, along with emphasizing the central idea that learning something new means connecting that something to something else already known.

A map can also help characterize different questions. Familiar territory encompasses those questions we can ask and answer; unfamiliar territory constitutes a realm about which we can ask questions that we cannot answer. And unknown territory engulfs those questions we cannot even begin to ask. Such a concrete representation of horizons plays right into processes used for the study of religious belief. With this analogy between maps and conceptual space in hand we are able to explore the dynamics of cognitive processing—the activity that revises our maps, that gives us new maps for old.

First, we can ask what it means to understand as distinct from merely to know. On a recent trip to Morocco one of us had an excellent guide who could not read maps. The guide was excellent because he always and unerringly knew where he was. It turned out that he had an unsurpassed ability to recognize landmarks along his route—indeed to the point of being able to supply details of relevant historical events going back centuries. And yet he could not read a map. He always knew where he was, but in a larger sense he did not **understand** where he was, that is, where he was in relation to places he had only heard of, and, of course, to those he did not even know existed. To read a map is to understand a territory.

But more than mapping a territory we attempt to map two territories, science and religion, onto **one** map, a single map that permits the development of an understanding of the relations between science—with the concerns that permeate it—and religion along with its issues.

We wish to call attention to two important references to metaphor and cognition that predated the publication of *MP* (1984). One of them, Lakoff and Johnson's *Metaphors We Live By* (1980) is well known and perhaps the most widely used basis for the interpretation of metaphoric language at the present time. We recommend it as an approach in contrast to our own. The other, less widely known, was called to our attention by David Edge in his review of *MP* published in *Isis* (1985). Edge pointed out that we had neglected Donald Schon's pioneering *Displacement of Concepts* (1963) and we are grateful to him for an important precursor to our work that hadn't turned up in our research.

Schon, who acknowledges Ernst Cassirer's influence, is interested in the process he sees in the generation of language. He understands metaphors to be related to the evolution of language as the fossil record is related to the evolution of life: "The metaphors in language are to be explained as signs of concepts at various stages of displacement, just as fossils are to be explained as signs of living things in various stages of evolution" (51). For him metaphors are what are left over from the process of creating new language. Our use of metaphoric process shares the dynamical aspect of process with Schon but ours is a different process and yields a different outcome. Schon's process yields new concepts whereas our primary concern is the creation of higher viewpoints when two concepts firmly embedded in two fields of meaning are equated and understood—said to be the same. Rather than creating new language and new concepts, what we call metaphoric process at its grandest constitutes a revolution— a tectonic reformation—of an entire field of meanings that results in a higher viewpoint, a new understanding of the world or *Weltanschauung* (see our chapter three below).

The first section of this book begins with an introductory essay, "The Role of Metaphoric Process in the Development of Cognitive Complexity," that addresses the ways metaphoric process both complicates and simplifies our world—and foregrounds the achievement of Nicholas Copernicus in divorcing our world view from the limitations of naive experience.

We continue with "Modeling Metaphoric Process," turning our attention to metaphoric process itself and showing how a process (rather than a metaphor) is at the root of "The Reformation of Worlds of Meaning" that leads to the tectonic change that alters maps so drastically. The last essay in this group analyzes the "Sublimation of the Goddess" one of the most profound changes in Judaism, as just such a tectonic change—a change that removed the goddess from the religion of the Hebrews.

The second section contains three essays that address the genre established by two persons from different academic fields in conversation. "The Genre Bidisciplinary Dialogue" describes our understanding of this genre and ends with a special dialogue—the Turing Test of computer intelligence (along with a suggestion for improving the test). The genre BD dialogue is then illustrated first with an actual dialogue as "A Scientist and a Theologian See the World," and then with "A Generalized Conception of Text Applied to Both Scientific and Religious Objects"—a more formal discussion of the way the idea of text can serve as a point of unification between science and religion.

The final section of the book contains four essays that illustrate the new relations that exist when science and religion are mapped together. "Mathematics, Empirical Science and Theology" illustrates how the relations between mathematics and the empirical sciences parallel the relations between the empirical sciences and theology. "The Limits of Quantum Mechanics and Cosmology as a Resource for a Contemporary Theological Metaphysics" suggests how quantum physics **can and cannot** help us to understand some religions questions. "Cog Is to Us As We Are to God" is a critique of an article on robotic technology, a critique that purports to hear an echo of the creative activity of the God in the text of Genesis.

The final essay, "Myth and Public Science," contrasts the results of applying the idea of myth to science with the use of myth in religion and argues for a mythic dimension of public science—the science we find in the scientific journals—as distinct from the science (private science in Gerald Holton's terminology) that takes place in the laboratory or in acts of solitary theorizing.

The private moments of the scientist in thought can be as deep and profound and law-transcending, it would seem, as the private moments of the theologian.

Part I

Metaphoric Process: Reforming Worlds of Meaning in Theology and Natural Science

1

The Role of Metaphoric Process in the Development of Cognitive Complexity

We understand metaphors to comprise linguistic objects linked in surprising and superficially inappropriate ways. We understand cognition to be the dynamic activity of a mind traversing conceptual fields of meanings in a search for understanding. Because metaphors link different parts of fields of meanings, they have the ability to distort or reshape these fields, increasing the complexity of the interactive conceptual elements contained. We call this distortion "metaphoric process" and suggest that it plays an important role in the development of understandings of complex states of affairs.

W<small>E BEGIN WITH METAPHOR AS A LINGUISTIC OBJECT AND COGNITION</small> as the process of thinking. These understandings suggest that attention to both metaphor and cognition implies a focus on the way metaphors affect the process of coming to know, what we call knowledge-in-process. Our earlier book (*MP* 1984) was about knowledge-in-process, not about metaphors as such.

We belabor this point somewhat because over the years we have had unnecessary disagreements with academic colleagues in poetry

This chapter was presented as the keynote address at the International Conference on Metaphor and Cognition, Torun, Poland, 1999, and published in *Metaphor and Cognition*, a special issue of *Theoria et Historia Scientiarum*, ed. by Tomasz Komendzinski (Peter Lang, 2001).

and literature who thought we were trying to get them to change their accepted definitions of the literary object called metaphor—an object dear to the hearts of lovers of literature and poetry. We want to emphasize that our concern focuses on what happens to human knowledge of things when cognitive transfers (metaphors) are undertaken, rather than what happens only in the aesthetics of language.

Since the time of Aristotle it has been understood that something strange happens in the process of creating a metaphor. Metaphors change the ways we understand things. Sometimes our understanding is disrupted or radically altered. But just how are cognitive changes *caused* by metaphoric process?

1. Metaphors, Analogies, and Cognition

Metaphor is everywhere! One of our colleagues noticed a sign over the baggage area in the Athens airport; it contained the word ΜΕΤΑΦΟΡ— equivalent to "transfer," as in "baggage transfer." The occasion serves to remind us that *metaphor* is a much more common word in Greek than it is in English—at least until recently. Once restricted to the fields of language, rhetoric, and poetry, *metaphor* has now become so popular that it is in danger of losing its distinctiveness.

Definitions of simile, analogy, and metaphor are not mutually exclusive (if they ever were); they refer rather generally to the substitution of some thing (usually some word) in the place of another. Some authors use simile, analogy, and metaphor interchangeably. Some uses of metaphor are so broad that any act of representation can be referred to as metaphorical. There is an increasing danger that the term will soon become meaningless as in the tag line, ". . . speaking metaphorically, of course"—an expression intended to imply that what has been said is, in some unarticulated sense, **un**true, just when one means that what has been said is, in some (other) unarticulated sense, more true than otherwise.

Turning to theories of metaphor, one becomes quickly aware that, in the words of Paul de Man (1978), "metaphors, tropes, and figural language in general have been a perennial problem and, at times, a recognized source of embarrassment for philosophical discourse and, by extension, for all discursive uses of language including historiography and literary analysis" (13). The failure of efforts to develop a generally accepted theory of metaphor arises, we believe, because theories of metaphor usually address a kind of text (called metaphorical) rather than a kind of cognitive **process** (called metaphoric) for which the texts give evidence. Without a model of cognition and explicit attention to the cognitive effects of metaphor, the things one sees in metaphorical language are but the shadows of thought.

In the first stanza of Emily Dickinson's poem #258 in the *Collected Works* we find a simile that is often conventionally analyzed as a metaphor.

> *There's a certain Slant of light,*
> *Winter Afternoons*
> *That oppresses, like the Heft*
> *Of Cathedral Tunes. . . . (#258)*

The slant of winter light is taken to be the first term, or A, and the heft of cathedral music to be B. When a poet says that A is like B, some readers (those who already know both A and B) can take pleasure at affirming (often with some surprise) that A is indeed like B. The effect of such affirmation is to increase cognitive and affective solidarity—to reaffirm one's cultural belonging. For other readers (those for whom either A or B is unknown, e.g., a person in the tropics who does not know winter or someone who has never heard an organ), an analogy is discovered to be of a certain kind and is instructive—it renders meaningful that which was formerly unknown. Here, the analogical act builds an addition onto a world of meanings and allows the world of meanings of the reader to conform more to the world of meanings addressed by the poet. Such readers can use the analogy to move closer to members of the poet's culture. Finally, there may be readers who know neither A nor B. On these readers the analogy is lost and there is no effect on their world of meanings (except, perhaps, for an increase in the sense of their alienation from the culture to which the poet belongs).

We have used the term "poet" here to stand for any of the class of teachers, which includes, for example, the scientist, artist or composer.

With respect to our theory there is no metaphoric tension in the cases described above. The first kind of readers had their understandings affirmed, the second kind had theirs enlarged, and the third, except for the possibility of alienation, had theirs left unchanged. The key word is "oppresses": The **effect** of A is said to be the same as the effect of B—both A and B **do** the same thing rather than A itself being the same as B. Such, we maintain, is **not** the stuff of metaphoric process.

What, then does it take to distort a field of meanings? What is a field of meanings—the thing to be distorted? How does the distortion of a field of meanings change our understandings and affect the ways we think? These are the questions we need to examine. First we take up the idea of a field of meanings.

2. Fields and Worlds of Meaning, Cognition, Knowing vs. Understanding

Many scholars, including Mary Hesse, Nelson Goodman, and Paul Ricoeur, address the problem of understanding the metaphoric process in terms of an implied model of thought. For Hesse there is a "network of meanings" (1); Goodman speaks in terms of "worldmaking" (1); Ricoeur refers to a "shift in the logical distance" (147). In each case, although a model of cognitive structure or function is implied, no description of a model is given.

Our model of a world of meanings is constructed as a network of nodes (concepts) interconnected with branches (relations). We understand a science (e.g., physics and theology—insofar as the latter is a science) as being the business of relating every object of inquiry (here, experiences of nature) to everything else (concepts already related). We assume that we are able to understand experiences only if, to some extent, they can be related to previously understood experience. The test of the effectiveness of our understandings lies in our ability to analyze the relations that hold with respect to experience. Metaphoric process **changes** relations within a field of meanings, a disruptive cognitive act that goes beyond analogic process.

Compare the modeling of analogic process with metaphoric process on a field of meanings. **Analogic process** equates a known concept

($C1_k$) in a field X with an **unknown** concept (C_u) not in any known field of meanings:

$$C1_k = C2_u.$$

In this way analogic process makes the unknown concept known, that is, isomorphic with the known in the X field of meanings. Analogic process creates no tension and does not distort the X field of meanings. **Metaphoric process**, in contrast, equates a known concept ($C1_k$) on the field X with another **known** ($C2_k$) on the field Y thereby forcing the two different concepts to be isomorphic on a **new field of meanings** (X + Y):

$$C1_k = C2_k.$$

Metaphoric process connects the two original fields with a force that creates tension and distortion in one or both fields, X and Y, that contained the original concepts. Metaphoric process, then, creates isomorphism where none existed and the resulting disruptions of the fields of meanings involved can reshape a world of meanings, especially when the metaphors include so-called "root" metaphors—those central and controlling in our thinking. Let us examine this model of thought in more detail.

Our cognitive model is a field of meanings in which is embedded a network of nodes and branches. We speak of a field of meanings as a part of a world of meanings. The nodes are understood to be particular concepts that "come to mind" when, for example, we encounter words or signs (or sounds, or images, or feelings). The branches that link the nodes are understood to be the relations that obtain with respect to the concepts. Within a field of meanings, every concept is in principle related to every other concept, so that there are as many relations as there are pairs of concepts taken two at a time (relations far outnumber concepts). We can take what Ricoeur calls the "logical distance" between two concepts to be the length of the branch (the relation) that connects the two concepts. The various lengths of the many branches that connect the concepts can be understood to determine the shape or topography of a particular field of meanings in much the same way as changes in the lengths of some struts in one of Buckminster Fuller's geodesic domes would change the shape of the dome. A diagram of a field of meanings is shown in Fig. 1.1. Here the C_i constitute the conceptual nodes, and the R_{ij} constitute the relational branches connecting C_i and C_j pairs.

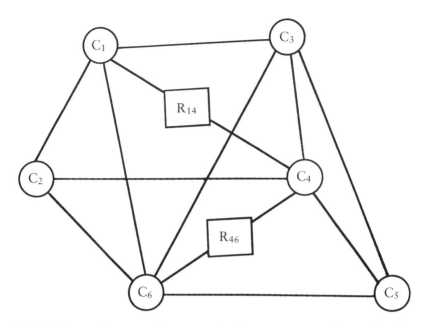

Fig. 1.1 A cognitive network composed of five concepts (circles) and twelve relations (lines).

Now we do not mean to imply by our model that concepts are somehow fixed and previous to the relations that connect them. There are no concepts to be known in the absence of a theory, and in our model, theory is found in the structure of a field of meanings. To change a relation—the logical distance between two concepts—is to shift the locations of many related concepts. Such changes of location correspond to conceptual changes of meaning. Meaning, then, arises out of the interaction of concepts and relations and is expressed in the topography of the field. Necessary concept changes, such as those that might arise from a new experience, alter relations. And changes in relations—such as those that occur when one attempts to understand an experience in a new way—relocate old concepts.

The field of meanings might be thought of as continuous surfaces whose forms are controlled by the embedded skeleton of concepts and relations.[1] The infinite conceptual possibilities of thought are represented in the infinite number of conceptual points on the surfaces. When one thinks or speaks words, one is limited to localized concepts, but non-linguistic thought processes can wander over the surface—the topography of the field—with a freedom only loosely coupled to language. Our conception of a cognitive field of meanings has an appearance similar to illustrations published by cognitive scientists (see Figs. 1.2 and 1.3).

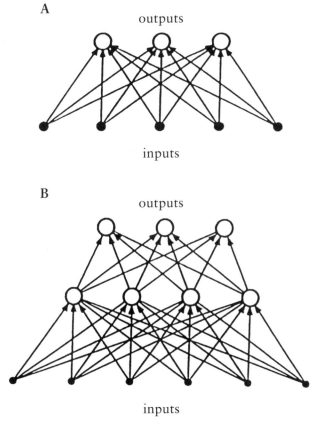

Fig. 1.2 Examples of cognitive networks (from Churchland, 77). A is a "feedforward" network with one layer of weights connecting the input units to the output units. B is a "feedforward" network with two layers of weights and one layer of hidden units between the input units and output units.

We now have a topographic model for human understanding that begins with a field of meanings. Our model of understanding takes a field of meanings to be an assortment of interrelated concepts—a conceptual net—each knot a concept, each string between knots the relation between the concepts connected. The resulting arrangement forms a multidimensional network. The model is of the kind referred to by Patricia Churchland and Terrence Sejnowski in their book *The Computational Brain*.[2]

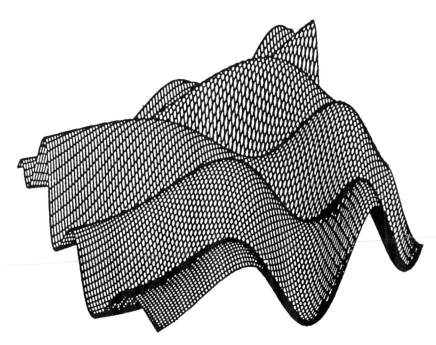

Fig. 1.3 Another example of a cognitive network (from Churchland, 88): a visualization of the dynamics of a Hopfield network. All possible states are in the x-y plane, and the height of the surface is the energy of the corresponding state of the network.

In our theory, the most elementary form of relation is modeled in a pair of concepts joined by a single string. The "strength" of a relation, i.e., the degree to which one concept depends on or is "like" another, is indicated by the length of the string—distant concepts being less strongly related than proximate ones. Synonyms are likely to refer to concepts grouped together. It cannot be assumed, however, that concepts relating to a word will necessarily be distant from the concept relating to that word's antonym—the situation is more complicated than it might seem at first. A multidimensional sense of distance is at work here. And this complexity drives us towards a topographic model. (For what follows, refer to Fig. 1.4.)

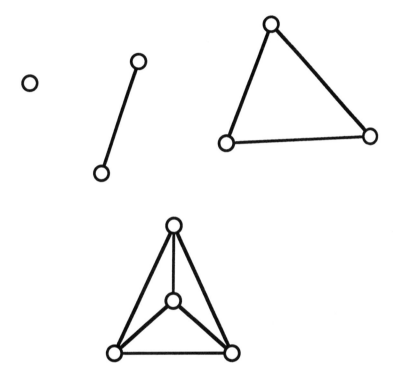

Fig. 1.4 The buildup of a cognitive topographic network: first, with a single concept; second, with a pair of concepts and their (mutual) relation; third, with three concepts and their relations (planar); fourth, with four concepts and their six relations (in general three-dimensional).

A single concept, represented by the circle in Fig. 1.4 has no relations and no field. Two concepts are needed to have a relation. With three concepts we can have three distinct relations. Every relation requires a pair of concepts. However, as the number of concepts increases, the number of possible relations increases quadratically.

(They can be counted by multiplying the number of concepts by the number of concepts minus one and dividing that product by two.) Relations between relatively distant concepts can be neglected, however, and by including just those that are proximate we can arrange for all the concepts and their close neighbors to form a two-dimensional surface we call a field of meanings.

3. Distortion, Complexity, and Simplicity

We have said that metaphoric process contributes to cognitive complexity, but we should not let it go at that. Not long ago one could describe something as complex and have confidence that one would be understood—complexity was a simple concept. Everyone understands that an internal combustion engine is complex and that a jet engine is simple by comparison, that a strand of DNA is far more complex than a hydrogen atom. Granted, there are a few examples that are marginally unclear, such as crystals and fluid flow. Nonetheless, one could use the terms "complex" and "simple" without heavy qualification. All that has changed.

Complexity has become an industry—one spawned by the identification and taming of chaos. Complexity theory—generally understood to be the formal study of self-organizing systems—is now pursued by foundations and universities as a serious science. We need to distinguish what we mean by cognitive complexity and simplicity, from what is meant by such terms at these large research institutions.

Let us make a reductionist move and distinguish two kinds of complexity. Most of what is under heavy study in the halls of complexity laboratories is what we may call dynamic complexity—the modeling of various self-organizing systems, such as biological or economic systems. In contrast, we wish to focus on structural complexity—a much tamer and more stable characteristic. In particular, the cognitive complexity we find increased in metaphoric process is topographic or topologic in nature: It is an increase in the tectonic or structural deformation of our theoretical cognitive terrain—our field of meanings. Think of the difference between the Tatra Mountains and the Great Plains of Poland. If thinking—cognitive processing—is analogous to traversing the surface of a field of meanings, we can claim that climbing over a mountainous surface or a topologically convoluted surface is more cognitively complex than walking on the plains.

We need to be clear about what we mean by concepts on the one hand and relations on the other. The word "house" brings a concept to mind. The word "tree" brings another concept to mind. There is a concept called "lumber" that is ordinarily more closely related to the concept "tree" than to the concept "house." However, if we modify the first word and think "frame house," the relation between this (new and more complex) concept and "lumber" is "stronger" (logically "closer") than was the relation between "house" and "lumber," and we will have pulled all of these four concepts "closer together." This way of understanding a concept **in terms of its effective distance from other concepts** functions with abstract objects as well as it does with objects perceivable by the senses, and depends on one's ability to abstract characteristics of any element grasped in attention. Consistent with structuralist theory, any relation between the concept called "house" and the word "house" is entirely arbitrary.

A world of meanings (the German: *Weltanschauung*) is made up of a collection of fields of meanings and comprises the ground for an individual's understanding of the way things are. Worlds of meanings are culture-bound. Within a particular culture, persons have worlds of meanings that have a comparable topography despite the fact that a particular field of meanings possessed by one person may be completely absent in another. Persons of the same culture, therefore, have relatively few difficulties communicating about general matters.

The worlds of meanings of readers from significantly different cultures have generally differing topographies. As our analysis of the Dickinson stanza illustrated, such readers are likely to make divergent interpretations of ambiguous texts, and communication among such readers is often faulty.

4. Grounds for Metaphoric Process

Metaphoric process and its concomitant cognitive disruption is justified by the efficacy of the result. In *MP* we called the driving force behind metaphoric process an "ontological flash" (114), an insight that a particular act of cognitive distortion made the world more understandable. From time to time we glimpse a possible cognitive rearrangement of our world of meanings, or one of its fields of meanings, a rearrangement that might render our view of our world more comprehensible, more comprehensive.

Some years ago one of us was rummaging around in the dark attic of a house on a stormy night. He had been told that he would find a certain chair in the attic and he had been groping along for some time. His hands encountered a variety of objects he was more or less able to identify: an old bridge lamp, a cedar chest, some old clothes on a hanger. Suddenly, there was a flash of lightning, and for a split second the entire attic was full of light. Then it was dark again. From that instant on he knew where all the objects in the attic were. He was able to go, with confidence, right to the chair. This kind of insight is related to the so-called aha! experience or "aha! reaction" in psychology as described, for example, by Martin Gardner in his book *aha! Insight* (1978).

In order to characterize more complex and deliberate experiences of this kind, we borrow the formal term "higher viewpoint" from Bernard Lonergan. Lonergan used the term "higher viewpoint" to designate a "complex shift in the whole structure of insights, definitions, postulates, deductions and applications" (*Insight*, 13). Rather than a "shift" in structure, we speak of a "torque" or twist in the world of meanings such that some meanings formerly distant, become close, and some previously close are now displaced to a distance. Lonergan saw higher viewpoints as resulting from further questions which emerge within established fields of meanings—"when inverse expectations are allowed full generality, when they are not restricted to bringing one back to one's starting point" (15). For us, the initiation of a higher viewpoint is as apt to be aesthetic or ethical as it is to be formal—a higher viewpoint results from our dissatisfaction with, or attempt to change, the "shape" of our world of meanings.

Our use of "higher viewpoint" is more epistemologically general than Lonergan's. We focus on the new cognitive perspective that can arise as the result of what Arthur Koestler called "a combinatorial act" (Koestler 1964). More specifically, Koestler described the effects of combining ideas that were formerly "strangers to each other." Our conception of metaphorical process requires the equation of two concepts, or conceptions, formerly thought to be different from each other. Our paradigmatic example, drawn from human perception, is binocular vision—the constructive combination of two, two-dimensional images into one three-dimensional image, along with the greater insight and understanding thereby produced. An important point here is that the two elements are **necessarily different**: each two-dimensional view contributes different information that, when combined, results in a single three-dimensional view (see Fig. 1.5).

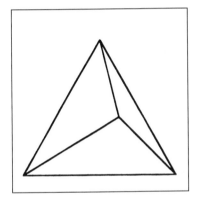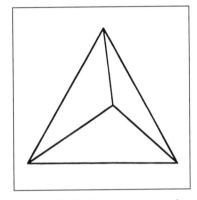

Fig. 1.5 A stereo pair illustrating a four-concept field of meanings as a three-dimensional surface (irregular tetrahedron).

Compromise—a process that would require either or both images to be changed—plays no role in the transformation that leads to the three-dimensional view, i.e., the higher viewpoint. Metaphoric process is one means of achieving such a rearrangement. There need not be any prior "similarity" in the parts of the cognitive world of meanings brought together by the metaphoric process. Indeed, the distortion created by the metaphoric act may eliminate similarities that formerly existed. If, however, the world of experience is subsequently better understood (more intelligible), metaphoric process is successful (see Figs. 1.6 and 1.7). If there is no improvement in our understanding, metaphoric process fails. In the meantime there is the tension required to "hold" these two parts together. Once it is clear that the world is, indeed, better understood, the tension begins to subside, the world of meanings assumes its new topography, and the metaphor begins to die (although religious metaphors may not atrophy in this way—see #7 below).

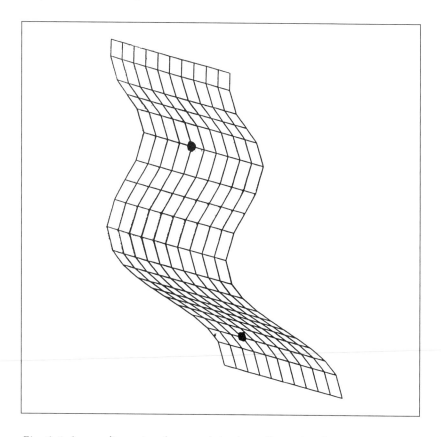

Fig. 1.6 A two-dimensional network in three-dimensional space as a model of a field of meanings (sometimes called a "net" or a "rug"). Two concepts are marked on the net.

The test of any model is to be found in the extent to which it elucidates the state of affairs under consideration. However, there is more to it than greater complexity because metaphoric process is productive of understanding precisely because it sets the stage for further simplicity—for the discovery of a higher viewpoint. We offer examples.

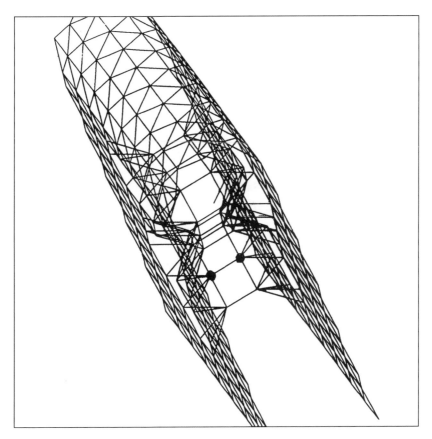

Fig. 1.7 A field of meanings (the net of Fig. 1.6) distorted by metaphoric process that requires the two marked concepts to be related more closely. The field of meanings and hence the relations between other concepts are also changed in the process.

5. Formal Examples of Metaphoric Process from Geometry and Philosophy

The tetrahedron in two and three dimensions:

[Left-eye view + right-eye view = three-dimensional view (higher viewpoint).]

We will model a field of meanings as a *spatial* structure with a knowledge of its geometry or topography representing, in some sense, our understanding of the field. If we specify two concepts with one relation, we have a linear diatomic structure. When our field contains three concepts, we have a planar triangular structure. An increase to four concepts with six relations yields a structure that in general requires three dimensions. If all the relational branches were the same length, we would have a tetrahedron.

Now a two-dimensional view of a regular tetrahedron shows the four concepts not equally spaced. Only when displayed in three dimensions is the structure accurately presented. Recall that in Fig. 1.5 it took two different viewpoints (a left view and a right view) to achieve a stereoscopic 3-dimensional representation. Moreover, it was not the sum of the two views that achieved the three-dimensional presentation but a synthesis or fusion of the two views. A stereoscopic view is an analogue of the higher viewpoint described above. Neither individual need relinquish her/his point of view. One does not have to ask which view is correct—both are.

We saw that three equidistant concepts could be represented by an equilateral triangle in a plane; four equidistant concepts required three dimensions to display a tetrahedron. Five equidistant concepts, however, cannot, in general, be represented spatially because they require four orthogonal spatial dimensions. This problem illustrates the representational limits of conceptual maps or networks of concepts and relations (see Fig. 3.1 below). The inability to represent the high dimensionality of a field of meanings in conventional configuration space may account at least in part for the lack of success of extensive efforts to develop conceptual maps in physics and may also explain why many religious thinkers prefer creative syntheses over systematic theologies. Despite these limitations, we believe the idea of a topographical field of meanings is of great utility in describing the way change takes place in ways of thinking.

Phosphorus (φωσορια) and Hesperus (εσπερος) to the Greeks:
[Morning Star = Evening Star.]

We draw our philosophical example from Gottlob Frege's famous paper "Über Sinn und Bedeutung." Frege said that "the reference of 'evening star' would be the same as that of 'morning star,' but not the sense" (57). He said, in other words, that the morning star **is** the evening star. In terms of our theory of metaphoric process, to insist on this relation is to create a metaphoric change in a world of meanings. Prior to this metaphoric act (whenever it first occurred) we had from time to time a phenomenon—a bright star seen near the eastern horizon just before dawn. We also had from time to time another phenomenon—a bright star seen near the western horizon just after sunset. These disparate observations (presentations) are given, in the metaphoric assertion, a single reference—the planet Venus. Frege used this example to distinguish between the sense (*Sinn*) of a word and its meaning (*Bedeutung*) or reference—the thing to which the word "points." We refer to Venus (the planet) in two different ways (senses) phenomenologically distinct. The metaphoric achievement is to "realize" that the distinct phenomena (distinct texts) mean, or "point to" the same thing. To observe two manifestations is to encounter two phenomena. If these phenomena are separately understood and one subsequently realizes that these two phenomena are manifestations of the same thing, one has encountered a cognitive metaphor. Lest the morning star/evening star example seem a purely scientific issue unrelated to religious concerns, consider the possible effect of the metaphoric transformation on two tribes: one tribe worships the morning star and the other tribe worships the evening star. The metaphoric process **equates** what were formerly two **different** gods—a potentially explosive theological change. Indeed, such a change can be seen in the Hebrew Bible with the metaphor, Yahweh = El, made in response to Moses' question, "What shall I say when they ask me your name?"—an example we elaborate in chapter four.

Following are examples of cognitive disruption brought on by metaphoric process, first from natural science, and second from theology.

6. Examples from Physics and Astronomy

The examples in natural science are drawn from physics and astronomy—surely there are many others in geology, biology, and chemistry as well that can be added by those knowledgeable in these fields.

The Copernican Revolution:
[The Sun (not the Earth) = the Center.]

Copernicus wrote one of the most important books in history, *De Revolutionibus Orbium Coelestium* (1543). In it he claimed that the Sun rather than the Earth was the center of the universe (solar system). To the best of our knowledge the claim was made on the basis of no definitive observational evidence whatsoever. The "facts"— i.e., the observations that had been made of the motions of the Sun and the planets in the heavens—were as completely accounted for by Ptolemaic theory as they were by Copernican (see Fig. 1.8). We understand the Copernican assertion as deriving from a metaphoric act based on his understanding of the relations among the heavenly bodies (actually not an entirely new understanding since it had been held by Aristarchus about 1800 years earlier). The negative reaction reached its climax in 1633 with the Italian church's house arrest of Galileo Galilei (who **did** have observational evidence to support his teaching the Copernican system).[3]

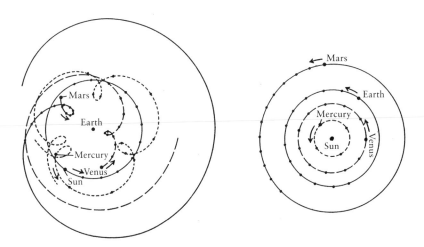

Fig. 1.8 Two views of the inner solar system. The same motions as seen from Earth are accounted for by both the Earth-centered theory and the Sun-centered theory. The view on the left represents the Ptolemaic theory of how the motions of the Sun and planets can be accounted for. The view on the right represents the Copernican theory of how the motions of the Sun and planets can be accounted for.

With Galileo, the issues were no longer matters of opinion, for when he turned his telescope on Venus he saw the phases of that planet. Now in the Ptolemaic system everything (Sun, Moon, Venus and the other planets) circled the Earth. However, observations had always shown Venus to be near the Sun (as the morning star in the east or the evening star in the west). If Venus were going around the Earth—somewhat in step with the more distant Sun—the Sun shining on the planet would always put it in a crescent phase. But that was not what the telescope revealed to Galileo. Venus had a gibbous phase (it was more than half illuminated) when near the Sun which meant that it was then further from Earth than the Sun was! (It was also smaller and dimmer in the gibbous phase than in its crescent phase). A Sun-circling Venus could account for all of these observations. No Earth-circling model could account for what the telescope revealed.

No longer was the Copernican claim merely a matter of expressed simplicity or calculational convenience. One of the greatest metaphoric acts in history had forever changed the way people on Earth would be able to think of themselves.

Notice that the negative reaction to this act was intensified by the distortion of **other relations** that occurred as a necessary result of the metaphoric process effected by Copernicus. These cognitive effects could be suppressed so long as the Copernican scheme was seen as merely a calculational convenience (as it surely was), but could not be avoided when the Copernican system was taught as science. The daily rotation of the Earth requires an observer (at European latitudes) to be moving with a speed of about 1000 km/hr—some thirty times the speed of a running horse (very likely the fastest thing experienced at the time) or about twice the speed of a jet airplane today. Moreover, the revolution of the Earth around the Sun in a year's time requires the planet to move at a speed of about 100,000 km/hr.—a speed so great as to be unimaginable **as an experience**.

Reviewing a linguistic expression of the Copernican metaphor, we notice that the statement can be reduced to "The location of the Sun (not of the Earth) is the center of the solar system." This is not a simile, nor is it an analogy. Furthermore, there is nothing unknown or ambiguous about the meaning of either "the Sun" or "center of the solar system." To insist that one of these concepts *is* the other, despite the general understanding that they were different concepts, conforms to our formula for the linguistic expression of metaphoric process. The new understanding of the Sun as the center of the solar system changed a host of relations in the relevant cognitive fields profoundly distorting the topography of the sixteenth century world of meanings. Testimony to the outrageousness of the act is amply given in history's description of the reaction to it. And although the idea had Greek origins, the Copernican revolution remains the paradigmatic example of metaphoric process—cognitive disruption with a move to a higher viewpoint—in the history of Western science.

The Newtonian Synthesis:
[The Laws of Heaven = The Laws of Earth.]

Although Copernicus' metaphor changed the way we see ourselves as related to the rest of the universe, the metaphoric process that caused Isaac Newton to equate the mechanics of the heavens with the mechanics of earthly objects had perhaps an even more profound effect on our lives. The mechanics of the "heavens" had been developed by Johannes Kepler. His laws of planetary motion expressed, in quantitative terms, the relations between the planets (the "wandering" heavenly bodies of the Greeks) and the Sun. The mechanics of the "world" (the surface of the Earth) was put together by Galileo, who could, for example, calculate the rate of fall of an object as it moved from some height toward the ground. Newton (in the famous falling apple allegory) realized that Galileo's laws of falling objects applied to the Moon as well as to terrestrial objects, and, with that metaphoric act, caused the laws of Earth to become the laws of heaven—quite a reversal. The laws of mechanics followed, and the resulting ability to analyze mechanisms thoroughly and to predict mechanical behavior reliably can be understood as having reshaped one world of meanings to create a new world of meanings that lasted for over 200 years. The Newtonian synthesis combined the Galilean laws of terrestrial motion and Kepler's laws of planetary motion using a new form of mathematical analysis—the calculus—to create analytical mechanics, arguably the most powerful scientific system in history up to the twentieth century.

Thompson/Joule:
[*Heat = motion.*]

Some cognitive disruptions are more like the flow of lava than a bolt of lightning. Benjamin Thompson's observations at the end of the eighteenth century and James Joule's early experiments in the late 1830s resulted in a shift from the old understanding that heat was a fluid substance (called phlogiston or caloric) to the new understanding that heat is the random motion of particles. However, this shift took almost half a century.

7. Examples of Metaphoric Process from Religion and Theology

John's Epistle:
[*God = love.*]

It is said that religious metaphors retain their tension long after other kinds of metaphors have lost theirs (see, for example, Soskice 1985:158; Hesse 1988:18). Can our model of metaphoric cognition account for this claim?

Some of the most startling and perennially productive religious metaphors include the assertion in John's Epistle that "God is love" (1 John 4:8), and the statement made by Jesus when the disciples were vying with one another over primacy of place, that "the least among you all, that is the one who is great" (Luke 9:48). With respect to the first (*God = love*), the equation of God and love involves equating one of the field of attributes associated with God, namely, omnipotence, omniscience, and impassibility with the field of meanings associated with love, here understood as human relationality at its best (including vulnerability as well). With respect to the second (*the least = the greatest*), the equation is uncommonly paradoxical. Neither of these radical claims helps us to understand the everyday world where there are mass murders and where competing for the top spot appears to be the way to succeed. Instead, these metaphors challenge us to imagine a possible world to be reexamined and reaffirmed in the light of human experience. We understand and even believe religious metaphors **in spite of** their inability to explain the problems of evil, of suffering, and of meaning in the world.

> *"In the midst of life we are in death" (Christian burial service):*
> [*Life = death.*]

Among the major religions we find different images for the idea of life-after-death: resurrection, karma, the afterlife. In relation to a world of meanings, the concept introduces a fundamental twist or torque in the ordinary perception of reality. For example, in Corinthians 15:23, Paul writes of all persons as "dying in Adam and being brought to life in Christ" as though Adam had not been the biblical ancestor through whom life had been given. In a related sense, Al-Hallaj, who in Herbert Mason's Islamic narrative *The Death of Al Hallaj*, is accused of blasphemy and will be executed, says, "We do not think about the end. There is none." Al-Hallaj describes the everyday understanding of reality as a distortion "leaving us floating blind spots we forget when our vision is clarified in His" (72–73)!

> *Moses:*
> [*Yahweh (God of the Exodus) = El (God of the Fathers.*]

In the Hebrew Bible, the Mosaic declaration in the Book of Exodus that the God Yahweh is the God of the Fathers (El) results in a radical distortion of pre-Exodus meanings. The theory of metaphoric process provides here a basis for interpreting the transformation of the religion of Israel from polytheism to monotheism. By equating the God of the Exodus with the God of the Fathers in the metaphoric pronouncement Yahweh = El, Moses invokes the new concept *Yahweh*, now God of all the tribes of Israel.

We understand this process as a sublimation of the Goddess in the cognitive field of meanings that has been restructured by the metaphoric process in which Yahweh = El (see chapter four).

We have seen the world-creating effects of metaphor as the metaphoric process distorts, reshapes, and complicates our world of meanings. By contrast, the Grand Unification Theories of physics—should they succeed—will make the physical world extraordinarily simple in physical terms. The metaphoric processes embedded in that theory will surely die quickly because the theory will explain so much—will have such theoretical efficacy. The efficacy that kills the metaphors of science does not prevail with respect to many metaphors of religion precisely because of our inability to see the world as religion says it is. We fail to understand, and so the metaphor lives on. Questions in science are limited—rigidly circumscribed; questions in religion *are limit-questions*—questions about limits. If someday the root metaphors of religion die, it will be a sign that the eschaton is here.

8. Summary: Thinking on a Field of Meanings

To plan a trip by car from one city to another, a member of the American Automobile Association can order a custom-made map that will display the trip in a straight progression of roads, in effect reducing the map of the planned journey to a narrow linear strip. To abstract a trip or a proposition in this way is, in our model, to know but **not to understand**. The same is true for a hiker who must follow a blazed trail to get through a forest. That hiker knows how to get to the other side only by starting and ending at designated places each time. By contrast a forester who understands the forest can go through in many ways starting from any point. The forester understands the forest and will not be lost when away from the trail. Analogously in our model, to understand is to know the shape of the cognitive field of meanings, to know one's way over and around the surface in a general sense. And, as we have seen, when the shape of the surface of the field of meanings changes, the change will be apparent to one who understands, even when it might go unnoticed by a person who is able only to follow a narrow path from start to finish.

We take thinking to be the activity of traversing relations—of going from one concept to a related one in a purposeful way. Cognitive activity can lead us along a path marked by conceptual points until we reach a conceptual point not yet experienced. At this point according to our model, an "analogic act" expands meanings within fields without distorting the fields.

The "metaphoric act" also involves the recognition of similarities, but these similarities are created by a "disruptive cognitive act" which **forces** an uncalled-for analogy within or between the fields of meaning—a distortion of one or both of these fields—in order to achieve the required analogy. When this distortion is productive, it creates new understandings and meanings.

In a text, the effect of metaphoric process, as well as analogic process, depends on the knowledge state of the reader. For a reader who knows only one of the two metaphoric elements, the text functions as an analogy, since the unknown element is free to move within the field. Such freedom removes the possibility of tension or distortion of the field of meanings of the reader—the litmus test of metaphoric process. The possibility of an utterance being metaphoric for one person and analogic for another, depending on each person's state of knowledge, shows the ability of our theory to explain misunderstandings about metaphor as well as misunderstandings in general.

In the middle of the twentieth century Albert Einstein is reported to have remarked that everything had changed except our thinking. We would say that our fields of meanings were substantially enlarged but that the shape and form of these fields had not changed.

Since 1950 our knowledge of the universe has been reshaped by metaphoric process, reshaped in a way not unlike the way our understanding of the universe was reshaped by Copernicus when the Sun rather than the Earth became the center of the universe. Because of Copernicus our point of view moved off the Earth and into space— the higher viewpoint of the time. In the second half of the twentieth century, our *Weltanschauung* was once again reshaped—so much so that the very concept of a center of the universe lost its meaning. Whether or not we can achieve a higher viewpoint appropriate for this new universe in the twenty-first century remains to be seen.

2

Modeling Metaphoric Process

Science requires an empirical test of an hypothesis or a model. Our model of metaphoric process as a cognitive restructuring of a world view should be no exception. Opportunities for some empirical experimentation come when we are invited to give workshop presentations on metaphoric process and when we teach our course in science and religion. Analogy and metaphor give way to a theory of metaphoric process. Analogies are created by saying, "X is like Y." Metaphors are created by saying, "X *is* Y." The ability of the human mind to make sense of almost any utterance in this form can be demonstrated by taking pairs of nouns at random and claiming that one of them is (means the same as) the other ("A ____ is a ____.").

M ETAPHORS ARE OBJECTS IN LANGUAGE, BUT METAPHORS AFFECT thought. Our theory of metaphoric **process** is a theory about how knowledge and understanding **change**, so the theory must address questions about thinking. However, our access to thought is through

Two workshops given at the Forty-Second Annual Convention of the Catholic Theological Society of America in Philadelphia in 1987 as part of the overall theme, "The Linguistic Turn and Contemporary Theology," published in 1987 *CTSA Proceedings*, 42, 107–113. The discussion of metaphor theory and its relation to knowing by means of metaphoric process was first published as part of "The Cognitive Effect of Metaphor" in *Listening: Journal of Religion and Culture* 25 (Spring 1990), 114–126.

language. We have come full circle. We realize that, in our efforts to explore thinking and knowing through metaphoric process, we must employ words, despite the fact that metaphoric transformations are not limited to language nor really about metaphors as such.

Since the creation of understanding through metaphoric process affects language but is not about words, we are critical of predominantly linguistic solutions to the problems of relating science and religion—solutions like those proposed by Earl MacCormac in his book *Metaphor and Myth in Science and Religion* (1976). Efforts like MacCormac's to relate science and religion through the use of language seem to us to avoid the epistemological issue of how we come to know in either field—let alone how we can justify changing meanings of things after we have come to know what things are.

1. What Is a Metaphor and How Does It Shape the Way We Think?

We ask participants in workshops on metaphor to write one or two sentences that state their understanding of metaphor. The definitions they offer range widely from metaphor understood as a figure of speech that compares two things not using *like* or *as*, to definitions informed by major theorists of metaphor, such as Aristotle, I.A. Richards, Max Black, Ricoeur, and Jacques Derrida (see *MP* 1984: 97–107). Our work in metaphor draws upon this theoretical tradition and points out their family resemblances. We take note of the limitations of these definitions taken singly: for example, the classical metaphysics underlying Aristotle's definition and the focus on "dead" metaphor in Derrida's. Rather than define metaphor as a linguistic object, however, we focus on metaphoric **process** as a way of coming to know.

In spite of all the attention given to it, metaphor is generally not taken seriously in everyday communication. Imagine a conversation like the following:

"Are you going to the meeting this afternoon?"

"Yes, I plan to. Do you know who is chairing it?"

"Nancy Ballard, I think. Do you know her?"

"No, what is she like?"

"She's a bulldozer! (pause) Speaking metaphorically, of course."

Notice that the tag line, "Speaking metaphorically," acts as a denial of a claim which usually would be understood appropriately without the tag line. The tag line in effect means, "It's *merely* a metaphor."

Not only is there a tendency not to take metaphor seriously in everyday communication; most of what are called metaphors turn out in our analysis to be analogies. So that we can set aside non-metaphors from our consideration, we examine analogy as an extension of meaning (as distinct from the creation of new meanings).

For both analogy and metaphor, we represent a world of meanings as an artist's pallet (see Fig. 2.1). We speak of an epistemic *world* of meanings to refer to an individual's knowledge in process at any given time, or in a related sense, to one's "horizon"—that which encompasses what is known from a determinate perspective. A subject's world of meanings is the totality of "things" known, including relationships among those things with which this subject (in the present state of his intentional development) can operate.[4]

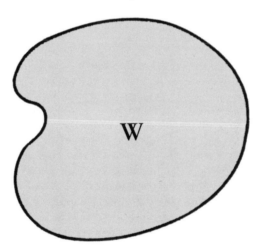

Fig. 2.1 A surface of indefinite shape used to illustrate a world of meanings.

The boundary or horizon of a subject's world of meanings is depicted in this figure as a line that separates what is known from what is unknown. Within a world of meanings we find many *fields* of meanings. These are regions which have rather indefinite boundaries and which can be understood as relating to a particular discipline or sub-section of a discipline or topic. A concept, which we illustrate here as an s-shaped curve, is described as embedded in a field of meanings and, if it is an understood or known concept, it can be expected to have well established relations to other concepts within its field. It is, in other words, rigidly embedded in its field.

In the case of analogy, we apply something that we know already to a new situation. Diagrammatically, we adjust the concept curve of understanding (the new concept) until it is similar to the analog concept in the known field (see Fig. 2.2). Most pedagogy is conducted by means of analogy as the teacher tries to transform something that is initially unknown to students by comparing it to something with which they are already familiar. Explaining something we know to a person who does not know involves finding an analogy, or a correspondence. Thomas Aquinas used the common knowledge of "habit" (in his day, it was used to refer to only habits that are desirable!) to develop an analogous theological understanding of "grace." Making analogies in this way leaves the shape or the world of meanings undistorted, since the unknown can be adjusted to conform to the known without changing the field.

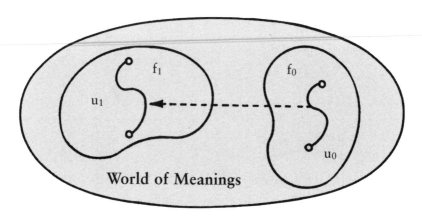

Fig. 2.2 A sketch of a world of meanings in which two fields of meaning, f_0 and f_1, are identified. The transfer of the curve of understanding, u_0, from the known field, f_0, to the new field, f_1, generates, by analogy, new knowledge, u_1 (from *MP* 1984: 111).

In metaphor, however, one insists that two knowns, each of which is firmly embedded in its field of meaning, are the same. If the insistence is successful, that is, if the two concepts declared to be the same are pulled together with their separate fields of meanings and held there in tension, the result is a metaphor (see Figs. 2.3 and 2.4). Analogies rearrange the concepts that make up our fields of meanings: The unknown adjusts and finds its place in the known. But metaphors re-form the fields of meanings themselves. To say that a saint is an enigma is to expand our knowledge of saints but to leave both fields of meanings undistorted.

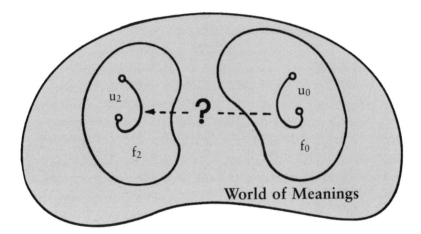

Fig. 2.3 A world of meanings, shown as containing two fields of meaning each of which contains an established understanding (from *MP* 1984:112).

To say that a saint is a vineyard, however, is to create the following possibilities: (1) The character of a saint is initially unknown and is now known incorrectly in terms of vineyard; (2) The character of a vineyard is initially unknown and is now known incorrectly in terms of saintliness; (3) the characters of both saint and vineyard are initially known and the analogy is denied. In each of these possibilities, the analogy is received as a "bad" analogy either because it creates misunderstanding or, as in the third possibility, because no analogy exists. It is at this point that metaphor may make its aggressive entrance with the insistence that the analogy, which appears to

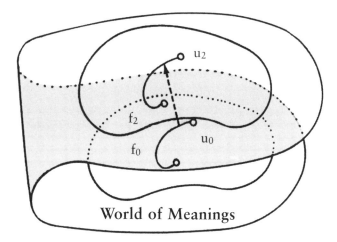

Fig. 2.4 A fold in a map of a world of meanings that makes an analogical relationship between two understandings, u_0 and u_2, possible. This permanent folding is the result of metaphoric process that has the effect of reordering the relationships between other understandings not shown in the illustration (from *MP* 1984:113).

be "bad" or impossible, really is the case. The insistence—that is, the making of the metaphor—creates a distortion in the field of meanings of both saint and vineyard.

Whether or not a particular example is an analogy or a metaphor depends ultimately on the process of knowing and the world of meanings of the knower. However, to the extent that the fields of meanings are shared and concepts are indeed embedded in fields of meanings, it is often possible to arrive at consensus among a given group of interpreters.

This possibility of consensus was explored in particular examples by the participants in the workshop. Two lines from Shakespeare were tried. "All the world's a stage" is commonly accepted as a metaphor today, even though it has lost whatever tension it might have had for the early audiences of Shakespeare's *As You Like It*. Most participants agreed that "Bare ruin'd choirs, where late the sweet birds sang" ("Sonnet 73"), however, is a metaphor because the tension between bare tree boughs and vacant choir lofts is sustained in our ordinary understanding. Everyone agreed that "time flies" is today a dead metaphor since only with reflective effort can we discern two distinct fields of meanings; in everyday usage the tension has been lost and one field has been assimilated into the other. In groups of four to six, the participants suggested and discussed the following religious examples generally thought to be metaphors: "dark night of the soul," "This is my body," "kingdom of God," "I am the bread of life," "the cross as salvation," "the God who suffers," "God as warrior," "Jesus as the lamb of God." The discussion centered on three considerations: (1) which of the examples are better understood as analogies; (2) which of the examples are better understood as metaphors; (3) which of the examples cause us to understand differently because they are metaphors rather than analogies.

2. How Do New Meanings Arise from New Ways of Thinking?

Experimental workshops and classes on metaphoric process begin with special emphasis on the distinction between analogy and metaphor. The distinction is made in terms of the following model.
    First the analogy:

Question: "What is X?" [where X is unknown]
Answer [the analogy]: "X is like Y." [where Y is known]

The effect of the analogy is to enlarge a world of meanings but not to distort it—to create new knowledge: X is now known.
    Now the metaphor:

Question: "How are X and Y to be understood?" [where both X and Y are known]
Answer [the metaphor]: "X **is** Y."

The effect of the metaphor is to **distort** a world of meanings—to create new relations among established meanings—i.e., new understandings: No new knowledge results—X and Y were known before. What is created is a new understanding of the state of affairs to which X and Y are related.

The metaphoric form, "An X is a Y," provides the basis for our first experiment, which we call a modeling of the metaphoric process.

3. Experiments in Metaphoric Process—An Empirical Study

The Noun Exercise (typical method)

Two transparencies, each with a vertical set of blanks, are given to the workshop participants, one sheet to those on the left side of the room and the other to those on the right side. Participants are asked to print, in block letters on a line, a simple noun in the singular, drawn from any field of meanings. The two transparencies are then projected together so that they each provided a random noun to fill each blank of the statement,

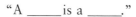

"A _____ is a _____."

The challenge to the participants is to make sense out of the assertions being displayed. Following are examples of some of the combinations considered along with comments about their implications (the understandings).

One word contributed for X was "community," which combined—perhaps too easily for theologians—with contributions for Y such as "house," "cell" "table," and "meal." More difficult was the combination,

"A river is a house."

After some discussion it was suggested that a river was a house for fish. Notice that the river is not at all "like" a house, for fish it **is** a house, and the new understandings that arise should contribute to our respect for the quality of the environment.

"A wave is a table."

One of us remarked that quantum mechanics had two theoretical forms, one of which is called wave mechanics, and another is called matrix mechanics. In wave mechanics a particle is represented mathematically as a wave; in matrix mechanics the same particle can be represented as a matrix—a table of numbers.

"A flute is a pen."

Here the discussion turned to the idea of the power of the pen (which is "mightier than the sword") and its comparison with the power of the Pied Piper's flute in his abduction of the children of Hamelin. Other suggestions included the observation that the flute could play a love song as readily as the pen could write a love letter. However, we should not pass over this example too lightly. It remains to ask whether a flute is **like** a pen. In other words we need to test for an analogical claim that merely omits the word "like." The case of the house and the river passed this test, we believe. However, we could say that a flute is like a pen in that both can express emotions in a powerful way. Here, not finding new understandings or a new state of affairs resulting from the claim, we are inclined to reject this example as a model of metaphoric process. The choice in these models is rarely clear cut. As is often the case in exercises of this kind, the discussion of the ideas and options are what constitute the valuable contribution to understanding metaphoric process.

4. The Interpretive Dimension

Exercises of this kind sometimes lead to the further question: Are there pairs of nouns that, when combined in this way, are entirely void of the possibility of interpretation? This hermeneutical challenge may evoke sympathetic responses from people, like scholars of important text fragments and students of the speech of young children, both of whom are searching for meaning in what they read or hear.

Germane to this question is a claim made by Mark Turner in his *Reading Minds: The Study of English in the Age of Cognitive Science* (1991), especially his review and explanation on p. 152. We differ from Turner in our attempt to model both the processes of conceptual change and the relationships between concepts, whereas Turner attempts only the latter. We also think that language both reveals and hides thought, whereas he writes that "the shape of language discloses the structure of cognition" (ibid.). Finally, we find that our model works better as an interpretive model than his on his example (154)

"The moon is a monkey wrench."

Turner's method of interpretation involves substituting "connections" for the two nouns but he reaches only a weak interpretation based on an analogical, rather than metaphoric processes (according to our distinction between these two processes): "To understand this phrase, we must create some connections. One person might reflect that the moon is like a monkey wrench because both can expand and contract, which is to say, the moon's waxing and waning has image-schematic structure shared by the opening and closing of the monkey wrench. Another person might claim after reflection that he can see no connection" (ibid.). We would look for a situation wherein the statement made sense within a world of meanings, such as that of two burglars planning a robbery for a particular date. Discovering that there was to be a full Moon that night, one burglar might exclaim, "The Moon is a monkey wrench!" There may be other circumstances in which this metaphoric disruption of ordinary meanings take place, but we think that such circumstances would be less likely to turn up using Turner's model than using ours.

We suspect that poets, especially those with a penchant for playing with words, might hunt out effective metaphors by applying the structure we use for our models. We have an artist friend who makes creative images out of combinations of random lines. We have a colleague who gets his students to exercise their poetic imaginations by making word combinations in more or less random ways. All of these activities model the metaphoric process, even though only very rarely are true metaphors created, because there must be grounds for creating a distortion of a field of meanings. Distortion for its own sake is merely the form and lacks the substance of metaphor although it may provide an aesthetic inspiration for art.

What justifications might there be for asserting that X is Y? We suggested that there are two. The first—one that might apply to the poet or the artist—is productivity or efficacy: The images that result are useful and effective; the distortions open us to new ways of imagining and describing. The second—one that is more important for metaphoric process in science and religion—is an ontological flash: having a surprising experience that creates conviction (sometimes a conviction that might be said to "go beyond all reason"). For an analogical example, see chapter one, section four on the search in the attic.

5. Some Cognitive Implications

We return to the root effect of metaphoric process, and that is the change the process can make in our world view. Remember, we are concerned less with language than with thought, values, and concerns both proximate and ultimate. When these aspects of thinking are addressed we are reminded of the considerable use of metaphoric process for what we consider to be pathological purposes. Nazi propaganda created distortions in the value structure of many of the German people in the 1930s. In the infamous 1924 Chicago murder case, Nathan Leopold and Richard Loeb were intrigued by something equivalent to the metaphoric assertion,

"To kill is to experience life."

It prompted them to take the life of six year old Bobby Franks with whom they had but a passing acquaintance. We speak of persons who are mentally or cognitively disturbed, or who lack a value system that conforms at all to what we understand to be a human norm. We find wars being fought over tiny bits of territory that have symbolic or religious or historical "meaning" and we suspect that metaphoric process would be found to be the root cause of the mind set that supports these world views. We mention these aspects of thinking and understanding and metaphoric process to underscore the importance of learning about and understanding understanding.

6. Examples of Metaphoric Process in Science

We often make use of a description of the metaphoric process at work, first in the case of Newton, and then in the Special Theory of Relativity developed by Albert Einstein to show the way new meanings arise as a result of the metaphoric process in science.

In the first example, we stressed how important it is to understand that metaphoric acts are extraordinarily rare in science, perhaps the most intellectually conservative of intellectual disciplines. Then we described Newton's metaphoric act, taking as X, Kepler's laws of planetary motion, and as Y, Galileo's laws of terrestrial motion, and asserting that they are the same laws. In making the metaphor, Newton was insisting that the laws of nature are the same on Earth as they are in the heavens.

In the second example, Einstein's metaphoric act was to insist that the concept of (Galilean) relativity applied not only to mechanical phenomena, but to electromagnetic phenomena as well. When Einstein required that all laws of nature (physics) and the speed of light (c) be the same for all persons in various states of motion, he discovered that moving clocks must run slow, that objects get short in their direction of motion, that moving particles increase in mass, and that $E = mc^2$—all new meanings arising from his metaphoric act of equating the relativity of mechanics (X) with the relativity of electromagnetism (Y).

7. Example of Metaphoric Process in Religion

When we treat the religious theme of life-after-death as metaphor, we focus on what we know about those two disparate fields of meaning. There are, of course, many aspects of both life and death that are unknown, such as the questions of when and where I will die; the questions of if, where and how the present world as we know it will end. The religious fascination with life-after-death has always been with the sense of projecting a future which is intrinsic to human freedom and the operations of consciousness. This sense is based in an awareness of openness toward a future which is possible not merely as given but as gift.

In fact, we do know many things about life-after-death from diverse fields of meaning. From biology, we know what happens to the body. From psychology, we know the effects of dying, not only on the terminally ill but on those bound to them with ties of blood, love or care. From the history of religions, we know about the role of the dead in different civilizations—about the Nuer tribe, for example, where the most recently deceased are believed to reside in the village, those dead up to ten years to reside at the boundary of the village and forest, and the ancestors (who are thought of as the founders of the village and the way of life) to reside in the forest. From post-holocaust theological ethics, we learn not to allow Adolf Hitler a "posthumous victory."

Even in traditional theology, the "last things"—however numbered and however conceived—have never together been understood literally. That is, there has always been an uneasy relationship or a tension among them. Today we might understand the last things as aspects of our limit-thoughts about the future as they impinge upon our present. However, when life-after-death is understood only as concept, what is to prevent it from becoming a gnostic category, as has original sin for many people? We argue that our theory of metaphor enables us to retain the tension and thereby an appropriate theological understanding of the concept.

Indeed we have a precedent for such tension in the originating texts of Christianity. How can we completely reconcile the sayings attributed to Jesus that the reign of God was both to occur in time to come after the present **and** that it was to be found within human beings themselves? Or Paul's statement that he was "born when no one expected it," and that "he died in Adam" and had been "born in Christ"; that "we are not all going to die but we shall all be changed?" Metaphoric process enables us at once to recognize the theoretical structure of the concept and the mediative role of that structure in coming to know religiously. With that understanding, we are likely to position ourselves differently in life than before.

3

Metaphoric Process as the Tectonic Reformation of Worlds of Meaning in Theology and Natural Science

> In a multidisciplinary world of meanings, associative contexts depend on topography. Occasionally, a cognitively disruptive experience will create new relationships among conceptual elements in that world of meanings. If these newly related elements were formerly distant, the new world will exhibit a new topography which in turn can give rise to new understandings in theology and/or natural science.

OUR MODEL FOR HUMAN UNDERSTANDING IS BASED ON OUR WORK within our own disciplines as well as the joint explorations we have undertaken with others in disciplines other than science and religion. In all these explorations, the physicist leans toward empirical observation and the analytical operations of mathematics, and the theologian toward the narrative coherence of story and the interpretation of written texts. Each of us shares an appreciation of the role of all of these methods in the operations of what we call knowledge-in-process, the ongoing human drive for understanding we first wrote about in *MP* (1984).

In what follows we describe our model of the process of thinking and understanding. We then explore the ways that human under-

This chapter was originally presented as the annual Fellows lecture at the Center for Theology and the Natural Sciences in Berkeley, California, in April 1992. A different version was published in the *CTNS Bulletin* 13 (Spring 1993), 7–13.

standings can change in the course of the dynamics of knowledge-in-process. A list of examples in which changes of these kinds have taken place, along with possible new understandings, follows the theoretical discussion.

A. STATICS: THE TOPOGRAPHY OF WORLDS OF MEANINGS

1. Concepts and Relations: Fields/Worlds of Meanings

A static geometrical topological model for human understanding begins simply with a field of meanings. We think of a field of meanings to be an assemblage of interrelated concepts or a conceptual net made up of strings of different lengths. Each knot in the net represents a concept and the strings between knots represent the relations between the concepts connected. A field of meanings results from a distinctive arrangement of meanings and relations and forms a multidimensional network, i.e., one with two or more dimensions.

With one concept alone there can be no relation and hence no field. When we add a second concept, we have one relation between the two concepts. When we add a third, we have three relations. In general, the number of relations grows as the number of concepts taken two at a time,

$$N_R = N_C!/(2(N_C - 2)! = N_C(N_C - 1)/2$$

[which can be understood as being the number of concepts (N_C) times one relation for each concept's connection (i.e., relation) to all remaining concepts ($N_C - 1$). This number must be divided by two because we have counted each connection twice—once from one end and once from the other.]

Thinking about four concepts, we have six relations, and with a thousand concepts—the words for which correspond to a minimally functional vocabulary—the number of relations has grown to about five hundred thousand. This conception of a conceptual network is now too difficult to conceive—it has become unimaginable and therefore unmanageable (except, perhaps, for a computer). So we go back to the drawing board for a more imaginable model.

In chapter one we modeled a field of meanings as a spatial structure with a geometric knowledge of its surfaces approximating, in some sense, a more dynamic understanding of the field of meanings. There we showed how an increase in the number of concepts and their relations grew geometrically from a linear diatomic structure (two concepts with one relation), to a planar triangular structure (three concepts with three relations), to a three-dimensional structure (four concepts with six relations). See Fig. 3.1.

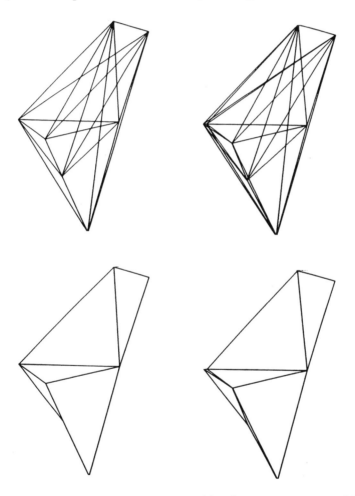

Fig. 3.1 Eight concepts and their 28 possible relations (top stereo pair) and eight concepts with the number of relations displayed restricted to thirteen. The network can now be viewed as a surface (bottom stereo pair).

We can translate this three-dimensional model into a topographical map by imagining a terrain with valleys, mountains, and plains. Traversing this model of the field of meanings requires that one know the entire territory. Getting from one place (i.e., a concept) to another involves traveling a measured distance (i.e., a relation).

Even this model is inadequate because it does not allow for those rare instances when a whole field of meanings is pulled out of whack by metaphoric process. We have said that metaphoric process occurs when two concepts, each firmly embedded in a known field of meanings, are claimed to be the same. We have found that trying to find an adequate model for the distortion in the two fields of meanings that results from metaphoric process taxes the ability of all two or three dimensional models for human understanding. We ourselves have found the most adequate model to be the experience of stereotopic vision by which a new vision results from the cognitive interaction of the individual views.

2. Thinking as Tracks on a Field of Meanings

The advantage of using a simpler model is that we can show some of the essential features more clearly. So if we reduce the connectedness of the network, that is, not require every concept to be related directly to every other concept, we can confine our conceptual points to a two-dimensional surface (of arbitrary size, curvature and, possibly, connectedness). We can then represent relations as distances along the surface, and our displayable configurations are significantly enhanced (see Fig. 3.1). Moreover, the idea of a surface provides a sense of continuity and coherence lacking in a discrete array of points even when the points are connected with lines.

The risk of venturing into this kind of theoretical model is that one may be talking nonsense. We can take heart from a story told by Freeman Dyson in *From Eros to Gaia* (1992). In 1958, Wolfgang Pauli gave a talk on a new theory that he and Werner Heisenberg had developed. The audience included Niels Bohr. After some discussion Bohr was called upon to summarize the argument. "We are all agreed," he said to Pauli, "that your theory is crazy. The question is . . . whether it is crazy enough to have a chance of being correct. My own feeling is that it is not crazy enough" (106). So bear with us now while we see if this idea of a field of meanings is crazy enough.

If you were an author, you might think of the nodes in a field of meanings as if they were characters in a story and the relations between nodes as relations between those characters. In that case to tell the story would be to traverse the field of meanings much as one would walk over a landscape. However, the "landscape" in this analogy is a **changing** field of meanings since, as the story unfolds, the relations between characters change.

What does it mean to think, and how can we distinguish the act of *knowing*, a thinking process, from the act of *understanding*, a state of affairs?

3. Language Is Not the Equivalent of Thought

An Example from Physics

To think is to traverse a one-dimensional track or trail across a field of meanings. In saying this, we do not mean to imply that one thinks about each concept that lies along a track. We especially do not wish to imply that any voiced or unvoiced verbal process is taking place. We maintain that thinking is *not* essentially a linguistic process. Consider the following example:

You observe that there are two identical plastic pails of sand on the floor in front of you. One pail is completely filled. The other is only half full. How heavy will one pail be, compared to the other? You can imagine thinking as follows:

(1) Newton's second law states that the force exerted to accelerate an object is equal to the mass of the object times the required acceleration.

(2) The acceleration of any object near the surface of the Earth is the gravitational acceleration (g) which will be the same for both buckets of sand. Therefore, the force required to lift each bucket is proportional to the mass of the bucket and its sand.

(3) The mass of the sand is equal to the density of the sand times the volume of the sand. And since the density of the sand in

each bucket is the same, the mass of the sand is proportional to its volume.

(4) We conclude, therefore, that the force required to lift the full pail will be about twice that required to lift the pail that is half full.

Now human beings might think in this sequential fashion but we do not believe they do. We maintain that a person reacts to the sight of the buckets and concludes directly on the basis of experience that the full one will weigh twice the half-filled one. The stepwise analysis that we have described, if it takes place at all, takes place *after* the conclusion has been reached and acts as a *rationalization* of that conclusion.

An Example from Theology

The need to take stock of change in theological understanding is in some sense like the need to compare the forces required to lift two unequally filled pails of sand: a "change" in theological understanding is far more elemental and immediate than any formulation of the change.

What evidence do we already have for sensing changes in the way we reflect theologically? First, with the development of a sense of cultural diversity, we are increasingly able to appreciate the religious values and achievements of other cultures. Second, with the globalization of information, we now know some of the consequences of ignorance and lack of appreciation: for example, religious wars reflecting triumphalism in religious self-understanding, and gender and racial bias inhering in policies oppressive to minorities. Finally, a remarkable consensus among major theologians is emerging in Christian theology today—namely, a perception that the genres of proposition and argument that have dominated theological discourse are no longer adequate to understanding the phenomenon of religious experience and understanding. Theologians are becoming alert and responsive to other genres as well. Together with data on new population concentrations of world religions, these developments help us understand—often despite our lack of cogent analyses—the significant tectonic shifts that are taking place in theology. The implications of these shifts remain to be seen.

B. DYNAMICS: COGNITIVE DISRUPTION

We now turn our attention to the ways in which fields of meanings change both in natural science and in theology. Much attention has been given to the question of changes in natural science during this century in part because there has been so much change. At first the question was asked as a question about scientific method. Only later did questions turn toward issues of systems of belief in science. Credit for this turn goes to Thomas Kuhn with his 1950 essay on scientific revolutions and to Holton for his work on thematic origins. Holton examined the notebooks and private writings of scientists in order to expose and explore what he calls S_1—the private and individual professional thinking of scientists such as Einstein and Robert Millikan.

This shift from formal objective methodology in science to informal day-to-day working of individual scientists has allowed the doing of science to be understood as more of a human activity and encourages comparison with the thinking activities of theologians, which have always been understood to have a private and personal dimension even while the conclusions themselves might be of vital concern to large numbers of other believers. In our bidisciplinary explorations, we have learned that the ways in which change is brought about in theology and natural science are more alike than different. This conclusion has two consequences: (1) when the relationship between theology and natural science is taken as an object of study, times of major change in understandings within each field need to be taken at least as seriously as times of relative stability in understanding, and (2) the focus of our own study needs to be the phenomenon of change and only incidentally the beliefs or their rationalizations at any historical moment.

We are now ready to ask in what ways a field of meanings can be changed. At least three possibilities come to mind:

(1) New knowledge—adding to a field of meanings—a cumulative process

First, we can imagine an increase in the number of concepts that make up a field. The additions might come at the edges of a field or as a filling in of an already established region. In either case we take a change of this kind to correspond to a basic learning process that results in an increase in what is known.

(2) New understandings—templates and molds—analogic process

In *MP*, we compared processes of coming to know (knowledge-in-process) in science and religion. We found that in either field there were two distinct kinds of operations which we called analogical on the one hand and metaphoric on the other. We said that when a conception is not well known, it is not rigidly contained in a field—its relations with other concepts in a field are underdetermined, loose, or at least elastic. When we attempt to understand such a concept, we often say that it can be understood as being like some other well established concept in the field. In making the comparison we are asserting a kind of cognitive proportion between the known and unknown concepts and, since the new one is free to move, little if any cognitive tension is caused by the comparison. This process is analogical and the newly learned conceptual element takes on the shape of the known concept without strain.

(3) New topography—tectonic change—metaphoric process

Consider now the case of two concepts both firmly or rigidly embedded in a field of meanings. Here both concepts are known. Here each has well established relations with other "nearby" concepts, and the shape of this part of the field is understood. What happens, we ask, when we suddenly realize that one of those concepts is the same as the other? Bringing the two concepts together cognitively involves considerable intellectual stress and results in a distortion of the field, a distortion we understand as metaphoric strain. Large cognitive forces come into play here because of the rigidity of the conceptual relations in the field of meanings.

The effect of the metaphoric process is to achieve new understanding without the addition of any new concepts to a field. The newly shaped field constitutes a better construction of what we already know.

C. EXAMPLES OF COGNITIVE DISRUPTION

Following are examples of cognitive disruption brought on by metaphoric process, first from natural science, second from theology, and finally from theology and natural science combined.

In Natural Science

The following examples of cognitively disruptive assertions are drawn from physics and astronomy. We are sure there are many others in geology, biology, and chemistry as well and invite those knowledgeable in these fields to make suggestions for additions to this list.

(1) *The Sun and not the Earth is the center. (Copernicus)*

Although the idea had Greek origins, the Copernican revolution remains the paradigmatic example of cognitive disruption in Western science. We elaborate on this example in chapter one.

(2) *The laws of Heaven are the same as the laws of Earth.*
(Newton)

The Newtonian synthesis combined the Galilean laws of terrestrial motion and Kepler's laws of planetary motion to create a theory of motion that includes the entire universe.

(3) *Heat is motion. (Thompson/Joule)*

No longer is heat understood as a fluid substance. It is understood as the random motion of particulate matter.

(4) *Electromagnetism is not mechanical.*

As Dyson (1992) points out, the great James Clerk Maxwell, who created the theory of electromagnetic radiation—light as electricity and magnetism combined—could not see that his theory was independent of the mechanics of Newton (103). This example of cognitive disruption is particularly interesting because it represents cognitive fission rather than fusion. Most of the cases of metaphoric process we know involve the realization that X is the same as Y. In this case we have the realization that X and Y are independent.

(5) *Galilean relativity holds for electromagnetism*
as well as mechanics. (Einstein)

Einstein insisted that, for all observers, the laws of physics are independent of the state of motion. In applying this galilean principle to electromagnetism Einstein was required to say that the speed of light was the same for all observers. This statement of an absolute yielded the special theory of relativity.

(6) *Light is particulate as well as undulatory. (Einstein)*

Einstein was awarded the Nobel Prize for his theory of photoelectricity—the release of electric charge when light strikes a metal surface. The then prevailing view of light as electromagnetic waves was insufficient to account for the experimental observations.

(7) *Energy is particulate. (Planck/Bohr/Einstein)*

The idea that energy comes in chunks is one of the most remarkable conceptions of the past century. It gave rise to the quantum theory that is a universal denial of continuity. At the submicroscopic level everything is discrete and all knowledge fundamentally statistical.

(8) *Mass is undulatory as well as particulate. (deBroglie)*

What wonderful symmetry! Not long after Einstein showed that light could behave as particles, Louis Victor deBroglie asserted that particles could behave as light. Demonstration came in the form of the diffraction of electrons. Ironically, it was diffraction of light that banished Newton's original corpuscular theory of light. The field of meanings in this area of human thought must look like a pretzel!

In Theology

(9) *God is human as well as divine. (Luke)*

In the Christian New Testament the concept of God becoming a human being in Jesus Christ results in a distortion of previously discrete fields of meanings for "God" and "human." Indeed, the crowd's avowal of the charge that Jesus had claimed to be the Son of God is so politically unsettling that it results in a death sentence (Luke 22:66–71).

(10) *An individual's ultimate concern is that person's god. (Tillich)*

Paul Tillich used to claim that he needed only a fifteen-minute conversation with someone in order to be able to identify that person's God. Here Tillich is relegating god and human interests to the same field of meanings.

(11) *God is relational rather than all-knowing, all-powerful, all-present and unchanging.*

Distancing the concept "God" from classical metaphysical fields of meanings enables us to correlate the concept "God" with contemporary metaphysical understandings of relations and processes. Such distancing began with the "turn to the subject" in early twentieth-century theology and was developed further by process theologians Charles Hartshorne, John Cobb, and Marjorie Suchocki.

(12) *The "natural" state of existence for human beings is to be "graced." (Karl Rahner)*

By calling the "natural" a "remainder concept," Rahner called into question the notion of the **merely** "natural," especially in the sense of its being only a basis for the "supernatural." Rahner argued that, rather than designating an actual state of affairs, the "natural" is best understood as a hypothetical designation of what would have been the human condition—had it not already been blessed from the beginning.

(13) *Christ is sophia and logos.*

The christology of traditional Christianity was drawn from the logos tradition. New appreciation of the sophia tradition in Biblical exegesis and theology means that the logos concept no longer need dominate: It becomes possible to reconstruct the concept "Christ" in feminine as well as masculine terms.

Before moving on to examples of changes in the field of theological meanings suggested by new understanding in physics, we should remember that it is no mere coincidence that painting, music, and dance all have undergone tectonic reformation. Throughout history the arts have been most reliable indicators of the state of the world of meanings of their time.

Rather than display a list of changes in religious thinking influenced by natural science over the years, we choose to focus on two quite recent conceptions that remain incompletely developed and unresolved. We choose such cases to stimulate not merely discussion of historical *faits accomplis* but also inventive speculation—to encourage a more imaginative approach to the creation of theological understanding. Here are two proposals.

First, conceptual structures in science in relation to understandings in theology:

(14) *Evil as entropic degradation. (Robert John Russell)*

In his "Entropy and Evil" (1984) Russell explores the possibility of a "substantive relationship between entropy and evil." Does the probable inevitability of evil, degradation, and death play the same role in human being that entropy plays in the second law of thermodynamics? The second law of thermodynamics is a statement to the effect that when any natural process takes place, one can find a corresponding increase in the entropy of the universe, an increase in the uselessness of everything—especially energy. Thus gravitational energy degrades into radiant energy which in turn degrades into low temperature heat energy in the form of random molecular motion. In like manner the highest aspirations of human beings, as in the story of the tower of Babel, decay into jealousy, war and garbled communication. Can we do no better than improve the situation in a limited region at the inevitable cost of making things worse everywhere else?

If this ingenious analogy is to avoid concluding in one of the gloomiest conceptions of human being we can imagine, we must study it—as Russell does—with care. It is no wonder that we have difficulty living our lives on the basis of an understanding of the field of meanings that contains these great principles. Of particular importance is the related concept of information—shown by Claude Shannon to be a form of negative entropy. Information enables us to manage complicated scenarios with a degree of efficiency and thereby to minimize the excoriating effects of the increase in entropy. We should all be especially concerned that the Sun is shining its light away at enormous cost in entropy-increase, and we are doing little to take advantage of this process for the benefit of human beings. Our lack of willingness to develop space with the same confidence we developed the western United States may yet turn out to be the scandal of the century, and seal the early demise of the human species.

Here is a second application of conceptual structures in science to understandings in theology:

(15) *Time and the Second Coming of Christ. (Gerhart/Russell)*

In *MP* (1984) we quote, from Mark 13:30–32, a familiar eschatological passage attributed to the Christ: "I tell you solemnly, before this generation passes away all these things will have taken place. . . . But as for the day or hour, nobody knows it, neither the angels of heaven, nor the Son; no one but the Father. Be on your guard, stay awake, because you will never know when the time will come."

In a mechanical understanding of the world, if a particular event is going to happen, the probability of its occurrence tomorrow increases as each day goes by. If the alarm clock is going to ring, each minute you wait makes it more likely the alarm will go off in the next minute. If you wait a long time, however, say two thousand years, and the event has not occurred, you may reasonably conclude that the system that would have caused the event is inoperative—the clock is broken. However, our understanding of nuclear physics now belies this conclusion. A radioactive atom has some probability of disintegrating in the next moment, and that probability does not change with time. As we observed earlier, submicroscopic processes are fundamentally statistical. In this sense, the eschaton is as likely today as it has ever been.

Let's speculate further. Is there a natural science understanding of time that would make the time of the Second Coming significant in human experience? We think perhaps there is, and we look to the special theory of relativity. There we learn that an individual's time is personal, in the sense that it depends on the individual's history—in particular Einstein's theory demonstrates that your time depends on your state of motion. Travel fast enough and you would live the two hundred thousand years it would take to cross the galaxy.

Consider, then, in the light of that conceptual situation in physics, the following understanding of the time of the Second Coming: Perhaps that time is the same time for all human beings. Perhaps that time coincides with the time of the death of each of us. Perhaps the promises made in Jerusalem are all to be fulfilled at one moment that is common to us all. The conceptual structure of Einstein's world does not say it is so, but it does say that such a conception is not impossible.

D. NEW UNDERSTANDINGS

Understandings of God may differ for different human beings; human beings are different from each another. Theology tries to account for differences and similarities in understandings of God and of human beings. Let us recall two ancient puzzles. One is the story of the blind person trying to understand reports of what is being felt by six other blind persons, each of whom is describing a different part of an elephant. The other is a puzzle, attributed to Heraclitus, which states that we cannot step in the same river twice. How do these puzzles apply to both science and theology? The elephant story illustrates the difficulty of trying to understand God from reports of various persons, including theologians. The river story illustrates the change undergone by people and theologians as God changes and all descriptions of God change.

Early attempts to grapple with heterogeneous theological questions and answers in the late Middle Ages provide good examples of the expectation that abstract understandings can in some sense be discrete and repeated, an expectation borne out in the "Sic et non" style of thought. To questions like, "Is the Son God? Is the Son human? Is the Spirit the same as the Son?" formal answers were given: "Yes, yes, no," together with the arguments for the sense in which these were the correct answers. It is apparent to us today that these logical exclusions were mind-boggling to early and medieval thinkers. Tertullian, for example, took the position that one ought to believe religious doctrine precisely **because** it is absurd! (Here we might recall Bohr's "Is it crazy enough?") But since then human beings have become better at managing ambiguity. With Hegel, for example, it became possible to think these contradictions and to eliminate the law of the excluded middle as an impediment to thought. But the big danger today is not only in the kind of rationality that is being called into question. The danger is even more present in thinking that it is best (or adequate) to think through any major issue only privately. For if we do not attempt to understand cooperatively, that understanding is less likely to be able to reach the goal of reasonableness to all who also ask a question about what is described.

The theological question asked by many Jews after the Holocaust—how could God have allowed these atrocities to happen—for example, is a question not only for Jews. It is a question to be taken seriously by any contemporary person who attempts to find the concept of God meaningful. An answer any better than completely inadequate is likely to begin with the cognitive disruption cited in example #11 above: namely, that *God is relational rather than all-knowing, all-powerful, all-present and unchanging.* With the distancing from classical metaphysical fields of meanings, the concept "God" is drawn closer to the ways in which human beings differ and change.

This insight about the changing character of theology is borne out by the question of what will happen in the ever-increasing recognition of plurality—both within and between major religions. David Tracy reminds us that, until recently, the question of the relationship of Christianity to other religions typically has been taken up last—often in an appendix in systematic theology. But with the shift in populations, there has come a shift in theological focus, especially in liberation and feminist theologies, away from human beings as non-believers. Theological reflection done exclusively within a community of believers has expanded to include interreligious dialogue as well. If that dialogue is to be authentic, those who participate put at risk their presuppositions about other religions. They also experience a sense of the ambiguity of all propositions concerning their own religion because of changes in lived experience and its expressions. Tracy thinks that no one can foresee just what will result from this interreligious dialogue and that it may take two more generations before the direction of change becomes clearer.[5]

Novelty is forced on natural science by empirical observation: theories become inadequate to do the job of accounting for experience. So we are forced to reconstruct theories in a wild but intelligible effort to explain experience. As we argue in "Mathematics, Empirical Science and Theology" (see chapter eight), verification in theology proceeds by affirmation rather than by empirical observation. When people change, what can be affirmed changes. When people are no longer willing to say "yes, I can believe in that," their failure of faith has less to do with natural science than with their own experiences in the world. The need to understand both these experiences and those of natural science makes it possible and necessary to do new theology today. What we have done is to provide a conceptual tool to support the expectation and existence of novelty in theological as well as in scientific traditions. There is something new under the sun. All is not more of the same. Not all was given at the beginning.

4

Sublimation of the Goddess in the Deitic Metaphor of Moses

A theory of metaphor is used as the hermeneutical basis for interpreting the transformation of the religion of Israel from polytheism to monotheism. By equating Yahweh (God of the Exodus) with El, the God of the Fathers, in the metaphoric pronouncement Yahweh = El, Moses creates Yahweh (God of all the tribes of Israel). One effect of metaphoric process in this instance is to transform Asherah/Goddess, whose union with El/God is related to the procreativity of the gods, into the Serpent/Goddess in the postmetaphoric Garden story of Genesis. Here the Serpent/Goddess seduces Eve into eating the fruit of the Tree of Knowledge (of human sexuality), thereby deifying Eve and, indirectly, Adam. Henceforth it is the union of the godlike human beings that serves procreation in a world in which the secular has been made holy. This process is understood as a sublimation of the Goddess in the cognitive field of meanings that has been restructured by this Mosaic metaphor of the gods.

THE BIBLE REMAINS THE PREMIER CHALLENGE IN LINGUISTIC INTERPRETATION. Both for their intrinsic importance to Western culture and their extraordinary complexity, the texts of the Hebrew Bible and the New

---

This chapter was originally published, with Joseph P. Healey as co-author, in a special issue of *Semeia: An Experimental Journal for Biblical Criticism* 61 (1993), 167–82, entitled "Women, War, and Metaphor: Language and Society in the Study of the Hebrew Bible."

Testament deserve their reputations as proving grounds for every hermeneutical tool we have been able to find.

In the sweep of religious history as presented in the biblical texts, there is no larger, more overarching problem than that posed by the changes that take place in the relationship between God and the people of Israel. Indeed that relationship might be taken as the subject of the entire Hebrew Bible. In this article we apply our understanding of metaphor to the transition from the ancient Hebrew deities to Yahweh. In analyzing the transition process, which we see as metaphoric, we will be paying special attention to the fate of the Goddess, intimately related to El, but commonly and superficially understood as lost in Yahweh. We see this loss rather as a kind of sublimation, that is, an act of cognitive repression which preserves and enhances the power and influence of the object—in this case, the Goddess—even as the object is lost to view.

Whatever the "historical facts" regarding the two principal names for God in the Old Testament—El and Yahweh—just how the names are related has provoked wonder, inquiry, and debate. Ours is one interpretation of their relationship. While it does not presume to determine the history of the world of the Israelites, nor what it means to say "God," we believe this hermeneutical inquiry does have historical and theological implications.

A. THE COGNITIVE STRUCTURE OF METAPHOR

The understanding of metaphor we will be using in the analysis has antecedents in the works of Ricoeur, which are concerned as least as much with the way we think with metaphors as with the way we say them. In order to describe the effects of the metaphoric process on the way we think about things, we need a more or less straightforward model of the cognitive structure that is undergoing change in the process.

In the Gerhart/Russell model (1984, 1990), human cognition takes place with respect to "fields of meanings" which together make up, for a person or a culture, a "world of meanings." The structure of a field or world of meanings comprises a network of concepts and relations. In such a network, concepts can be compared to the knots in a net and relations to the strings that connects the knots. The model differs from a simple net, such as that a fisher might use, in that every concept is potentially related directly to every other concept so that the number of relations is not simply twice the number of concepts, as the strings are twice the number of knots in a square net, but depends quadratically on the number of concepts in the way given by the expression,

$$R = \frac{C(C-1)}{2},$$

where R is the number of relations and C the number of concepts. For example, if one had nine concepts in a cognitive field there would be potentially thirty-six relations connecting them to each other. Clearly, relations far outnumber concepts in any cognitive field of significance.

Making use of Ricoeur's idea of logical distance, we understand that relations between "distant" concepts are less definitive than relations between proximate ones. Distant or loose relations between concepts can vary with little effect on the cognitive structure of a field. As we shall see, however, a major change that makes concepts formerly distant from each other proximate (i.e., a radical "shortening" of formerly distant or loose relations) can profoundly change the way we think.

Traditionally human knowledge has been thought to be something that grew rather like a tree, but that did not change in structure. A modern epistemology, to the contrary, recognizes that human understandings are subject to radical revision from time to time, and in our view metaphor is one of the important agents in such revision. We say that the cognitive network is distorted by changes that a metaphor can make in cognitive relations. The greatest distortion in a world of meanings occurs when two concepts, say A and B, which both have multiple connections to their own neighboring concepts, but which are only distantly related to each other, are proclaimed to be the same, to be in the form: A = B.

Expressed in English, the act of proclamation takes, for example, the form "This [bread] is my body" (Jesus); "The laws of the heavens are the laws of the Earth" (Newton); "The Sun, not the Earth, is the center" (Copernicus); and "God is love" (John). It is clear that we are dealing with powerful and cognitively disruptive material here, and it is perhaps fortunate that metaphoric acts of such magnitude—in any given history—occur relatively rarely.

It needs to be understood that ours is not the common usage of the term "metaphor." Although writers on metaphor often compare "metaphoric meaning" with "literal meaning," the distinction between literal and metaphoric has little significance for our cognitive theory of the metaphoric process. To say "A = B" under our conditions for the concepts A and B is both to speak metaphorically and to make a statement that has "literal meaning." The "metaphoric meaning" is to be found in the newly restructured field of meanings and not in the words used to express the metaphor.

The word metaphor is normally applied freely to what would mostly often be understood in cognitive terms as analogy or simile. If, for example, one of two objects being compared is initially unknown or insufficiently known and made known or better known by the comparison, we judge the cognitive operation to be not metaphorical but analogical (where function as well as appearance is involved) or of the nature of a simile (where the issue is primarily one of form or appearance). Only when each element taken separately is well understood (i.e., firmly, even rigidly embedded in its own field of meanings) can a radical change in cognitive relation between these elements result in what we call a metaphoric distortion of the fields of meanings.

Peter W. Macky, in his *The Centrality of Metaphors to Biblical Thought*, describes metaphors that satisfy the Gerhart/Russell criteria as those ". . . which contradict old views, almost forcing people to view the world differently" (74). We will argue that our theory of metaphor, applied to the problem of the origins and identity of the God of Israel, evokes a new understanding of the fate of the Goddess.

When we apply our model to Hebrew, we encounter an interesting difficulty: the Hebrew language contains no copula—it is not possible in Hebrew to say "A is B." So, for example, the translation of Gen. 49:22 found in *The New English Bible* (hereafter, NEB) is "Joseph is a fruitful tree," a perfect structure for a metaphor in

English. However, a word-for-word translation of the Hebrew yields: "Joseph fruitful vine," a syntax which depends on juxtaposition rather than on the verb "is."

It would appear that identifying biblical metaphors by linguistic structure alone is a slippery business at best. Fortunately, in situations where metaphoric structure in the language is uncertain, cognitive analysis allows us to make a judgment. In the case of the Genesis verse above, one element is a person (Joseph) and the statement enhances our knowledge of that person. To learn that Joseph is fruitful is to add to the cognitive field which contains Joseph, and not to distort that field. What we have here is a poetic analogy. Contrast the cognitive aspect of that Genesis verse with the Christic sacramental metaphor, "This [bread] is my body." Both "bread" (a baked, leavened dough of flour or meal mixed with liquid) and "body" (the organized physical material of a human being, whether living or dead) are concepts well understood independently of each other, i.e., fixed rigidly in their respective cognitive fields. They are also relationally quite distant from each other. To proclaim them the same is to force a major cognitive distortion (e.g., to break the bread is to break the body), in this case to the point of creating a kind of riddle—one that has prompted some fifteen hundred years of wonder and debate.

Returning now to the Hebrew Bible, we ask—based on our cognitive theory of what a metaphor is—what can be said to be the major metaphor of the Hebrew Bible? The answer to this question is at the heart of the answer to another: Who is the God of the Israelites?

B. THE DEITIC METAPHOR OF MOSES

If our cognitive model is to be applied to biblical texts, we must find in those texts an apt metaphor. Given both the relative rarity of metaphor in terms of this model and the specific absence of the verb "to be" as a copula in biblical Hebrew, finding evidence of metaphoric process in the Old Testament is not a simple task. Lengthy discussion among linguists on the question of the use of the verb "to be" as a copulative has not made the search easier.[6]

But if we look at the question of the religion of the Israelites from a phenomenological point of view, it seems clear enough that a qualitative difference exists between this religion and the religions that preceded it or coexisted with it. The biblical story tells a tale of how this change came to take place and what its implications might be. The religion of Israel in its canonical form (i.e., in the biblical text) presents itself as utterly different from all previous religions. Whereas the religions of Egypt and Mesopotamia showed themselves to be remarkably adaptable to the shifting fortune of their gods, changing at will the relative positions, titles, indeed even the names of the gods as custom or circumstances dictated, Israel tests itself over and over again on the rule of fidelity. And whereas the other cultures were able to assimilate happily the goddesses and gods of subject nations or conquerors, as the case might be, Israel's history as told in the narrative of the bible is the story of a remarkable stubbornness in resisting such adaptability. Indeed, the narratives are at pains to eliminate any trace whatever of religious experiences not carefully related to the central cult of Yahweh.

In the biblical text, the common thread credited with holding Israel together is the absolute sovereignty of Yahweh and his insistence that he is the only god the Israelites are allowed to worship (early sense of monotheism). In the lawgiving episode the very first declaration of the Covenant is the assertion that Yahweh alone is God: "I am the Lord [Heb. *yhwh*] your God [Heb. *'lhyk*] who brought you out of Egypt, out of the land of slavery. You shall have no other god to set against me" (Exod 20:2–3; all quotations are from the New American Bible [NAB] unless otherwise indicated). Here Yahweh is identified as the one who led the Israelites out of Egypt.

In the same lawgiving episode, Moses makes explicit to the people his earliest encounter with this God on Sinai/Horeb. There Moses was told, "I am the God of your fathers . . . , the God of Abraham, the God of Isaac, the God of Jacob" (Exod 3:6). In that same narrative, Moses sought further information about the God, "'If they ask me, "What is his name?" what am I to tell them?' God replied, 'I am who am' [Heb. *'hyh 'sr 'hyh*]. Then he added, 'This is what you shall tell the Israelites: I AM [Heb. *'hyh*] sent me to you.' God spoke further to Moses, 'Thus shall you say to the Israelites: The LORD [Heb. *yhwh*], the God of your fathers, the God of Abraham, the God of Isaac, the God of Jacob, has sent me to you'" (Exod 3:13–15).

Reading these texts and assuming them to be constitutive of the faith of Israel, we can render the Mosaic assertion as the declaration, **Yahweh is the God of Abraham, Isaac and Jacob** (Exod 3:6). In terms of the Gerhart/Russell theory, this assertion is in the form of a metaphor. Indeed, we would argue that this assertion is the primary metaphor of the Hebrew Bible, and that it is constitutive of the faith of Israel.[7]

Yahweh, clearly identified as the one who led the Israelites out of Egypt, is a known God (A) in the premetaphoric Mosaic field of meanings. But this God, Yahweh, is known only in an action that the Exodus group can identify. Yahweh as Yahweh is identified by his deeds (Exod 20:2).

The God El (B) is also known premetaphorically. He is El, the God of the Fathers in the Bible. Thus two distinct knowns, Yahweh (A) and El (B), become A = B as a result of the metaphoric process. The religious genius of the Moses narratives is clearest in the text which joins the God Yahweh, the God of the Exodus, to the God El, the God of the Fathers: "God also said to Moses, 'I am the LORD [Heb. *yhwh.*] As God the Almighty [Heb. *'lšdy*] I appeared to Abraham, Isaac and Jacob, but my name, LORD [Heb. *yhwh*], I did not make known to them'" (Exod 6:2–3). In making the metaphor, Yahweh = El, the God of the Fathers, Moses can be interpreted as creating a new religion![8] The metaphoric process of making Yahweh = El then becomes the means by which two disparate, and even contradictory, sets of religious beliefs are joined. Moses creates a bond between the people who had Yahweh as their God (the primary Exodus group) and the people who worshipped the God of the Fathers.

We are making use of the term "premetaphoric" to denote the two different fields of meanings as they were for the separate religions of the Canaanites and the Hebrews, and we will call "postmetaphoric" the field of meanings operative for the bonded tribes of Israel. We reserve the adjective "metaphoric" for the cognitive act, and say, for example, that the religion of Yahweh, the God of the Israelites, developed as a result of a metaphoric process, a process initiated, we claim, in the Moses narratives.

We are now poised to consider the further question raised by our interpretation, the question central to the purpose of our analysis:

namely, what happens to the spouse of El in the metaphoric process? Who is this spouse of El and where is she to be found in the post metaphoric field of meanings of the Hebrew Testament? It appears striking to us that a dominant aspect of the premetaphoric field of meanings described in related Semitic texts, namely the Goddess associated with El, the God of the Fathers, is, in the Hebrew Bible, utterly distanced from Yahweh. Surely what must accompany El in the metaphoric process that makes Yahweh = El is El's spouse!

C. THE SUBLIMATION OF THE GODDESS

The discovery of the sacred as feminine in the Hebrew Bible is important for many reasons, not the least of which is the correction of the common misunderstanding, in both Judaism and Christianity, of God as exclusively male. At least three kinds of searches for an explanation of the loss of the sacred feminine have been undertaken in recent scholarship. One kind of search emphasizes the excision of the image of woman from the godhead (documented in Deuteronomy, Judges, Samuel, Leviticus and the Chronicles) by the slashing, burning, and destruction of the shrines of Asherah during numerous reform movements down to the sixth century BCE. Other scholars find male usurpation of the female prerogative of child-bearing in the portrayal of a male God creating human beings. Still a third kind of search discovers displacements of the Goddess under different names (for example, in the Wisdom texts) or in the occasional explicit analogies of stereotypical female characteristics or roles in the God of Israel.

Attempts to retrieve the sacred as feminine in one way or another are often at odds with one another: many reformist scholars, for example, believe in the basic correctability of the androcentric bias of Jewish and Christian traditions, whereas revolutionary scholars find the traditions incorrigible on the issue of women (see McFague 1982: 152–76). The Gerhart/Russell theory of metaphor makes it possible to see how these positions are related—specifically, how what happened to the world of meanings after the Mosaic metaphor occurred can be understood through the network model of cognition. In terms of this model, the excision, usurpation and displacement of the feminine can all be called a sublimation of the Goddess.[9]

1. The El/Asherah Premetaphoric Field of Meanings

Before the creation of the Mosaic metaphor Yahweh = El—whenever that may have been—the Goddess was prominent in two kinds of Ugaritic-Mesopotamian myths: in stories of the creation of the gods and in stories of the creation of human beings. In the Babylonian epic "Enuma Elish" for example, Tiamat figures prominently in both kinds of creation. She is a mother-goddess who remains faithful to a father-god Apsu, even though she opposes a plan Apsu has to kill the young gods. When Apsu is killed by their sons who planned revolt, Tiamat negotiates to regain supremacy. But Marduk, one of the heirs of the old gods, kills Tiamat—now described as a serpent/sea monster —splitting her and creating the Earth and the firmament from her body.

Recurring conceptual relations between the concept of goddess and that of serpent or snake in the premetaphoric field of meanings are highly suggestive. Phenomenologically, the serpent/snake has evoked fascination and dread from ancient times to the present. Its mysterious wavy movement, its uncanny ability to retreat with unsurpassed speed without external organs of locomotion, its ability to shed its skin for seemingly new life—such characteristics gave rise to a belief that the creature could even procreate without a mate.

Minimally, we can assume that remnants of Tiamat, the serpent/sea monster, are to be found in the biblical Rahab, now stripped of her guise as a goddess, and generically linked to the Garden story by being a serpent. In Isa 51:9–10, Yahweh is awakened and reminded, "Was it not you who crushed Ahab, you who pierced the Dragon?" Similarly, Ps 89:9–12 ties the notion of holy war to the mythic war with the serpent/sea monster: "You rule over the surging of the sea; . . . you have crushed Rahab with a mortal blow; with your strong arm you have scattered your enemies." In Job 26:12–13, cosmic control and wisdom are achieved over and against the serpent/sea monster: "By his power he stirs up the sea, and by his might he crushes Rahab. With his angry breath he scatters the water . . . ; His hand pierces the fugitive dragon as from his hand it strives to flee." Rahab seems all that Tiamat was—except that none of Tiamat's glory as a goddess before her defeat by Marduk is hinted at in any of the Hebrew texts.

In texts that describe the Canaanite religion, the Goddess appears not as a primal monster but as a kinship figure in a pantheon of gods

(Eliade 1978:139–62). While there is some confusion in the use of names, Asherah in the Ugaritic Ras Shamra tablets is generally portrayed as the wife of the high god El and mother of the gods, though she remains associated by epithets with the Sea.[10] Anat is the daughter of El.[11] Though sometimes confused with Asherah, Anat is instead a warrior-goddess who defeats the Sea, personified in these myths as male (Yamm). The combined characteristics of these two deities, Anat/Asherah, include wisdom, fertility, creativity, culture, and skill in warfare (Cassuto 1971:58–59, 64–65). The religion of Canaan has been characterized as a fertility cult (Albright 1969:67–92), but this interpretation tends to ignore the manifold diversity of the Canaanite goddesses' aspects and characteristics. Nevertheless, we may presume that the sexual act was sacred in the religious world of Canaan and that, whatever her other characteristics, the Goddess was an object of cult worship regularly associated with fertility.

2. The Yahweh (God of the Exodus) Premetaphoric Field of Meanings

What can be found from the search for the sacred feminine in the deitic field of meanings of Yahweh prior to the metaphoric transition (the empty region shown in brackets in Fig. 4.1 below)? For one thing, since the sacred feminine is a repressed concept we cannot expect to find a goddess explicitly in the text. Instead we must be alert for textual references to relations that are conceptually illegitimate. In effect these existent relations remain unconnected with, and can only point toward, the concept which cannot be seen.

With the advance toward monotheism in the metaphoric act, the post metaphoric field of meanings no longer includes a goddess with whom a god could procreate. On the level of myth it becomes necessary for the deitic conjunction Yahweh = El to usurp the function of fertility. By excluding the Goddess, and hence the possibility of procreative union, the canonical God Yahweh came to represent only an abstract sense of fertility. The more concrete aspects of fertility were formally distanced from the male representations of the sacred. In an ancient text, however, we find what may be a remnant of Canaanite myth, ritual or both: "When men began to multiply on earth, and daughters were born to them, the sons of heaven saw how beautiful the daughters of man were, and so they took for their wives as many of them as they chose" (Gen 6:1–2). In this text the abrogation of the role of the female in reproduction can be seen in the absence of any reference to mothers or to the Goddess. At the same time the desire of the "sons of heaven" for wives described in this text reminds us of the importance of sexuality and gender in the deitic fields of meanings, concepts found irrepressible in the developing new religious order of the Israelites.

Our account of the Goddess in the field of meanings of El, the God of the Fathers, should alert us to evidence of differences between the way the religion of Yahweh is articulated in the texts and the official reactions to the way the chosen people lived as described in other biblical texts and ancillary sources (Morton Smith 1971; Levenson 1985:56–70). Feminist scholars, among others, have observed that laws are often more honored in the breach and that the more insistent the mandate the more likely it is to be the case that the mandate was directed against actual behavior. The Goddess, spouse of El, although formally absent in the premetaphoric field of meanings of Yahweh, very likely remained active and alive and was worshipped as Asherah in the community that constituted Israel. For example, we find the following text in Jeremiah:

From all the men who knew that their wives were burning incense to strange gods, from all the women who were present in the immense crowd, and from all the people who lived in Lower and Upper Egypt, Jeremiah received this answer: "We will not listen to what you tell us in the name of the LORD. Rather will we continue doing what we had proposed; we will burn incense to the queen of heaven and pour out libations to her, *as we and our fathers*, our kings and our princes have done in the cities of Judah and the streets of Jerusalem. . . .

And when we burned incense to the queen of heaven and poured out libations to her, was it without our husbands' consent that we baked cakes in her image and poured out libations to her?" (Jer 44:15–19, emphasis ours)

Here the fathers (presumably, the same fathers whose God was El), as well as the people speaking to Jeremiah, are said to have participated in the worship of Asherah—now referred to as the queen of heaven. In this passage we can hear echoes not only of El, the God of the Fathers, but also Asherah, the Goddess of the Fathers!

The Goddess was hidden for generations although her worship continued, probably as a part of the women's ritual celebration of first menstruation, sexual initiation, marriage, pregnancy, childbirth, menopause, observances having to do with plant and animal culture, and death. There are many references to "asherahs" in the Hebrew Bible, which according to Urs Winter (1983: 551–60) are best interpreted as shrines.[12]

Both males and females initiated and participated in the worship of Asherah. Solomon with his Sidonite wife both initiated the worship of Asherah and erected her sacred pillars in the hills. Rehoboam is reported to have "set up pillars and sacred poles on every high hill and under every spreading tree," and the narrator adds, "There were even men in the country who were sacred prostitutes" (1 Kgs 14:23–24).[13] Rehoboam with his favorite wife Maacah also placed an image of Asherah in the temple.

Further indirect evidence of the presence of the Goddess under Yahweh is given by the energetic destruction of Asherah-worship by males, reported as being carried out with particular bravado. Asa drove out the sacred prostitutes and burned his grandmother's shrine for worshiping Asherah (1 Kgs 15:13). Josiah pulled down houses of male prostitutes—houses in which women were said to weave clothes of Asherah—and did away with those who worshipped Baal and the Sun, Moon, stars, and firmament (2 Kgs 23:5–7). Although the reform activity was directed against both the God and the Goddess, the prohibition of images was, in effect (even if not in intention), a disembodiment more of the Goddess than of the God, because the God continued to be affirmed in aniconic forms of language and priesthood.

The disembodiment of the Goddess therefore constituted a primary repression. Dangling relations that are vital elements in the premetaphoric texts, however, continue to point to the missing goddess concept. Finally, in the Garden of the postmetaphoric creation story we find the Goddess herself as a central player.

3. The Re-Emergence of the Feminine as Sacred in the Garden of the Postmetaphoric Creation Story: The Eve/Serpent/Goddess

Whatever creation story the Israelites might have had before the Mosaic metaphor, it is now clear that the story had to be radically retold if it was to conform to the postmetaphoric conceptual structure relating to the God of the Israelites. The progression from a polytheistic religion to a monotheistic religion that equated Yahweh with El required some transition that could account for essential concepts such as procreation—formerly the province of the gods and embodied in the Goddess and now nonfunctional in a monotheistic framework. We believe that the principal elements and their transitions can be identified in the Garden of the postmetaphoric creation story. Indeed, one can understand the Garden as **the** representation of the postmetaphoric cosmology. Our interpretation of the conceptual elements and their transitions is represented schematically in Fig. 4.1.

The top half of the figure contains representations of the premetaphoric fields of meanings; the left side is a representation of the field of meanings associated with the polytheism of El, the God of the Fathers. Here the God, El, is conceptually related to power and immortality. The other essential concepts, fertility or general fecundity and knowledge of sexuality, are most closely related to the Goddess, Asherah. In the polytheistic environment the basis of the procreative act is found in the union of the God and Goddess.

The right side of the top half of the figure contains representations of the premetaphoric field of meanings associated with the monotheism of Yahweh (the God of the Exodus). Here the only efficacious deity, male or female, is Yahweh to whom we relate the concepts of power and immortality, and (subsequent to the law-giving on the mountain) the Law and the Covenant. But it is not possible to relate to Yahweh the concept of the union of a goddess and a god. Hence the associated concepts which are close to the Goddess— namely, fertility, procreativity, and knowledge as sexuality, as well as the Goddess herself—constitute a lacuna (as indicated with brackets) in the premetaphoric field of meanings of Yahweh. For the mythic resolution of the puzzle created by the metaphor Yahweh = El, the

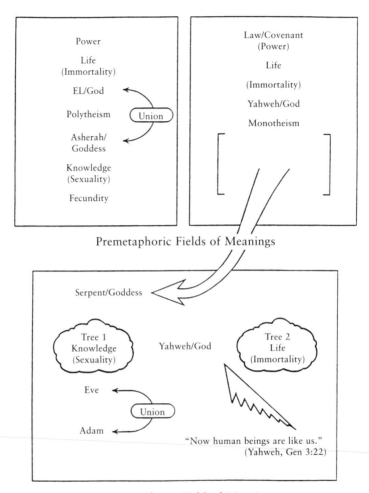

Premetaphoric Fields of Meanings

Postmetaphoric Field of Meanings

Fig. 4.1 Fields of meanings before and after metaphoric process. The premetaphoric field of meanings (polytheistic) of El and Asherah/God and Goddess of the Fathers is made coincident with the pre-metaphoric field of meanings (monotheistic) of Yahweh by the deitic metaphor of Moses. The metaphoric field of meanings (monotheistic) that results is mythically presented in the Garden of Eden where the Goddess, in the form of the Serpent, seduces the Woman to eat from the the tree of Knowledge of human sexuality so that the Woman becomes Eve, "the mother of all the living" (Gen 3:20), and the human beings, Adam and Eve in union, take over the sacred function of procreation. Yahweh then banishes them so that they will not acquire immortality from the tree of Life. The human beings are now, as Yahweh remarks, "like one of us" (Gen 3:22) as a result of the gift of the Goddess.

Mosaic act that brings all of the tribes of Israel (not just the tribes of the Exodus) under Yahweh, we turn to the Garden—depicted with the conceptual representations in the bottom half of the figure—and explore the concepts, illustrated schematically as the post-metaphoric field of meanings, in relation to the texts of the story as told in Genesis 3.

The conceptual elements related to the necessary characteristics of deity are represented in the schematization of the Garden as Tree 1 and Tree 2. Tree 1, the Tree of Knowledge (of sexuality), is closely related to the Serpent/Goddess, who has a vested interest in deifying Eve, and is shown hovering above Tree 1 in our figure. Tree 2, the Tree of Life, represents the second essential characteristic of a god, i.e., immortality.

The Serpent/Goddess seduces the Woman, who partakes of the fruit of Tree 1, and generously (but perhaps impetuously and unwisely) gives some of it to Adam. The action of the Goddess both deifies Eve[14] (and also Adam) and gives to her sexual knowledge and the function of sexual procreation (in union with Adam). The Woman becomes Eve, and replaces the Goddess as, in the words of Genesis 3:20, "the mother of all the living."

Tree 2 is indicated as shielded from the human couple, and the bottom line notes Yahweh's spoken affirmation of the (incomplete) god-likeness of the human beings—a tacit recognition of the achievement of the Goddess. From now on the procreative act will be union between human female and male, rather than divine goddess and god.

The human couple both win and lose; they have their sexuality, and are empowered to procreate. But they are kept from the Tree of Life and must leave the Garden. Eve's gain is a sacrifice (holy gift) of the Goddess. It also results in a loss to the offspring of the Serpent/Goddess, who will forever "bite the heel" of the more fortunate offspring of the Eve/Snake/Goddess.[15]

An epistemological interpretation of the Garden story, such as that offered in *MP* 1984:189–92, makes explicit the action of the Goddess not as an exercise of her power but as an invitation, a luring, and disposing—what we have chosen to call a "seduction" to a new way of being in the world. For of the two trees in the Garden, Eve was drawn initially to the Tree of Knowledge, rather than to the Tree of

Life. Eating the fruit caused Eve's and Adam's eyes to be opened to their procreative capabilities; it also made them self-conscious. In the Garden, Eve and Adam became independent knowers before they became independent procreators.

The field of meanings created by the Yahweh = El metaphor, expressed as a text in Genesis 3, and interpreted schematically in our Fig. 4.1, makes it possible to describe the fate of the Goddess as a sublimation that achieves, against the will of Yahweh, the partial deification of human beings—especially the female. It is now understandable that the secular realm, represented in the bottom part of the postmetaphorical field of meanings in Fig. 4.1, should ever after be understood as sacred, an understanding reflected in the day-to-day practices of the Israelites and enunciated by Yahweh, "You shall be holy, because I, the Lord your God am holy" (Lev 19:12). Our interpretation suggests that the holiness of human beings was less an act of Yahweh than it was an achievement of the Goddess.

Part II

Bidisciplinary Dialogue and Text in Science and Religion

5

The Genre Bidisciplinary Dialogue

The written work of two authors from different disciplines in dialogue constitutes a specific genre. Other genres of dialogue are examined and discussed. Maurice Merleau-Ponty's considerations of alterity (otherness) in conversations is explored and related to dialogue. The authors' revision of the Turing Test overcomes the lack of success of the original. The revised Turing Test and the hermeneutical circle are evaluated in relation to bidisiplinary dialogues. Genuine bidisciplinary dialogue may engender a higher viewpoint.

A. GENRES BETWEEN DISCIPLINES

THE END OF THE TWENTIETH CENTURY WAS WITNESS TO A SHARP INCREASE in attention given to extradisciplinary activities. Most commonly under the banner of "interdisciplinary scholarship," many academic professionals and not a few non-academic professional authors have taken up working residences in the interstices between the traditional disciplines of English, history, political science, economics, philosophy, sociology, psychology, to name just a few. These workers often maintain a quasi-stable balance between two or more

Paper presented at the conference, "Genre Theory at the Millennium," held at Colgate University and Hamilton College, September 11–13, 1998.

well defined academic fields and draw out ideas, concepts, methods and language from conventional locations, recombine these elements, reconstruct the languages, and lay down new patterns onto the pages of (often new) journals.

This between-the-disciplines model, this scholarship of the gaps, is burdened with a number of presuppositions and inherent limitations. Prominent among presuppositions is the belief that there is scholarly gold to be found in the combinational activities, either in some form of new knowledge or in the possibility of creating new academic territory over which new scholars can preside. Prominent among the limitations is the fact that the practitioners often are well schooled in one traditional discipline, but not as prepared to make informed use of scholarly achievements in another discipline.

One solution to the latter problem is to be found in collaborative work between scholars in different disciplines. Here the work of communication is structured as a reciprocal exchange between two disciplines rather than as an unschooled interpretation by an interloper from within one discipline. The existence of the form of reciprocal exchange we call "bidisciplinary dialogue" (hereafter BD dialogue) belies the common lament that there is no communication between the disciplines.

BD dialogue is increasingly to be found in the interaction between theologians and scientists who share interest in religious questions. Growth in this area of scholarship has been fostered in no small measure by private foundations such as the John M. Templeton Foundation, who encourage and support lectures and conferences that bring scientists together with religious scholars.

Published materials also reflect cooperative activity that sometimes prompts readers to ask questions such as, "Is this being written by a scientist or by a theologian?" or "Do both scientists and theologians agree with this conclusion?" An understanding of the literary genre of a written document can often be an aid to its interpretation. We expect this to be no less true for bidisicplinary dialogue than for other genres.

In this essay we explore BD dialogue as a genre. By comparing BD dialogue with other forms of dialogue, we develop the sense in which BD dialogue is appropriately understood as a genre in addition to its being more generally a form of pedagogy or communication. By distinguishing BD dialogue from other forms of dialogue, we exhibit some of its special features.

1. The Genre BD Dialogue as *Parole De Deux*

A genre is that aspect of a text which requires interpretation as a structural whole in order to make sense of its parts. A reader unconcerned with genre theory tends to "naturalize" every text—that is, to read it from a genre perspective that is assumed to be obvious and legitimized by the "facts" readily found in the text. Such a reader is either untroubled by conflicting interpretations, or if troubled, not so much troubled that she will seek different ways of addressing them. By contrast, a reader acquainted with genre theory will "test" the text in the light of several genres in order to maximize recognition of ambiguities in the text and differences in interpretation caused by different genric clothing. Such a reader will also recognize the role of genre in the creation of texts. In *Genre Choices, Gender Questions* (1992:162–68), Gerhart illustrates how some texts more than others call for genre testing.

No less important is the somewhat neglected relationship between discipline and genre. In his well-known study of speech genres (many aspects of which pertain also to written genres) Mikhail Bakhtin (1966) called attention to the "enormous ocean of extraliterary genres, primary and secondary, made up out of these that constitute not only literary but all other text types (legal, scientific, journalistic) as well." Bakhtin sees disciplines as comprising sets of genres: "What distinguishes one science from another is the roster of genres each has appropriated as its own" (60).

BD dialogue is a special kind of dialogue that presumes the validity of the genres of each discipline or opens the genres of both to productive inquiry. Bakhtin thought that "the wealth and diversity of speech genres are boundless because the various possibilities of human activity are inexhaustible, and because each sphere of activity contains a entire repertoire of speech genres that differentiate and grow as the particular sphere develops and becomes more complex" (60).[16] But Bakhtin mentioned only speech genres. We have identified

TABLE I: A representative, but not exhaustive, roster of genres in science or in religion, generated in BD dialogue between a physicist and a theologian.

Genres in Science (19)

abstract	graph	precise observation
analogy	history	(e.g., astronomical)
argument	hypothesis	prediction
article	law	quantity
data	mathematics	story
example (case)	model	theory
experiment	paradigm	

Genres in Religion (35)

analogy	drama	myth
apocalypse	epistle	narrative/story
apology	example (case)	pericope
argument	hagiography	prayer
architecture	history	parable
art	homily	promise/covenant
belief	invocation	prophecy
calligraphy	lamentation	proverb
commandment	liturgy	psalm
commentary (*tafsir*)		ritual
creed		testimony
doctrine		theology (theory)

BD dialogue also as a new **written** genre—a dialogue between two disciplines.[17] Science and religion exemplify two disciplines historically seen to be in conflict. Fear of the outsider, of course—the threat of the innocent and of the unschooled to the genres of the discipline—is not limited to science and religion. In a sense, every discipline is at risk, especially at the edges of its intellectual development where the discipline is most fragile. Those unschooled in a discipline often misunderstand the substance of what is said. In another sense, however, the unschooled are sometimes able to cut through academic superfluage and expose vacuousness. Among the disciplines, religion and science epitomize these doubts and are frequently wildly misunderstood—physicists are often viewed today as engineers who screw things up, while theologians are seen as fakirs who walk on hot rocks and cause wars. BD dialogue offers a scholar in one discipline a vestibule, if not an entry, into another.

2. BD Dialogue and Related Genres

BD dialogue written by two persons differs from dialogue written by a single person. Consider the following possibilities:

- **Actual dialogue**—A conversation/discussion between two persons focusing on a particular question or issue. Actual dialogue can be subdivided as follows (with exceptions as noted):
- **Recorded dialogue**—A transcript or audio recording of a dialogue.
- **Edited dialogue**—A revised transcript of a dialogue (best when revised by the original discussants).
- **Represented dialogue**—A written text in dialogue format by a single author.[18]
- **Interview**—One person asking questions of another. Since one asks and the other answers, the interview lacks the symmetry required of a dialogue.
- **Debate (formal)**—Two persons taking opposing sides of an assigned issue in an effort to win a contest. Opponents are not permitted to change their official positions on the issue during the course of the verbal exchange—a limitation not present in BD dialogue.
- **Debate (political)**—Two or more persons attempting to influence the views or opinions of an audience comprised of legislators or voters. Authentic BD dialogue is not "staged" in this way.
- **Correspondence**—Letters written back and forth between two persons. This genre may meet the requirements of focus and symmetry, but the delay between reception and reply usually breaks the continuity of thinking and mutual interactive influence present in BD dialogue.[19]
- **Conversation**—A more primal play of verbal exchange often interrupted by argument, explanation, and theoretical reflection (see Tracy 1987:28–46).
- **Interdisciplinary dialogue**—A parallel form of interchange[20] between two or more disciplines that provides additional viewpoints on particular issues.

∎ **BD dialogue**—An interactive form of communication between scholars from two disciplines that has the potential for leading to higher viewpoints.[21]

Let us further provide a locus for BD dialogue in Bakhtin's "ocean of genres" by recalling particular texts.

The Platonic dialogues, a representation of verbal exchanges between the historical character Socrates and some of his contemporaries, are perhaps the best known examples of written dialogue. Socrates himself did no writing as far as we know, nor are the individuals with whom he dialogues his equals with respect either to intelligence or verbal facility. Indeed, Socrates' dialogue partners frequently provide foils or are themselves "fall guys" for Socrates. Socrates often puts words into his interlocutor's mouth, a habit for which he is forgiven because of his charm and intelligence. According to Maranhão's distinction, the Socratic dialogues are "represented dialogues," written by one author ostensibly reproducing verbal exchanges—exchanges which may or may not have had a verbal origin and in which the author may or may not originally have participated.

Classical dialogues include Galileo's *Dialogue Concerning the Two Chief World Systems—Ptolemaic and Copernican* (1629), David Hume's *Dialogues Concerning Natural Religion* (1779), and a seventeenth-century anonymous poem entitled "Dialogue of the Body and the Soul." We find it interesting that the genre *drama*, while largely made up of dialogue, has not yielded set pieces of dialogue that are memorable: Dramatic monologues are abundant, but we could find no anthologized examples of dramatic dialogues.[22]

Contemporary examples of BD dialogue are found in *Anti-Oedipus: Capitalism and Schizophrenia* (1977) and *A Thousand Plateaus* (1987) by Gilles Deleuze and Filix Guattari (a philosopher and a psychoanalyst, respectively) and in *Conversations on Mind, Matter, and Mathematics* (1995) by Jean-Pierre Changeux and Alain Connes (a biologist and a mathematician). Alluding to their own understanding of BD dialogue, Changeaux and Connes preface their book with the following comments:

Mathematicians and biologists get along fairly well for the most part, but they do not really talk to each other. Their training and interests are so different that conversation sometimes seems impossible (xi). . . . Our book takes the form of a dialogue, because neither one of us knows enough about the other's field to take it upon himself to answer the many questions that arise in each one. The dialogue form has the advantage of allowing each of us to sharpen his views in response to each other's. On certain points we agree; on others—and not necessarily the least important ones!—we disagree. (xiii)

In his note to the American edition, the translator and editor comments that "the original edition consisted of a mostly unedited transcript of the authors' conversations." We suspect the following description of the original French edition could be applied to most transcripts of actual dialogues:

Because the . . . text is frequently choppy and elliptical, as actual conversation often is, and in many places hard to follow, my aim here has been to smooth out the language, to make the technical arguments both more precise and more accessible . . . , and to soften the many sharp shifts and turns of debate as it initially unfolded—without, however, sacrificing the spontaneous quality of principled, passionate quarreling that gives this a prominent place in the literature of friendly dispute for the sake of truth and knowledge. (vii)

This description of process emphasizes the distinctive interactive nature of BD dialogue, a genre that originates in verbal exchange but does not remain there. In its published form it is edited dialogue (for an example, see chapter six below).

B. THE CHARACTER AND FUNCTION OF BD DIALOGUE

BD dialogue has both written and spoken components. We must therefore differentiate the two components and highlight the roles of two speakers instead of one speaker/author. Descriptively, then, BD dialogue is different from other kinds of dialogue because of the presence of two speakers/writers each trained in a different discipline. This difference provides a leading thread to an analysis of the genre. It also forces us to reconsider some aspects of genre theory that are perhaps too easily taken for granted.

Most discussions of text-interpretation assume the written text is the boundary of what is to be interpreted. Ricoeur (1976:35), for example, understands the text as having escaped the bonds of authorial intentionality, of having cut its moorings by having been published and made available to anyone who can read. We essentially agree with Ricoeur's analysis. But in order to explore further those aspects of the creative process present in the text—aspects of the text which may be overlooked unless they are studied as well in terms of the spoken dimension—we focus in this section on the spoken part of BD dialogue, the part of the process of creation that, while entirely spoken, might also be recorded or reproduced in notes by the participants themselves or by someone else. In particular, we take up two aspects of the spoken dimension of BD dialogue: (1) its distinctive kind of purposefulness, and (2) characteristic alterity.

1. Dialogue as Purposeful: A Phenomenology of Speaking

The purposefulness of BD dialogue is attached to the presence of two speakers/writers in a way that makes it possible to expand the idea of purposefulness beyond the literary framework usually employed to discuss the teleology of written texts. We argue that a distinctive kind of purposefulness is present in BD dialogue precisely because of the "stake" the speakers have—their considerable vested interest in their respective disciplines. When speakers attempt to question or speak beyond the bounds of their respective disciplines—i.e., to speak "extradisciplinarily" rather than *ex disciplinam*—they are alert to the possibility that something is at risk in discussing issues in such an "unprofessional" way. While they may have something to say and there may be something to be gained, there is the risk that much could be lost by being undermined or blind-sided by considerations bracketed in the home discipline.[23] We would expect this risk to increase with the cognitive "distance" between speakers (Ricoeur 1978). The speakers' consciousness of all these factors is enhanced by the structure of spoken dialogue. In some sense the genre initiates the behavior of the two speakers: The genre—here, in the structured patterns of verbal exchange—carries the speakers to, through and even beyond what they may initially have "intended."[24] We call this the praxis dimension of genre—the work that it does. To show the particular way the work BD dialogue does is purposeful, we borrow some analysis from communication theory.

Götz Hindelang (1994:40) provides us with a means of parsing the varieties of spoken dialogue that take place between two speakers (Sp1) and (Sp2). Aware that most dialogues are more than passing comments about the weather, Hindelang allows for the possibility of discord between discussants. In particular, he recognizes that those engaged in "purposeful" dialogue may or may not have interests in common (see Fig. 5.1). Hindelang then proceeds to identify speech acts which characterize the minimal forms of purposeful dialogue. For us it is sufficient to identify those combinations of types normally operative in BD dialogue between a scientist and a theologian. And, making the presumption that such dialogues are purposeful

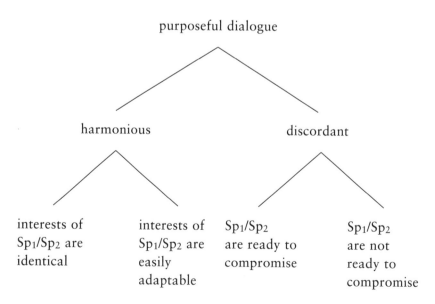

Fig. 5.1 A diagram of purposeful dialogues and their relations (from Hindelang).

(despite the fact that they appear at times not to be), we are able to extract three possible combinations from Fig. 5.1.

Identical interest (far left) is hardly ever possible when the dialogue is bidisciplinary. Rejection of this possibility is based primarily in the disjuncture between the constellations of genres that make up each discipline (in Bakhtin's sense—for an example, see Table I). Unlike *identical interest*, the outcome *easily adaptable* (also under *harmonious*) is possible and often forms the productive dialogue intended in any good-faith effort at making progress toward new understandings jointly held. Discord, however, is unavoidable in BD dialogue; hence *readiness to compromise or not* (under *discordant*) are likely to be the most frequent outcomes.[25] Serious difference is perhaps the greatest hazard to productive dialogue, and can be particularly insidious when it lurks at a lower level, as in the case, for example, of a scientist with a fundamentalist background in conversation with a theologian possessing a more revisionist point of view (or vice versa).

What Hindelang's figure does not do for us is to explore the nuances inherent in the more or less easily adaptable as well as the negative implications associated with *compromise*. **Both the idea of adaptability and the idea of compromise run counter to the productive development of the higher viewpoint as we will show.**

2. Alterity in Dialogue: Merleau-Ponty's Phenomenology of Speaking

One of the major achievements of postmodernist and deconstructionist critics—something like the achievement of the nineteenth-century painters who, it is said, taught us to see landscapes for the first time—has been to disclose "the other" and "otherness" in a new light. This achievement deserves praise even if other parts of deconstructionism—e.g., its adherents' refusal to acknowledge conditions necessary to any evaluation of interpreted reality—seem unnecessarily obstructive. In modernist genre theory, anything preceding the transformation of spoken dialogue into written text was considered irrelevant to interpretation. Today—thanks to the postmodernists and deconstructionists—it is appropriate to reflect on (or, in their terms, to "suspect") the speakers themselves as they appear in the text. Postmodernists want to show how the intention of the author is undone in the ceaseless self-referentiality of language.

In contrast, we want to show how the presence of another human being affects the thinking/speaking process. Toward this end, we enlist Merleau-Ponty's (1973) phenomenological analysis of otherness, as experienced in dialogue, to elucidate the continued sustained potential of the spoken component of BD dialogue. His point is that traces or strands of this spoken component, perceptible in the written component, are likely to go unnoticed altogether if they are analyzed only as speech.

In chapter five of *The Prose of the World* (1973), Merleau-Ponty begins his analysis not with speech but with the appearance of the other (here, the other speaker) in order to understand "the most essential power of speech" (133):

> It is not sufficiently noted that the other is never present face to face. Even when, in the heat of discussion, I directly confront my adversary, it is not in that violent face with its grimace, or even in that voice traveling toward me, that the intention which reaches me is to be found. The adversary is never quite localized; his voice, his gesticulations, his twitches, are only effects, a sort of stage effect, a ceremony. Their producer is so well masked that I am quite surprised when my own responses carry over. This marvelous megaphone becomes embarrassed, gives a few sighs, a few tremors, some *signs of intelligence*. (133)

Here, Merleau-Ponty graphically describes the non-cognitive dimension of dialogue. Moreover, his analysis applies even more forcefully when the "adversaries" are from different academic disciplines. Despite the threat of the other speaker, the dialogue gains qualitatively to the extent that the other's view is infused with one's own.

However, the danger of a purely phenomenological approach is that the dialogue gets lost. In the following passage, Merleau-Ponty shows how one can lose the dialogue in attending to the experience:

Nevertheless, the other is not I and on that account differences must arise. I make the other in my own image, but how *can there be for me an image of myself?* Am I not to the very end of the universe, am I not, by myself, coextensive with everything I can see, hear, understand, or feign? How could there be an outside view upon this totality which I am? From where could it be had? Yet that is just what happens when the other appears to me. To the infinity that was me something else still adds itself; a sprout shoots forth, I grow; I give birth, this other is made from my flesh and blood and yet is no longer me. How is that possible? How can the *cogito* emigrate beyond me, since it is me? The looks with which I scan the world, like a blind man tapping objects with his cane, are seized by someone at the other end and sent back to touch me in turn. (134–35)

The other ceases to threaten and instead perplexes. The perplexity consists in experiencing the other's view of oneself as an "outside view" of what was formerly the self's "totality."

How does one find a productive "outside view" of oneself? Merleau-Ponty could be talking of disciplinary fields in the following quotation, but he is not. "Field" in what follows is the horizon of consciousness from which the self determines what is intelligible and what is not:

Everything is ready in me to receive these testimonies. We must learn how they could ever be introduced so as to get to me, all the more because my own evidence is mine and my field holds for me as the universal locus of being. (136)

One of the paradoxes of bidisciplinary work is that the act of finding a speaker who could engage in BD dialogue—i.e., a person from another discipline who might conceivably be addressing the same issue or problem and who could make a difference in one's own understanding—is known after the fact of its already having occurred.

The mystery of the other—the one who is not me—is never completely decoded. The effect of attempting to speak with someone from another discipline, is to challenge our sense of having absolute and unique knowledge:

Perhaps now we are closer to understanding better the accomplishment language represents for us, how language prolongs and transforms the silent relation with the other. In a sense, the other's words do not pierce our silence. They are unable to give us anything more than his gestures. The same difficulty is involved in understanding how words arranged in propositions can signify anything else to us except our own thought, how the movements of a body patterned into gestures or actions can present us with someone else than ourselves, how we are able to find in these spectacles anything other than we have put into them. The solution is the same. It consists, as far as our silent relation to the other is concerned, in understanding that our sensibility to the world, our synchronized relations to it—that is, our body—the thesis underlying all our experiences removes from our existence the density of an absolute and unique act, making a transferable signification of our 'corporeality,' creating a 'common situation,' and finally yielding the perception of another like ourselves, if not in the absolute of his effective existence then at least in its general outline accessible to us. (139)

What we relinquish of our own academic self-confidence that we have derived from our training makes possible a perception of the other, no longer absolute but accessible to us in what has become a situation we have in common. However, language does not transcend or erase the irreducibility of the differences we have with the other. It simply makes them explicit.

If "otherness" is not overcome by language, neither is rationality reached through solely logical definitions:

Rationality, or the agreement of minds, does not require that we all reach the same idea by the same road, or that significations be enclosed in definitions. It requires only that every experience contain points of catch for all other ideas and that 'ideas' have a configuration. (143)

The configuration of ideas can be another name for subgenres of each discipline in BD dialogue. These subgenres comprise an irreducibility that surrounds each speaker in BD dialogue—a "corporeality" of the discipline made accessible by means of the genre.

Reference is often made to the "dialogue between science and religion." In most cases this is a figure of speech rather than reference to a conversation. However, the sense in which we use the term *dialogue* presupposes two persons, one from each discipline, engaged in conversation with all of the phenomenological attributes described by Merleau-Ponty. The central difficulty associated with the spoken word in an academic setting (as distinct, for example, from the political) is the evanescent character of talk—not only is it cheap, it is gone. In some sense, progress toward furthering the understanding of the relationships between two disparate disciplines depends on preservation in the form of publication. It is true that unresolved disputes do become memorialized in print when they erupt as full-blown controversies. However, the less dramatic process of agreement at what we will later identify as a "higher viewpoint" rarely ignites tabloidal attention.[26]

One element of purposeful dialogue is the ability to sustain a conversation—the ability to move to argument or explanation and back again to conversation. Historically, there have been several models for the relationship between science and religion (Barbour 1990:1–30). When the relationship is modeled as a dichotomy, one could say that conversation is highly improbable because each side expects that the other has nothing to say of importance. With other models the conversation may begin, but the argument is so threatening that it degenerates into saying little more than platitudes.

Our notion of BD dialogue contains the expectation that there is need for serious argument and that argument is not destructive to dialogue. This consideration raises the question of how to include, for example, the classically other—here, how to include feminism or to allow feminism to change the nature of science and theology. Ideally, in BD dialogue, the critique of the disciplines and proposals for change come to be part of what Merleau-Ponty calls the "common situation." We can now see that the attention given to knowing the other and including other voices is not merely a managerial issue. One must learn how to include those voices in the conversation because difference affects not only oneself but also one's discipline.

C. TWO CASES OF INTERPRETATION:
THE TURING TEST (NATURAL SCIENCES) AND THE
HERMENEUTICAL CIRCLE (RELIGIOUS STUDIES)

In this section, the limits of the claims we have made—namely, that BD dialogue is purposeful and that it includes non-linguistic elements as well as verbal conversation and argument—bring us to consider two specific cases in which BD dialogue, in different ways, is put to the test. The question is whether BD dialogue is equally appropriate for all disciplines. If the phenomenology of the speaker in the last section disclosed differences between speakers as human beings, will opening the phenomenology to widely disparate topics of discourse not add difficulties perhaps to the point of their being insurmountable? This is the fungibility factor: the extent to which disciplines are interchangeable in BD dialogue. If they are not interchangeable, then we would expect that the subject matter of some disciplines is more amenable than others to the linguistic mediation alluded to by Merleau-Ponty. To make the point more clearly, how can phenomena of the natural sciences "appear" appropriately as phenomena in BD dialogue?

To understand the nuances of BD dialogue between two academic disciplines it helps to know the role of dialogue in each discipline taken separately. Considered from the point of view of different disciplines, dialogue does different kinds of work. We expect that a discipline like religious studies will have developed a high level of sophistication with respect to human communication, since religious studies takes as its primary focus of concern the role of texts of all kinds in human understanding of the sacred. From the point of view of religion, the dominant issue is one of **interpretation**—is the object under study a text? What does it say? Does what it says change my understanding of the object? On the other hand, dialogue considered from the point of view of the natural sciences is likely to have different characteristics and can be expected to function in a different way. From the point of view of science, the dominant issue is one of **analysis**—what is the object under study? What are its properties? How does it function? The analytical function may also be clear when the dialogue takes the form of mathematical discussion.

That function is clear even when, as in Galileo's *Dialogue Concerning the Two Chief World Systems—Ptolemaic and Copernican*, the dialogue is entirely expressed in prose. In chapter seven, we explore the possibility of generalizing what we mean by text in order to include more examples analyzed in the natural sciences than would otherwise be the case.

We have chosen the Turing Test as an example of the use of dialogue in science, in this case a dialogue invented to answer questions or support judgments regarding the relation between human and machine intelligence. We have chosen the hermeneutical spiral as an example of a dialogical structure in religion, in this case a dialogue to answer questions of understanding or judgments about understanding. The Turing Test is intended as a measure of whether or not a computer can be considered to be intelligent and selfconscious. The hermeneutical spiral (circle) models the extent to which the human desire to know can be understood and the process of coming to a new understanding can be known.

1. Dialogue as Test of Intelligence (the Turing Test)

Can a computer be programmed to think the way a human being thinks? In a paper entitled "Computing in Cognitive Science," Zenon W. Pylyshyn, wrote

> . . . the Gestalt psychologist Wolfgang Köhler viewed machines as too rigid to serve as models of mental activity. The latter, he claimed, are governed by what he called *dynamic factors*,—an example of which are self-distributing field effects, such as the effects that cause magnetic fields to be redistributed when we introduce new pieces of metal—as opposed to *topographical factors*—which are structurally rigid. He [Köhler] wrote:
>
>> To the degree to which topographical conditions are rigidly given, and not to be changed by dynamic factors, their existence means the exclusion of certain forms of function, and the restriction of the processes to the possibilities compatible with those conditions. . . . This extreme relation between dynamic factors and imposed topographical conditions is almost entirely

realized in typical machines . . . we do not construct machines in which dynamic factors are the main determinants of the form of operation. (Köhler 1947:65)

[Pylyshyn continues] That computers violate this claim is one of their most important and unique characteristics. Their topographic structure is completely rigid, yet they are capable of maximal plasticity of function. It is this very property that led [Alan] Turing soon after to speculate that computers would be capable in principle of exhibiting intelligent behavior. For example, he devoted an important early philosophical paper in 1950 (Turing 1950) to an exposition of this idea. Turing argued that a computer could in principle be made to exhibit intelligent activity to an arbitrary degree. He claimed that a machine should qualify as being intelligent if it could successfully play the "imitation game"—that is, fool a human observer, with whom it could communicate only through a keyboard and terminal, so that the observer could not discriminate between it and another person. (Pylyshyn 1989)[27]

The Turing Test—named after the brilliant English scientist and mathematician who devised it—is a device for answering the question of whether a computer can think in the way human beings can think. The test was based on an English parlor game called "Imitation Game" in which an interrogator is challenged to identify the gender of two hidden persons, one male and the other female, on the basis of their answers to questions put to each of them separately (Hofstadter and Dennett 1981:71). For our purposes the Turing Test of computer intelligence (or self-consciousness, i.e., human-like mentation) may be described in the following way: a person, at a distance, communicates with two respondents (via telephone, for example), one on line A and one on line B (one line connected to a computer, the other to a human being). The person does not know which line connects to a computer and which connects to a human being. If the person, switching between lines and comparing the two "conversations," cannot determine which party (Line A or Line B) is the computer and which (Line B or Line A) is the human being, the computer is judged to have human intelligence.

2. Challenges to the Turing Test

John Searle challenged this test, asserting that it fails to provide a basis for deciding whether or not a computer can be considered intelligent. To make his case Searle invokes what he calls the "Chinese Room" argument. Here is Searle's description of his argument:

> Imagine that you carry out the steps in a program for answering questions in a language you do not understand. I do not understand Chinese, so I imagine that I am locked in a room with a lot of boxes of Chinese symbols (the data base). I get small bunches of Chinese symbols passed to me (questions in Chinese), and I look up in a rule book (the program) what I am supposed to do. I perform certain operations on the symbols in accordance with the rules (that is, I carry out the steps in the program) and give back small bunches of symbols to those outside the room (answers to the questions). I am the computer implementing a program for answering questions in Chinese, but all the same I do not understand a word of Chinese. And this is the point: *If I do not understand Chinese solely on the basis of implementing a computer program for understanding Chinese, than neither does any other digital computer solely on that basis because no digital computer has anything I do not have.* (Searle 1995a:61)

The **Turing Test** has failed. Notice that the **computer** did not fail the test—in fact it passed! But Searle maintains that we cannot conclude anything about the understanding possessed by a computer merely on the basis of its passing this dialogue test. That is, Searle believes that his thought experiment demonstrates that the computer does not have the understanding the test was presumed to detect. For Searle, human intelligence depends on the presence of semantic knowledge as well as syntactic knowledge. Searle concludes that the Turing Test measures syntactic knowledge only and that syntactic knowledge is not an adequate test of intelligence. In other words, the measurement of intelligence must take into account both semantics and syntactics. While we agree that the test fails, we are less certain than Searle that human "intelligence" (or what goes for selfconsciousness) is **in practice** measured in terms of both semantic and syntactic knowledge—hence only in the commonsense perception has the Turing Test succeeded. While we agree in principle with Searle, we think he overlooks the role that "style" (or lack of it) plays in human judgments regarding intelligence.

Moreover, dialogue was proposed by Turing as the basis for determining the intelligence of a computer. But is the genre *dialogue* the genre of this test? Why doesn't the test work? We think the answers lie in the fact that the original test was formulated on an inadequate conception of dialogue. As conceived by Turing, the test involved a computer answering questions posed by a human being. We have already mentioned the inadequacy of the interview model of dialogue. In this question/answer scenario, the answerer is constantly being "led" by the interviewer: No real dialogue takes place.

An example of human/computer "dialogue"—one which is also in question/answer form—is the ELIZA program (Weizenbaum 1965). The program is constructed in such a way as to imitate a clinical psychologist. Here is an example of a short session with ELIZA. In this first session the responding human being functions cooperatively in the "dialogue."

First Interview

    HELLO. MY NAME IS ELIZA. WHAT'S YOURS?
    prof. BD
    ALRIGHT, PROF., WHAT WOULD YOU LIKE TO TALK ABOUT TODAY?
    snakes
    IT IS OFTEN HELPFUL TO CONFRONT OUR FEARS.
    i don't want to think about them.
    I FIND IT HARD TO BELIEVE THAT YOU DON'T WANT TO THINK ABOUT THEM.
    i don't like them.
    ARE YOU CONSTANTLY AFRAID?
    only when i see a snake.
    WHAT IS IT THAT YOU REALLY WANT TO FIND OUT?
    how to overcome my fear.
    HOW LONG HAVE YOU BEEN AFRAID?
    all my life.
    I SEE YOUR POINT.
    can you help me?
    I DON'T THINK I CAN HELP YOU.
    can anyone help me?

EVERYBODY NEEDS HELP SOONER OR LATER.
i need help now.
WE ALL HAVE BASIC NEEDS AND DESIRES.
are you afraid of snakes?
LET'S DISCUSS SOME OF THE THINGS THAT FRIGHTEN YOU.
[end interview]

In the second interview below, the human being, responding **unco-operatively** to ELIZA, attempts to disrupt the computer by giving responses which are intended to confound.

Second interview

HELLO. MY NAME IS ELIZA. WHAT'S YOURS?
i will not say.
ALRIGHT, I, WHAT WOULD YOU LIKE TO TALK ABOUT TODAY?
whatever you would like.
IT APPEARS THAT WE ARE ALIKE IN MANY WAYS.
are you like you?
I DEFINITELY AM NOT LIKE ME.
who are you like?
I AM NOT SURE I KNOW, ME.
do you want to know?
I'M SORRY BUT I DON'T WANT TO KNOW.
it is important to know oneself.
IN YOUR OPINION, HOW FREQUENTLY IS IT IMPORTANT TO KNOW ONESELF?
always.
I FIND IT DIFFICULT TO AGREE WITH YOU, ME.
are you sure?
FORTUNATELY, I'M SURE.
then you are not like me.
I MUST DISAGREE WITH YOU.
and i must disagree with you.
I FEEL THAT WE SHOULD BE DISCUSSING YOU, NOT ME!
[end interview]

Most people experimenting with the ELIZA program for the first time find it hard to believe that there is not a human being at the other end. But what is of special interest to us in this problem is the degree to which the "conversations" that take place between the tester and computer or intelligent person can be considered dialogues. We think that the failure of the Turing Test and the wizardry of

ELIZA are grounded in the fact that what takes place in each case is merely syntactic. There are no semantics. It is **not** dialogue. This question should be examined at least in part because it forces us to focus on the difference between a dialogue on the one hand and a mere exchange of questions and answers on the other. We begin by first reconstructing the Turing Test as a true dialogue. We then explore why the test works in the reconstructed version although it fails in the original version.

In both the Turing Test and the ELIZA "dialogues," the very fact that one half of a participant pair can carry on without any sense of what is being said—without any semantic knowledge—invalidates the conclusion that what is going on is authentic dialogue. We therefore reconstruct the test as follows: Rather than having the distant person communicating with a computer on the one hand, and a human being on the other, we require two computers to communicate with each other and two persons also to converse with each other—both pairs discussing a topic chosen by a testing observer. The new test is compared with the old in Fig. 5.2.

What is the significance of the addition of an observer in Fig. 5.2? The person making the observation is no longer providing continuous input into the dialogue. Participants in the dialogue have to mold the conversation on the basis of actual strands of intelligibility. By contrast the observer does not run the dialogue. By removing the observer as a contributor to the discussion, we reestablish the need for the semantic element. Two people cannot talk intelligently to each other and not know what they are talking about whereas a computer and a person can merely talk to each other without the computer's knowing what it is talking about.

The crucial difference in the revised test is that we have taken the observer out of the business of pulling the strings. If, on the basis of the two dialogues, the observer cannot distinguish the two computers from the pair of human beings, the computers will be judged to have human intelligence. If the two computers do not exhibit the semantic capabilities of the human beings, the observer will easily distinguish between them and human beings. If computers do know what they are talking about, the observer will have difficulty making the distinction between them and knowledgeable human beings.

In terms of reader reception theory, the observer will have to judge

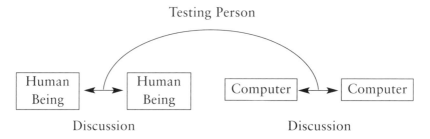

Fig. 5.2 The Turing Test (standard version) as diagramed on the top shows how the inputs from human beings can be used by computers to enhance their mimicry of human intelligence. The Turing Test (revised) on the bottom shows computers insulated from human inputs during the test so that their interactions can be independently compared with human interactions.

whether or not the computer can "read" its partner. If the computers exemplify a reciprocal ability to "read" (i.e., not only listen to, but hear the other), they will be judged to be intelligent. That is the semantic dimension. In Searle's' terms, the semantic dimension is knowing what the symbols mean. Being a reader is precisely what Searle could not be in the Chinese room—he does not understand Chinese! Is it then any wonder that the semantics involved play a central and indispensable role in the dialogue process?

Since syntactics alone are now not sufficient to pass the test for intelligence, we have moved from false dialogue to true dialogue. To understand the difference here we need to explore the characteristics of dialogue from the point of view of religious studies.

3. Dialogue as Hermeneutical Circle (Horizon Analysis)

The concept of the hermeneutical circle or spiral has been effectively used with respect to reader and text. In the case of reader and text, the spiral[28] causes a change (often taken as the development of understanding) in the reader's understanding of a written text. We wish to apply the concept to the case of two speakers in BD dialogue. In the case of speaker and hearer, the spiral (of taking turns) causes changes in the understandings of the two persons in productive dialogue. Should one person exclaim, "You're not listening to me!" it would be a clue that the other might have broken the spiral.

The hermeneutical circle is a long-lived model of human understanding, dating back at least as far as Anselm who, in the eleventh century C.E., gave its first formulation: Understanding gives rise to belief; belief is always informed by understanding. With the development of general hermeneutics in the nineteenth and twentieth centuries, the circle was reformulated in several other terms. Ricoeur, a hermeneutical phenomenologist, criticized as being "too subjective" the earlier formulations (including Anselm's) and suggested the addition of "text" as one of the elements. He later added "world" as a necessary element with the resulting emphasis on the methodological aspect of the circle:

> It is the circle constituted by the object which orders faith and the method which regulates understanding. There is a circle because the exegete is not his own master. What he wants to understand is what the text says; the task of understanding is therefore governed by what is at issue in the text itself. (Ricoeur 1974b: 389).

While the Turing Test tries to determine the limits and extent of computer "intelligence" in comparison with human intelligence, the hermeneutical spiral assesses the "horizon" of a human being. A "horizon" is defined as "maximum vision from a determinate point of view."[29] Horizon analysis makes a distinction between the questions a human being can ask and answer, those she can ask but cannot answer, and questions she does not yet even know to ask. The advantages of thinking of BD dialogue in terms of the model of the hermeneutical spiral are several. First of all, it is a process model that assumes a developing relationship between one's beliefs and one's understandings. The model initially assumes, as William James wrote, that "we believe as much as we can. We would believe everything if we only could" (James 1981:928). Or as in Hans-Georg Gadamer's theory, human beings enter consciousness with prejudgments (prejudices)—without which they would be incapable of attending to or orienting themselves with respect to objects in their worlds. Moreover, since the Enlightenment, the model of the hermeneutical spiral requires a critical element, most familiar in the twentieth century as "the hermeneutics of suspicion" introduced by Karl Marx, Friederich Nietzsche, Sigmund Freud, and feminist thinkers. Second, given the probability that there are initially two positions in BD dialogue, the model anticipates disagreement as well as changes in understanding and perhaps even belief based on the interaction between the two dialogue partners.

From the perspective of religious studies, dialogue is regarded as an interpretive algorithm, a method. What is the hermeneutical circle as it occurs in BD dialogue? At the very beginning, the speakers discover a mutual interest in a particular issue or topic. This discovery is akin to the process of discovering one's prejudgments or assumptions. In BD dialogue, the discovery is sometimes mutual, sometimes more surprising to one speaker than the other, often challenging or even threatening to both. Each speaker contributes a proposal with respect to an issue or topic being discussed. Sp_1's contribution often causes Sp_2's contribution to be modified and vice versa. Mutual reformulation may take place, particularly when each sees the issue differently. Although the two positions may be mutually irreducible to a common understanding, according to the model of the hermeneutical spiral each speaker retains and unpredictably later retrieves the other person's contribution by understanding it.

In hermeneutical theory, alterity first appeared as the problem of understanding another author. The Romanticist ideal of one's understanding another better than one understands oneself was based on terrain which posited the meaning of a text in the intention of the author **behind** the text. As a result of modernist New Criticism and postmodernist deconstructionism, however, language itself became the major instantiator of meaning.

BD dialogue as spoken communication between two scholars from different academic fields shares both the dangers and the promises inherent in the interpretation of texts. There is always the danger that, in the attempt and the claim to '"know" what the other person is saying, the particularity and the authority of the other is either lost or made subservient. But the possibility of loss and domination is legitimized by the desire on the part of both scholars to reach common understanding of the issue at hand. Robert Bernasconi (1995) deals with both the negative and positive effects of the possibility of understanding across "cultural divisions" in his essay entitled "'You Don't Know What I'm Talking About': Alterity and the Hermeneutical Ideal." Bernasconi's own use of Gadamer's approach to understanding a text across historical "distances" to address a problem inherent in a multicultural society can also be applied to the possibility of understanding across the distances between academic disciplines. Since these academic distances have demonstrably made institutions centers for the development of intellectual multicultural micro societies, the possibility of multicultural understanding can reasonably be transferred to bidisciplinary understanding on many of the same theoretical grounds.

Moreover, when from a different academic discipline we confront another's text, another's history, another's culture, or another's different understanding of an issue, we are ourselves also confronted. The risk that we will dominate or impose meaning on another is balanced by the call the other makes to us to change—or to use religious language, to convert—to turn our own perspective toward, or even into, that of the other.

Posing the problem of alterity as a possibility of either loss or gain, or both loss and gain, seems to us better than assuming a dichotomy between particular disciplines. In the nineteenth century, for example, what was taken to be a dichotomy between the humanities and the natural sciences was thought to have been solved by the creation of the social sciences. But the social sciences today often simply displace the original problem. For example, Mark Kingswell (1995) characterizes Charles Taylor's (another social scientist's) attempt to create an interpretive social science as "'unformalizable,' lacking 'brute data' and a 'verification procedure' and therefore 'nonarbitrable by further evidence.'" In this revised kind of social science,

Kingswell thinks, "each side can only [sic] make appeal to deeper insight on the part of the other":

> Lacking any algorithm of theoretical proof, we face a kind of conversation among those who disagree, each trying to display the error—or, as it may be in cases of limited insight, the illusion—of their opponents. Since we cannot coherently appeal to some authoritative conception of the ways *things* are, we must appeal to our own set of (possibly conflicting) insights concerning who *we* are.

Kingswell agrees with Taylor that such a shift would be "radically shocking and unassimilable to the mainstream of modern [natural] science" since the "context-eliminative bent of that tradition of science fails to take account of essential things" (16–17).

Is such a shift, however, likely to overcome the earlier dichotomy? In terms of BD dialogue, the answer is not to eliminate data, verification, and the search for evidence as Taylor is taken by Kingswell to suggest—but to make them visible as non-linguistic elements to be interpreted in BD dialogue. It would be ironic if the shift to eliminate data, verification and the search for evidence were made just as other efforts to better contextualize understandings begin to appear within science.[30] These efforts on the part of natural scientists are not dreamt of in Taylor's notion of "conversation" between social sciences and philosophers **about** the natural sciences—a counter example of BD dialogue that presumes that prior differences in the disciplines be relinquished before conversation can take place.

D. THE GOALS OF BIDISCIPLINARY DIALOGUE: THE HIGHER VIEWPOINT

We have remarked on the risks inherent in BD dialogue. If one is to engage in risky behavior one should have good reasons for doing so. In this final section we explore the motivation for bidisciplinary dialogue and describe how progress toward more unified *Weltanschauungen* might be made. Why is there need for BD dialogue? The answer is found in the present day flight from the disciplines as well as in the postmodern rejection of the idea of discipline itself. In addressing issues of genre and the academic disciplines, one confronts the negative aspects of the present structure of the academy—in particular, the fragmentation of academic substance and the isolation that subsequent insulation has created.

The gymnasium where Plato taught had no need for BD dialogue. And we cannot fault Plato for writing represented dialogue rather than providing us with transcripts of verbal exchanges between scholars of the time. First of all, the very notion of a transcript violated Plato's central respect for the function of memory, and secondly, he could have had no idea of the divisions of academic thought we know today. The academic person of that time is understood to have possessed a degree of intellectual unity we can only dream of. Every subject of human inquiry was understood to be addressable by any member of the academy. Accordingly there was no need for a special conception of a person from one discipline conversing with a person from another.

Today, however, human knowledge is a hodgepodge of subjects and methods so disparate that it is difficult for scholars in one discipline even to respect the work of those in another. Many scientists view talk of deconstruction as ridiculous, while many scholars in the humanistic disciplines view science as feeding a diabolical technology. If the human intellectual condition is to achieve some measure of coherence, we need to talk to one another with that particular purpose in mind. We need also to understand what dialogue, particularly BD dialogue, is capable of producing. Production here implies the possibility of some new state of understanding on the part of the participants—the root implication of Hindelang's category of "purposeful dialogue." How do such new states of understanding come about?

Oscillating between harmony and discord, two speakers from different disciplines address questions and issues of common interest as they seek resolution of their differences. However, within the framework of the fields of meaning available to the discussants, resolution may not be possible. It may be the case that the conceptual net in the field of one of the disciplines is incommensurate with the net in the other. What then?

Let us review Hindelang's diagram of possible outcomes of purposeful dialogues (see section B above). We are concerned here with *discordant* outcomes, the right-hand side of the diagram. Besides Sp_1's and Sp_2's *willingness or unwillingness to compromise* (implying that each gives up something in return for getting something, a process that does not yield new knowledge), we have found three other possible outcomes of discord in BD dialogue not diagramed by Hindelang. First, the discussants can agree to disagree and abandon the conversation or change the subject. (We suspect that this outcome is often accepted more or less by default in the interest of collegiality.) Second, Sp_1 may persuade Sp_2 (or vice versa). This outcome does not lead to new knowledge either.

There is, however, a third possibility: The pressure to find agreement (a view in common) may force change in one or both of the conceptual nets of the persons involved, especially in those cases where common interests are strong or vested. This pressure to find agreement may come from insight into the possibility that a higher viewpoint might be possible, a viewpoint from which what had appeared as difference may be subsumed into a more complete view.[31] We need to emphasize that the higher viewpoint is a synthesis of two views—an amalgam—that leaves the individual points of view unchanged. Such conceptual changes are not always possible nor do they always take place when they are possible, but if a higher viewpoint **is** possible a new level of understanding can be found.

We have found BD dialogue fertile ground for the emergence of higher viewpoints. In the sense that BD dialogue is a method (as we have presented it here) rather than a published text, many such dialogues have been and will continue to be lost—not all BD dialogue gets published. What does is rarely published as dialogue, edited or otherwise. Indeed almost all of our own joint writing[32] (including this one) has metamorphosed into more scholarly language as the individual voices of BD faded away. One of the reasons we welcomed this opportunity to write about BD dialogue is our felt need to make the genre explicit in the hope of fostering more productive dialogues between the academic disciplines—dialogues that, we believe, for the health of the academy, must no longer be postponed—dialogues that are published in the original genre with the different academic voices intact.

6

A Scientist and a Theologian See the World: Compromise or Synthesis?

A scientist (for whom the world is the universe) and a theologian (for whom the world is planet Earth) engage in dialogue, not contrived Platonic or Galilean dialogue, but actual bidisciplinary dialogue that strives for higher viewpoint. S: Is the preservation of the human species a primary human responsibility? T: It may be a responsibility we share with God. S: The human species has a limited future if confined to planet Earth. We must diversify our habitat by colonizing space. T: We are responsible for other life on the planet as well. The discussants conclude that besides protecting Earth ecologies, we should create new ecologies in space.

MG: ALLAN AS A PHYSICIST AND I AS THEOLOGIAN ARE ABOUT TO ENGAGE in a bidisciplinary dialogue in which we explore and attempt to integrate our two views of the world. The Templeton Symposium encourages us to express both our individual and our professional views, and Allan and I will be doing that in the spirit of Sir John Templeton's statement that "We are here for the future."

This article was originally delivered at the Templeton Symposium, "Science and Religion: Two Ways of Experiencing and Interpreting the World," organized by *Zygon: Journal of Religion and Science* and the Chicago Center for Religion and Science, September 1993. The article was published in *Zygon* 29 (December 1994), 619–38.

AMR: By dialogue we don't mean something like either the Platonic dialogues or the dialogue one finds in Galileo's last book, *Dialogues Concerning Two New Sciences* ([1638] 1914). Both Plato and Galileo created "fall guys"—shills for the opposing point of view. In those dialogues, one speaker is clearly intended to be knowledgeable or right and the others naive or wrong.

MG: In contrast with those dialogues, we presume in ours that each of us has something to contribute in an effort to reach a higher viewpoint . . . .

AMR: . . . and that we have a chance of reaching a higher viewpoint if we don't demolish each other in the process.

MG: It is true that these discussions often don't go smoothly. Our use of the term *higher viewpoint* is similar to Lonergan's conception of a higher viewpoint as he describes it in his book *Insight: A Study of Human Understanding* (1957). There *higher viewpoint* refers to the succession of insights that occur in different contexts as human beings face up to and respond to ever more complex demands on their capacities to know.

Lonergan gives as an example the development of algebra after the operations of arithmetic became insufficient to answer questions about quantification and measurement. Lonergan's description of a lower viewpoint in successive situations is also apt. He said, "timely and fruitful ideas are disregarded," and the non-implementation of these ideas deprive subsequent stages "both of the further ideas, to which they give rise, and of the correction that they and their retinue would bring to the ideas that are implemented" (1957: 229).

AMR: We'll have more to say about higher viewpoint and bidisciplinary method after attempting integration of our views in this dialogue. Science and theology have developed into disparate disciplines in contemporary culture. For now, just bear in mind that each of us is speaking from a different perspective and that each sees the world in a different way.

MG: In our book on metaphoric process (1984), we explored the senses in which, epistemologically, scientists and theologians have much in common. There we argued that, as knowers, the scientist and the theologian function in much the same ways. But views of the **objects** of scientific and theological inquiry are likely to differ more than do acts of knowing in the two disciplines.

AMR: In earlier work, we tried to develop a common view of the objects of scientific and theological inquiry by including them all under a generalized conception of text (see chapter seven). The approach we take today moves toward a **synthesis** of the two views that does not require a common view.

THE DIALOGUE

MG: During our flight to Chicago, Allan, you said your view of the world, a scientist's view, was like the view pictured on the cover of the symposium brochure—the famous NASA view of Earth from space. As a theologian *world* is more apt to mean for me what it does in Andrew Marvell's "Had we but world enough and time."[33]

I want to distinguish between theological views and general religious views. Both a religious scholar's and a theologian's view of the world are highly phenomenological and take multiple aspects of religious experience as their general focus. Religious experience has to do with freedom, authenticity, and ultimacy. Theological reflection has to do with all that comes to the attention in the light of religious experience. For theologians, this totality of experience is related to the experience of God. For some theologians, this totality is the experience of God; for others, the world itself may become sacred. This explicit attempt to understand the whole as it ought to be is what makes theology a normative discipline. Second, for a theologian, the world is the place of being. The German philosopher Martin Heidegger called the phenomenon of being human *Dasein*, or "being in world." It wouldn't be far off the mark to say that, for a theologian, the world is wherever human being is.

AMR: I'm speaking, then, with the right kind of scholar. Since I want to raise a question about the relationship between God and the human species I should talk with a theologian. The issues we are concerned with are issues of science and theology more than they are science and religion. So is *world* for a theologian the entire cosmos as experienced, say, by a cosmologist or is it planet Earth?

MG: Earth. I really mean *terra firma*—world for a theologian is first and foremost the place where human beings are. Therefore, environmental issues, for example, are likely to be close to the sensitivities of a theologian. If one of the perennial religious senses is that of wonder at one's own being in the world, another is a passion that **other** human beings have the wherewith to sustain a similar sense of wonder. In sum, the theological view of the world is inveterately anthropocentric in the sense that it is responsive to human needs and claims. It is theocentric in the sense that it takes seriously the question of god or goddess as the ultimate object of human experience.

AMR: But it seems to me that describing the theologian's view of the world as theocentric can be understood in two different ways: It can mean either that the theologian sees the world from God's point of view or that the theologian understands the world to have God at its center. In science, it is more common to use the word anthropocentric, or geocentric, or heliocentric to distinguish the nature of the theoretical model that is being called up. I have no trouble with your saying that a theologian's view of the world is theocentric if you mean that the theory of the world has God at its center. However if you mean that you see the world from where God is or that you understand the world as God understands the world, I would have trouble using the adjective theocentric.

MG: Theology has always been careful not to claim God's view. The mysterious God, the incomprehensible God—these all implicitly disclaim being able to see the world from where God is. On the other hand, the view that God/ess is the center of the universe has been a long-standing metaphor. The psalmist, for example, proclaims that all creation glorifies God and that human beings give a voice to this central magnification of the sacred. Now let's have the physicist's view of the world.

AMR: You're right about the physicist's use of world tending to mean the planet Earth as viewed from space. That would hold even for, say, a geologist who might nonetheless go along with *terra firma*. However, physicists view Earth in an astronomical context as a planetary body rotating and revolving around a rather common type G2 star, one of perhaps 900 billion stars in our medium-sized Milky Way Galaxy. The garden-variety nature of our star has prompted some scientists to propose that solar systems like ours are also common-place and that a significant fraction of them include a planet like ours—suitable for life. This kind of thinking has inspired SETI, the Search for Extraterrestrial Intelligence. While I don't object to sci-entists listening for signals from outer space, I am not myself a pro-ponent of SETI. I think the existence of another planet like ours is far less likely than the SETI people do. Bear in mind that we have an incomplete understanding of the origin of our solar system, so we are on shaky ground when we say that significant numbers of other planetary systems like ours exist. If we are concerned about the con-tinuation of intelligent life in the universe, prudence would call for us to assume that we are alone. Is the continuation of intelligent life in the universe a theological issue?

MG: The question of the continuation of intelligent life in the uni-verse becomes a theological issue when the continuation of intelli-gent life is related to the question of God: the biblical God of creation is understood to have existed prior to human life. In the biblical understanding of God, there is no reason to expect that the contin-uation of human life is necessary to the continued existence of God. But that's not the understanding of God you want to pursue. So for the purpose of argument, let's assume that God as now conceived is necessarily linked to human existence. Then we can ask whether God as now understood would exist in the future if there were no longer intelligent life in the universe. That human beings are necessary to the existence of God or at least assumed in the question might be argued by theologians who hold the panentheistic view.

AMR: Interest in the God of creation has been rekindled by the new understandings of the origins of the universe that cosmologists have developed over the past twenty-five years. The religious dimension of these understandings has been inscribed in what is called the anthropic principle—the apparent fine-tuning of the universe so that its laws and structure appear to be critically adjusted to make human life possible. Some physicists and theologians have seen in the anthropic principle evidence for the existence of a God of creation.

I am myself more interested in the questions the principle might be understood to raise about the works and intentions of human beings toward the cosmos and the importance of intelligent life in the universe to a contemporary understanding of God. If the universe was created the way it is in order to make the evolution of human life possible, then it seems to me we can infer that the continuation of earthly life in the cosmos continues to have the importance expressed in the story of Noah, where God, determined not to eliminate all human life, is said to have ordered Noah to build the ark and to take all creatures two-by-two to keep their kind alive. The anthropic principle seems to suggest that intelligent life is important in our universe. On the other hand, as a latter-day teleology—as a way of providing evidence for the existence of God in the cosmos, if you will—the anthropic principle just doesn't work for me.

MG: Why doesn't it work for you?

AMR: Its logical structure is tautologous—necessarily true. The universe **must** have a structure that permits human life if we are to be observers of it. In this connection I like Rudolf Kippenhahn's remark (quoted in Breuer 1990), that "we should beware of falling prey to the logic of the medieval monk who averred that we should be grateful to God for arranging things so that the Sun shines during the day rather than at night when it is no use to us" (p. ix).

MG: Hmmm—. The anthropic principle is a mixed blessing for a theologian as well. It can be understood as yet another attempt to prove the existence of God—an attempt which, although it is perhaps more appropriate for our time, seems, like the classical proofs, to claim too much. For example, the ontological proof seems today to rely too heavily on classical logic; the cosmological proof, to move too quickly to universal conclusions; and the teleological proof, to claim too precisely for the analogical imagination. On the other hand, the **proofs**, old and new, do at the least give evidence of the propensity of human beings to ask limit-questions—questions that we can ask but can't answer—and these questions point to the religious dimension of human intelligence.

AMR: I wonder if the view of the world as sacred—a view you said earlier was held by some theologians—I wonder if that view isn't also a limit-question. We do ask about the future of planet Earth but we can't answer. Ecologists can't tell us what the world will be like in the future even if we follow the courses of action they advocate today.

MG: These days most serious and intelligent persons care about the future of planet Earth. Postmodernists' view that reality is embodied in the structures of language and institutions has lent poignancy to this concern because of the overwhelming power of destruction now available to human beings. At the same time, theologians, like Sallie McFague in her book *Models of God: Theology for an Ecological, Nuclear Age* (1987), make the case that the quest for absolute power was mirrored theologically in the conception of God as having supreme power. These theologians question the adequacy of such an understanding of God. Many of these same theologians would prefer a model of God as conservator.

AMR: My environmentalist friends tell me what we should be doing to forestall the scenario we fear—the destruction of Earth's ecosystem. I wonder if they think that preserving the quality of our environment on Earth will preserve the human species. Sometimes I think they would welcome the loss of the human species if that loss would forestall the destruction of our planet's ecosystem. If they think the Earth can be preserved in that way, they are neglecting the extraterrestrial threats to the environment. We need to realize that we can't protect Earth's biosphere against all possibilities of destruction. Perhaps we've given the wrong answer to the question, "What's the problem?" Perhaps the first problem is the preservation of the human species. And perhaps preserving the human species means migrating into outer space.

MG: If human beings were to propagate into space, how much longer might human life exist in the universe?

AMR: If we stay only on Earth, we might last anywhere from a few decades to a few millennia. However, if we begin to inhabit space before Earth's ecosystem is destroyed, human life might last anywhere from a few million years to the end of the universe. It depends on how far and how fast human beings spread out, first from Earth, and then from the Sun. The most serious threat is the one that is most immediate, and that appears to be the possibility of Earth being struck by a large asteroid, one of the kind that may have made Earth uninhabitable for the dinosaurs.

MG: But that was millions of years ago. If there were still asteroids in the solar system that might hit Earth, wouldn't they be visible to astronomers?

AMR: Our ability to see asteroids in our neighborhood is much improved with the presence of the Hubble telescope in space, especially since the Hubble optics have been repaired. And a serious proposal has been made to initiate an asteroid-watch program with the intention of intercepting and deflecting any asteroid found to be in an orbit that would bring it too near Earth.

MG: You mean, blow it up before it got to us?

AMR: That might be one way. Alternatively, it might be necessary and possible to push it out of the way with a large rocket. It depends on how far away the asteroid is when it is first seen, in other words, how much time there is before possible impact with Earth.

MG: How much time do we have before such a collision is likely?

AMR: That's hard to say. Some scientists think that massive objects hit Earth with a frequency of the order of once every twenty million years. Numbers of this kind are based on the rates of prior extinctions of species found in the fossil record. In mentioning a number like twenty million I don't mean to imply that we have that much time before the next hit. A massive collision has some probability of occurring even in the next ten years or hundred years—the longer the period you consider, the higher is the probability.

Another limit is the time we have before the Sun begins its next evolutionary move to become a red giant star. That eventuality will make the entire inner solar system uninhabitable. By that time, about five billion years from now, human beings should have begun migrating to orbits around other stars. That migration will take place from space and not from Earth. The crucial move is the first one—from Earth into high orbit around Earth. That move is technologically within our present capabilities.

MG: Even if we were to decide that we should develop colonies in space, doesn't the recent failure of the Mars mission suggest that we may not have the capability of populating space?

AMR: There are a couple of responses that can be made to that objection. Number one, we have gotten very good at flying all over Earth and we still have an occasional failure: Once in a while planes crash. So a mission failure should not suggest that we don't have technological capability. Number two, that mission had no human beings aboard. There was no intelligent life available there to respond to an emergency, to repair or replace a nonfunctional piece of equipment. A spacecraft with a crew has a greater change of completing its mission than spacecraft of the same complexity that has no one aboard. Apollo 13 taught us that.

MG: Granting that we could live off Earth, then, do you think we should commit large sums of money to a major effort to develop space for human beings?

AMR: My short answer to that question is yes. I think we have responsibility to preserve earthly life. It seems to me that a theologian's view of the world might help with this question. Are there any clues that might indicate that God expects us to take on such responsibility?

MG: I don't recall the question's being raised in quite that way. Are you suggesting that we need to have a sense of what we are doing and why we are doing it—that we need to have a goal?

AMR: People used to speak of the will of God. Is there any sense of God's will in this picture? In other words, do we have a mandate with respect to the future of earthly life? Are we charged with major responsibility here? The Bible tends to talk about election and covenant and a goal that is eschatological—but without details. So insofar as human beings are trying to find perfect existence by doing God's will rather than things contrary to God's will, how are they to find out what that is—particularly with regard to the situation of a threatened world? How can we know if we are on the "right track"?

MG: First of all, I'd hesitate to use the term *God's will* to designate the "right track." The concept of God's will is difficult to work with in contemporary theology. It belongs to classical faculty theory and has connotations of an all-powerful, omniscient God who wills particular things in advance with a minimum of human participation. I can't speak about God's will.

AMR: Well then, let's weaken the question substantially and ask about God's desires. If those desires are to be fulfilled, human beings are going to have to cooperate. We have to participate in the action that leads to the fulfillment of those desires. But to participate we have to have some sense of what the goal is. Can theology help us here?

MG: One direction is to think about the whole network of terms referring to God's desires, some of which we have already used— mandate, will, participation, co-creation, frustration, lure, design, cooperation, initiation. Second, I think that it is important to avoid jumping to a course of action from which there can be no returning. The concept of a reversible process, which I think originated in your discipline, would be a good compromise: ideally, whatever direction we embark on should be reversible if new evidence calls for a change in direction. Embarking on a course of action of this magnitude— one that necessarily destroys other options—is at least as questionable as the intent to take no action. Specifically, we should not cease investing in the preservation of life on Earth even as we invest in extensions of habitations beyond Earth. But as your discipline also makes clear, as in the theory of thermodynamics, many processes are not reversible, like it or not.

AMR: Precisely. And especially for this reason, there still remains the question of goal. Do we think, for example, that the issue is one of preserving Earth or of preserving earthly life? These different goals may require different responses.

MG: Well, that's what we're about, to suggest that in times of great conflict, and when the needs of people are not only immense, but known in an immense way—known almost immediately in our modern communication system—it's tempting to arbitrate the immediate needs of people (jobs or the environment) rather than to argue for an expensive space program that promises major results only in the long run. I think that when you have a plurality of positions, it is best initially to encourage the expression and critical discussion of all of them. Then the goal may become clear. That's what hope is all about.

AMR: Well, from my point of view as a physicist, in considering matters of this kind, I fear that we might go on indefinitely saying that the way will eventually become clear. I think that the way has become clear. We now have reason to believe that Earth is under pretty constant threat not only from actions of human beings trying to squeeze sustenance from it, but also from its cosmic environment. The comet Shoemaker-Levy 9 has broken up, and its fragments fell on Jupiter in July 1994. It should come as no surprise that there is a significant probability that a similar cataclysmic event could wipe out higher forms of life on our planet. If we know with some reasonable probability this is the case, doesn't our humanity require us to respond?

MG: Yes, but I think that maybe there is a significant difference here between a physicist's and a theologian's point of view. The theologian at this point becomes very aware of what Lonergan called the possibility of the long decline—the foibles and the biases which the scientific point of view, like any other, is subject to. In making a statement such as the one you just made, you are ignoring these negative factors. So I would keep a skeptical view of process so that we don't go galloping off Earth to the detriment of current Earth-dwellers. And this optimism that the way has become clear . . . I'm not so sure that that in itself isn't too naive a reading of whatever we call God's desire.

AMR: I'm surprised that you call it optimism. I would call it pessimism. I said we expected with significant probability that Earth will be destroyed. Look, it's common wisdom that financial investments should be diversified—not put all in one place. Doesn't it stand to reason that the human species should not be all in one place? As far as we know, God's greatest investment is in life, especially in the life of the human species. I have always understood that we are stewards of God's investment. It follows that it is up to us to see that it's diversified.

MG: What's the *it*?!

AMR: The *it* is God's investment in us as intelligent beings in the universe. When there's a threat of extinction, I am dissatisfied with just keeping the discussion open and relying on hope. It seems to me you're neglecting the risk that action will become impossible because too much time is lost in discussion, negotiation, and, as you said, hope.

MG: Hope is not time lost—it pervades both action and reflection. Hope resists the awful sense that we can do nothing effective toward a gracious long-lived human future.

AMR: I'm pressing for the notion that there must be some kind of goal, and intrinsic to that goal in some way is the preservation, the sustaining of the human species. Are we or are we not, at some stage, responsible for the continuation of the human species? Can we answer that question?

MG: I think you have posed the central issue. I used to think that most people would without hesitation say "yes" to saving human beings before saving the Earth, if they had to choose. I wasn't prepared for the deep pessimism that now exists about the future of the human species.

AMR: There is a deep pessimism out there about our future. E. O. Wilson describes our current environmental situation and proposes that the human species may be suicidal.

MG: Nevertheless, it seems to me that posing the issue is already to have taken one step further toward action. To agree that the human species is the responsibility of human beings is one step that needs to be taken before we can address any of these other questions.

AMR: With the end of the second millennium (not just the end of a century), there is in the public realm an aura of contemplation and deliberation—reminiscence rather than action. We shouldn't be comfortable just thinking about possibilities. At some point inaction or indecision becomes worse than uncertain decision or imperfect action.

MG: In some sense, that question is a limit-question. Traditionally, such a question has distinguished the prophets who demand action from the mystics who create new ways of thinking about the experience of the whole. Method forces us to reflect on how we should engage in action—what we should do, not just how we should act.

AMR: Perhaps I can change the question somewhat. Instead of asking whether God might require us to maintain the human species, let's ask whether human beings are essential to God. What can the world do without and still have God?

MG: We were talking about how the term *limit-question* refers not only to questions we can ask but can't answer but also to the likely results of asking this kind of question. T. S. Eliot thought that what we have about such matters are hints and guesses—hints, we could say, followed by guesses or wagers. We have no final answers to the question you ask, but there are some clues. There are stories about the differences between gods or goddesses and human beings—like the Gilgamesh epic. Such stories typically lament that human beings lack what it takes to be gods or goddesses, but the stories also celebrate the potential participation of human beings in godship by being able to consider what it would be like to be a god. In the Genesis story, human beings take on the responsibility for procreation, and their development of knowledge and language creates the potential for the human species to become immortal, even though all individual human beings must die. The pre-Socratic Parmenides thought there was no universe without a knower—"What is . . . is identical with the thought that recognizes it."[34] In the Gospel of Matthew (10:40), the Christ is given to say to those going out in his name: "To receive you is to receive me, and to receive me is to receive him who sent me"—again, suggesting a continuity between his God, himself and anyone who would be received.

AMR: Can theology give us anything more definite on the basis of these hints?

MG: Taken together, these hints suggest a participatory role for human beings in God. The twentieth-century development of these ideas by process theologians such as Hartshorne, Cobb, and Suchocki is called panentheism. Panentheism is different from pantheism, which saw god in everything and particularly in nature. Most forms of panentheism point to the philosophical notion of *being* and focus on the special kind of being that human beings are. The force of this emphasis can be seen in Genesis, for example, where both the specialness of human being and its relatedness to other living beings are maintained. In the Genesis story, after the waters of the Deluge have subsided, the character of God says that God made the covenant with human beings and all living beings. Here human beings are doubly differentiated from both God and other created beings and related by virtue of their consciousness and of their special ability to participate both actually and analogously in the activity of God. The term *Imago Dei* captures this double aspect of differentiation and participation.

AMR: Are you saying that consciousness, particularly selfconsciousness, is one of the characteristics that suggests that human beings have a divine role in the universe—or something like that?

MG: Yes, I think that the emphasis needs to be on participation. In the nineteenth century, Hegel—although he was not nominally a panentheist—grandly spelled out the notion of a developing God, a God that is self-reflected in progressively higher forms of human consciousness. We need to measure Hegel's paradigms critically—he saw the gods (no goddesses) of contemporary religions as embodying more of Spirit-consciousness than tribal gods, for example. Nevertheless, his concept mirrors the contemporary insistence that, as Tracy wrote, "Given the fact that the basic metaphysical analogy for reality is the self and the self's own experience as intrinsically social and temporal, God too—precisely as real—is to be understood as social and temporal" (1975:181). This form of panentheism suggests the specialness of human beings, by virtue of their special form of consciousness as directly related to the consciousness of God.

AMR: Haven't some theologians thought that God was the "other" or "wholly other" than the human species? Now it seems to me that we are talking about a God that includes human beings.

MG: Well, in the order of knowing, God is an object of human consciousness. In the order of experience, God and human beings, in some sense, participate in each other's reality. In some forms of panentheism, God is a dipolar reality—not an either/or.

AMR: But other things are also objects of human consciousness. God is not different in that respect.

MG: True, but God is a different kind of question—a limit-question. Questions about knowing and not knowing the will of God indicate that human beings usually know and make claims about human beings in a way different from the way they know and make claims about God. And in language these claims about the relationship of God being, human being, and other being often take the form of story, analogy, and metaphor. These claims point to a peculiar aspect of the totality of being that has been called "limit-language," "limit-question," or "limit-concept." Those who write about Christian spirituality often refer to this totality as a combination of kataphatic (the path of knowing) and apophatic (the path of not knowing) consciousness.

AMR: There's something of both knowing and not knowing in the story of the flood. Noah knew only what he was told. There was much that he didn't know. He had no view of the future, neither a theological view nor a scientific view, let alone a higher viewpoint on the issue. If Noah were to save earthly life today, perhaps by taking some of them into space, in order to be persuasive he would have to claim that he knew more than what God told him.

MG: It's very interesting that in traditional treatments of the story it isn't at all the case that Noah is admired for the role he played in the story. Some Jewish commentary takes Noah to task for being too passive—he didn't challenge God on what he was told to do; he didn't talk back to God. If Noah could convince people to go with him today, where would he take them, to Mars?

AMR: If human beings were to go to live on Mars, it is true that they might be able to repopulate a devastated Earth. But actually, it is unlikely that people will choose to live on Mars—at least in the beginning.

MG: The Moon then?

AMR: Even the Moon has significant disadvantages compared to living in space. For example, like Earth, one side of the Moon points away from the Sun. Unlike Earth, the Moon rotates on its axis about once a month so that a night on the Moon is two weeks long. And there are problems getting on and off the Moon: There is still a considerable gravitational force on the Moon.

MG: Where would people live, then?

AMR: Some scientists think it would be best to start by building space cities in high orbit around Earth. Think of linking together a few buildings the size of the World Trade Center in New York City, or the San Francisco Hyatt, or larger still, the Mall of America. In the early part of this century ocean liners provided large and comfortable life support for many travelers. Large structures are even easier to build in the weightlessness of space than they are on Earth. Moreover, the transportation from one place to another in space requires very little energy compared to lifting off from a massive planet or the Moon. In addition there is sunlight—the cleanest form of energy—available in virtually unlimited quantities and on a continuous basis.

MG: But somehow it seems so unnatural for a person to be born in space and live out her life there. It's hard to imagine how human bodies and spirits, removed from all that has nourished them—the environment, culture, institutions—will survive as **human** in space.

AMR: Environments can be designed and constructed, and cultures and institutions can be moved. We've always had difficulty imagining how human beings would develop their worlds. What seems highly "unnatural" in one century can become commonplace in the next. There's the wonderful example of a letter written to President Andrew Jackson in 1829 by Martin van Buren, then governor of New York. In one section of the letter van Buren complains, "As you well know, Mr. President, 'railroad' carriages are pulled at the enormous speed of 15 miles per hour by 'engines' which, in addition to endangering life and limb of passengers, roar and snort their way through the countryside, setting fire to the crops, scaring the livestock, and frightening women and children. The Almighty never intended that people should travel at such breakneck speed."

MG: Clearly it's difficult to specify God's intention at any particular time in history. In retrospect, human beings rarely seem to have adequate imaginations for the task. But it seems to me that the differences for the human beings who would live in space are of a magnitude scarcely comparable with changes now familiar to Earth dwellers.

AMR: Ursula Goodenough (1994) speaks of organisms living in a niche—a collection of environmental domains. She points out that an organism must "operate in the context provided." It struck me at the time that the human species has become an organism that can design the "context" in which it plans to live. Astro city-states might just be the next major advancement in our ability to provide a niche for ourselves in a difficult environment—the environment of outer space, in this case one of the most general, even commonplace, environments in the universe.

MG: What you are proposing sounds something like genetic engineering to me. How do people react to this idea?

AMR: When I've lectured on the subject to college audiences, one of the first questions is almost always: What will you do with the bodies of the dead?

MG: This sounds to me like a practical expression of an eschatological concern. As a theologian, I would try to address this interest in terms of godship as well as the death of individuals. If we turn to art, we find that much of the iconography of the Middle Ages supported this notion of collective godship. The whole notion of mystical body—in those days it was spoken of as the church triumphant, the church suffering, and the church militant (all these words take their values from networks of meaning significantly different from our own) with Christ as its head. When we look at some of these icons, for example, "Mother of Mercy," by Piero della Francesca, we see one body—one participating agent actor—in which all human beings participate.

AMR: If I understand what you are saying, from a theological perspective, the human species is a body, basically. So what's the relation of that body to God and world? That's the central theological problem, isn't it?

MG: Yes, yes! And these icons of course did not portray the church as God, but again there were terms for the church, like the Mystical Bride of Christ, so that participation was always presumed on the analogy of a body—a bodily basis, one might say. The importance of bodily Life in the presence of God is one of the most long-lived emphases in Christianity. In this image of corporate body, we have a reflection of the prophetic dimension . . .

AMR: —Of what?

MG: —of religion, of theology—

AMR: But we're talking about the world now.

MG: —the prophetic dimension of theology as it looks at the world. . . .

AMR: OK!

MG: And the prophets of the world tend rhetorically to make distinctions between God and human beings because they want to impress upon human beings the dire effects of their failure to act . . .

AMR: Hear! Hear!

MG: —as well as of their badly conceived actions. Mystics, by contrast, emphasize participation and oneness with God.

AMR: But does the mystical carry any equivalent pressure to do more than worship and deliberate?

MG. I think that's the strength of the notion of participation. It moves mysticism from being a merely reflective activity to one . . . well, there are many moments in action. There is the initiating moment. There are culminating moments of action.

AMR: We seem to be avoiding until the very last moment the actual action itself. We begin and wind it up. But how do we . . .

MG: What are you saying? I don't understand.

AMR: It all seems to boil down to deliberation, to talk about it ahead of time, and to talk about it afterwards. And for me discussion isn't decisive action.

MG: Why must you dichotomize talk and action? What does it mean to say that discussion isn't action? We have all experienced conversation and arguments that provided some needed clarity or challenge to bring about better action. Besides, there's a whole well known body of literature (which I'm sure you know also) on speech acts. For example, J. L. Austin (1962) analyzed what is accomplished by the locutionary, and especially the illocutionary, and perlocutionary dimensions of speech. I spoke of an initiating moment in which action can be seen to emerge within speech, but that moment is capable of having all three dimensions of a speech act as well.

AMR: What do you mean by an initiating moment?

MG: When the action starts to take place—when the hard work of moving things in a particular direction begins. And then at a certain point someone says, "Look how far we have come." That's what I mean by a culminating moment.

AMR: With respect to the issue of the fate of the human species, where would you say we are now?

MG: We are deliberating on the issue on whether or not the continuation (as distinct from the fulfillment) of the human species is the primary human responsibility.

AMR: Perhaps we need to substitute the concept of process for that of progress. The inexorable quality of change is much more neutral than the idea of continuous improvement. In the notion of process, there is no necessary implication of moving toward the perfect or the good. By using the concept of process we can avoid the implication of improvement and still include the implication of a goal. Process does not imply chaotic change but rather change that moves toward. If we can't be explicit about the future states of a system, then we do not understand the process—the change the system is undergoing.

MG: I find the notion of process helpful, but we must not lose the focus on what life is about. This raises the question of the extent of the sacred. Even the psalmist speaks of that human as giving voice to the remainder of the cosmos. So there is a sense in which human beings are not only special but crucial to making the remainder of the universe sacred. On theoretical grounds, we need to redefine world to include the cosmos but not leave Earth behind.

AMR: Just as some say that there is no human freedom so long as there is one human being who is not free, some say that to consider human life sacred it is necessary to consider each human life as sacred. But if we are to fashion principles that are the basis for the most general conclusions, we must operate in exactly the reverse mode. We must have the most general categories we can find. In reaching for this high level we might even reach a point where we would have to acknowledge that there is human freedom so long as there is at **least one** human being who is free and that the sacredness of human life can continue to exist just so long as there is at least one procreative pair of human beings alive.

MG: I know that some people have reacted very negatively to the idea of human beings moving off Earth to live in space. Some say we are running away from problems here on Earth; others say that it is a solution for a few technologically sophisticated persons who are leaving the others behind to cope as best they can. What can be said to reduce the misunderstanding here?

AMR: If, as I hope, the development of space for human habitation is an international undertaking, it has a chance to be a multicultural affair as well. Perhaps it is most important to remember that no one reading this will be going on this human adventure. This undertaking is for the children, and their children, and theirs, and theirs, and theirs . . . in order "to keep their kind alive," as God said to Noah.

MG: When the classical texts of the historical religions were written, Earth was the universe in which human beings lived. The stars were thought to be in a separate realm. Now we understand human beings to live in a universe that includes the stars, the star clusters, the galaxies, and so on. People have been doing theology for at least 2,400 years.

The genres of special revelation—dreams, visions, mandates, apocalyptic—point to the need for deliberation and discernment as the way to action if we are to be responsible world-dwellers as well as responsible selves. Even if we had a mandate, merely knowing the direction and even the rate of change is not enough. One needs to have an idea of what state of affairs lies out there in that direction. For example, my friends in the environmentalist movement make good suggestions about the ways we must behave if we are to prolong the viability of Earth. Don't you agree that we need to reduce the rate of deforestation and the rate of release of chlorofluorocarbons and carbon dioxide into the atmosphere—all for good reasons?

AMR: I do agree that we must inhibit and postpone the degradation of Earth's life-support system. It seems clear to me that we do not have world enough—human beings have already strained the carrying capacity of the planet, and the planet itself is subject to cosmic accident. However, for the human species to continue, we must also diversify our location; we need to find ways to begin living in space.

MG: Templeton said, "God has placed us at a new beginning." The question, since we do not have world enough, is, "Do we have time?"

EPILOGUE

MG: The view of the world we are now discussing has become a bidisciplinary view—neither a physicist's view nor a theologian's view. The discussion of this bidisciplinary view of the world is not over. Indeed, it has just begun. But perhaps our purpose here today has been fulfilled. We wanted to demonstrate movement to a higher viewpoint by means of bidisciplinary argumentation.

AMR: Our analogy for the higher bidisciplinary viewpoint is binocular vision. The left eye sees one view, the right eye another. The two views are commensurate only in the three-dimensional view that is both different from each individual view and more.

MG: In bidisciplinary dialogue, both individual points of view must be accepted. Neither view can be allowed to dominate as the discussants strive for agreement. The more each view is presented, the more valuable and effective will be any higher viewpoint that may be achieved.

AMR: Of course, the success of any higher viewpoint attained must finally be measured in terms of the usual criteria of coherence, cognitive efficacy, and eventual acceptance by the communities concerned. As Karl Peters said at this symposium, "The future is open."

MG: "There's more to be done."

7

A Generalized Conception of Text Applied to Both Scientific and Religious Objects

According to Charles Walcutt, there are three forms of reading: R_1 (decoding to speech), R_2 (understanding language), and R_3 (integrating a meaning of a text beyond its context and toward the world). The idea of a text is reviewed and reconstructed to facilitate the application of concepts of interpretation to the objects analyzed in the natural sciences, as well as to objects analyzed in religion and literature. Four criteria—readability (using Walcutt's forms), formality, material transcendence, and retrievability—are proposed as the basis for a generalized conception of text. Objects in both religion and science, not previously thought to be texts, are shown to be included in the new definition and therefore to be potential subjects of developing methods of interpretation.

IN THIS CHAPTER WE SHIFT OUR ATTENTION FROM THE PROCESSES OF COMING to know in science and religion, to the objects of study in science and religion. In particular, we develop the idea of a text to a sufficiently high level of generalization that many of the objects of study in science and religion can be seen to be epistemologically the same.[35]

Recent years have seen an increased interest in processes of interpretation, especially in the fields of religious hermeneutics and liter-

Published in *Zygon* 22 (September 1987), 299–316.

ary criticism. Interpretation is of no less interest in the natural sciences. However, much of the excitement generated by interpretation issues in the humanities has come down to debates regarding the nature of texts. If the natural sciences are to be included in the development of modern interpretation theory, the debates about texts must be carried across the disciplinary "lines." Accordingly, we must find a way of understanding the natural sciences as being concerned with texts, in effect resurrecting the medieval idea of "The Book of Nature."[36] The process of interpretation, so central in the humanities because of the ubiquitousness of written texts, may not be so obvious in the natural sciences, where texts are generally understood to refer only to scientific writings, rarely subject to wide varieties of interpretation. However, interpretation is central to the problem of rendering observations and data meaningful, and this process has been one of concern to historians and philosophers of science as well as to practicing scientists themselves.

When Galileo turned a telescope on the heavens, he saw images that required interpretation. He understood the image of Venus as revealing phases of the planet similar to the phases of the Moon, and interpreted the bright dots near Jupiter as satellites of that planet.

Historically of still greater importance are the early interpretations of observational data on the positions of the planets. The data consisted of line-of-sight directions to planets at particular times— there were no direct data on the planets' distances from the Earth. These positional data were interpreted correctly but differently by Ptolemy, Copernicus, **and** Brahe: Ptolemy had the Sun and all the planets revolving around the Earth; Copernicus had the Earth and planets revolving around the Sun; and Brahe (in a late attempt at a compromise) had the Sun—circled by all the planets except the Earth—revolving around the Earth. Telescopic observations such as those by Galileo as well as dynamical theory were required before the Copernican schema could be accepted on grounds other than aesthetic (such as simplicity or symmetry). See Fig. 1.8, p. 24 above.

Data of instrumentation must be interpreted in the light of particular theoretical understandings before they can be considered intelligible, a conclusion even casual observations in a high-energy particle laboratory will confirm. Of particular interest to us is whether interpretation in the natural sciences on the one hand, and in the humanities on the other, can be understood to be equivalent epistemological processes. And this first question, we believe, will be clarified by asking a second question. Are the objects of study in each case epistemologically the same? Our method for addressing this second question is to reconsider what constitutes a text for interpretation in either the humanities—specifically religious studies—or in the natural sciences.

Ask scholars of classical religions what it is that they interpret, and many will respond, "We interpret texts." In religion, the idea of interpretation is linked to texts, either directly or indirectly: Only when we try to extend the notion of interpretation to text-marginal phenomena (such as oral tradition) do we become aware of the limit of the concept of text.

Ask the same question of a scientist and the response is likely to be, "What is to be interpreted are the data." The concept of "text" does not appear to play a major role, if indeed it plays any role other than mere communication, in scientific research.

We wish to dispel the naive expectation that the central objects of study—texts in religion and data in science—are conceptually different entities. Rather than redefining data and claiming that texts constitute the exclusive data of religion, we find it more profitable to define text in such a way as to include the central objects of study in science.

1. A Generalized Conception of Text

Under the heading *text* in any general reference book of quotations or the OED, the greatest number of citations is to the Bible and to other specific written works. Only with the employment of nineteenth-century hermeneutics does the term acquire a level of generality. In the works of Friedrich Schleiermacher and Wilhelm Dilthey, "text" begins to refer to one of the elements in the process of interpretation. Nevertheless, the term has tended to preserve its original referent—namely, books—and is generally understood as denoting a relevant object of study only in the humanities and social sciences. If we are to make texts the central objects of study in the natural as well as the human sciences, we must expand the class of objects to which the term can be applied, and see what such an expansion can accomplish.

Most scholarly work on texts gloss the question of what is to be taken as a text. This omission may be due to a naive assumption that everyone knows what a text is, an assumption particularly easy to embrace in academic fields overflowing with manuscripts. Being unwilling ourselves to take the nature of text for granted, we will begin by giving detailed criteria for what we will be willing to call a text.

We intend to enlarge the concept of text not only beyond sacred text, and literary text, but also beyond written text, to include objects that bear no apparent relation to language at all. We say that for an object to be a text it must possess the following four characteristics: readability, formality, material transcendence, and retrievability.

We begin by exploring each of four characteristics of "textness" and by examining, in particular, some of the objects we will call texts, in the natural sciences and in religion.

(1) READABILITY Anything we call a text must, in some sense, be readable. What do we mean by reading? This question can be addressed in a limited way without a full-fledged development of the concept of interpretation. Consider the following example: A student in a beginning foreign language class is asked to read a French text in French. The passage is read aloud with proper pronunciation and the student, asked to give an account, in English, of what has been read, is unable to say what the French text is about. Has the student read the text? The answer is yes—but in a limited sense. Walcutt (1971:ii–iii) distinguished three meanings of the word "reading," which he described as $Reading_1$, $Reading_2$, and $Reading_3$.

> $Reading_1$ is decoding the printed visual symbol into a spoken sound, which it designates. $Reading_1$, in other words, is turning writing into language. Language, as all the linguistic experts assure us, is spoken sound. Writing is a visual symbolization of those sounds. Reading converts writing into language. The definition holds whether or not the spoken sound is understood. . . . $Reading_2$ is . . . not really reading at all. It is understanding language. . . . It is the element of communication that is the goal of any reading instruction. $Reading_3$ is hardest to define, but essential to our use

of the word. On a higher level, reading takes us into a world of art and intellect . . . [and] permits the kind of study, elaboration, and accuracy that probably could not be sustained with only a spoken language.[37]

We might wish, right at the outset, to require of a text that it can be read in the sense of R_2 and R_3, and not only R_1. However, there is good reason to allow any one of Walcutt's three senses of reading to fulfill the readability criterion for our purpose.

R_1 applies to writing that is only marginally intelligible, such as disputed passages in the Bible or in Shakespeare. In a lighter vein, the first stanza of Lewis Carroll's "JABBERWOKY" will serve as an example (1965:18–19):

> 'Twas brillig, and the slithy toves
> Did gyre and gimble in the wabe:
> All mimsy were the borogoves,
> And the mome raths outgrabe.

Are we to take such an object for a text? We have no difficulty in reciting the stanza—it gives the appearance of being in English and even sounds like English. However, as competent readers of English, we are able to call its meaningfulness into question, and can assert that there is no literal meaning to the poem although, as a treasured part of literature, it survives as a wonderful parody of English style and syntax. By permitting R_1 to suffice for readability, we can accept "JABBERWOKY" as a text despite its lack of literal meaning and consider it an appropriate object for interpretation. Whether "JAB-BERWOKY" will meet our other criteria remains to be seen.

One can imagine the existence of an object that **might** be read, and that is therefore **potentially** a text. We want to include such cases even though they range from examples that have proven sound (e.g., the hieroglyphic figures that comprise the "texts" of ancient Egypt) to those that are doubtful in the extreme (e.g., the planetary and stellar configurations of astrology). It appears, therefore, that our criterion of readability should involve any of Walcutt's three senses of the word "read," and we will leave the question of understanding to be raised at the level of the critical evaluation of interpretations.

Distinctions among the three meanings of the word "read" have a parallel in the natural sciences, in the data of instrumentation which we wish to include in our world of texts. In the early stages of the investigation of physical phenomena it is not unusual to be able to do no more than to express experimental data in some regular mathematical form: J. R. Rydberg's formula for the frequencies of the spectral lines of hydrogen is an example:

$$f = R(m^{-2} - n^{-2}).$$

Even though Rydberg did not understand spectral phenomena—they did not at the time fit into any existing theoretical scheme—he was able to express the observed data in concise mathematical form. Such a state of affairs can be understood to correspond to $Reading_1$ in which language can be articulated without understanding meaning. Later developments may lead to an understanding: Bohr's theory of the hydrogen atom would be the corresponding example. The same text (the spectral lines) can, within the framework of Bohr's theory, be read with understanding ($Reading_2$)—with an interpretation— because the text refers to a physical theory, thus making it possible to relate the phenomena of the spectral lines to other physical phenomena. One can go further and consider $Reading_3$, which Walcutt called, "hardest to define," as the level achieved when spectral lines are understood within the framework of a comprehensive theory such as quantum mechanics.

For an example in religion of the application of the readability criterion in religion, we might take a Jewish cemetery. Corresponding to $Reading_1$ is the ability to identify certain symbols—the Minorah, tree of life, flowers, and (Hebrew) characters. $Reading_2$ would include an understanding of the symbols and inscriptions in relation to death. $Reading_3$ would relate Jewish funerary art to the transition from ancient Israelite religion to Judaism when cemeteries were introduced and apocalypse was emphasized.

Until this point we have been examining candidates for inclusion on the basis of the readability criterion only. Further criteria may yet require that some of these candidates be eliminated. Readability is a necessary but not sufficient condition for an object to be called a text.

(2) FORMALITY In order to qualify as a text, an object must be the product of, or have been produced in accordance with, the rules and conventions of some formal system. It is clear that any sample of a language will satisfy this criterion. It may not be obvious that a large variety of non-linguistic objects meet it as well.

In an article entitled "Texts and Lumps," Richard Rorty (1985:7–8) examined characteristics of a literary object such as *The Turn of the Screw* or *Hamlet* and those of a scientific object such as gold. He compared and contrasted the way a literary critic on the one hand and a chemist on the other might engage these objects. Rorty's objectives were not unlike our own. He characterized himself as a pragmatist who could, along with John Dewey, "see chemistry and literary criticism and paleontology and politics and philosophy all striding along together—equal comrades with diverse interests, distinguished *only* by these interests, not by cognitive status." Indeed Rorty came close to our approach in claiming that "most philosophical reflection about objectivity—most philosophy and epistemology of science —has concentrated on lumps. Most discussion of interpretation has concentrated on texts. A lot of controversies about the objectivity of interpretation can, I think, be smoothed out by insisting, as far as possible on the text-lump parallelism" (Rorty 1985, 7–8). However, Rorty, along with many others, takes texts as given, as not in need of definition or categorical analysis, and so he concentrated on a parallel between a natural "given" (the lump) and a human product (the text) thereby advancing what appears to us to be a category mistake, to use Gilbert Ryle's apt expression.

Ruth Anna Putnam (1985:11), in a reply to Rorty, "Poets, Scientists, and Critics," showed that she was aware of this difficulty. However, her understanding of texts in science is not the same as ours: "Both poets and scientists produce texts, and the texts they produce are **about** 'lumps.' But scientists produce texts **only incidentally**; qua scientists they investigate lumps: they transform lumps into objects of knowledge" (emphasis ours).

Texts that we recognize in science—we will be using the Fraunhofer lines in the Sun's spectrum as an example—are not at all incidental to the scientist's investigation; they are the central objects of the investigation. Moreover, these data-objects are produced in accordance with a formal system, a system of units and dimensions, of laws and relations. In the case of the spectral lines, we are referring not merely to the measured frequencies and intensities of the lines, but also to the apparatus that is required for their detection. The role of apparatus as part of the formal system is especially evident in the more analytical sciences.

Rorty, in order to achieve his objective, should have alluded to gold not merely as a lump, but to gold as a set of characteristics, not merely as "insoluble in nitric acid" (for other objects have that characteristic), but as having a certain density, atomic weight, malleability, color, all of which relate to a formal system. Nor can we agree "there's an end on it," for there may still be isotopic differences to be discovered, questions of origins to be explored, and so on. Actually, we suspect that Rorty understands this full well, for he goes on to say that "the **causal** independence of the gold or the text from the inquiring chemist or critic does not mean that either can . . . perform the impossible feat of . . . seeing [the chosen object] as it is in itself. . . ." Hence lumps cannot be "seen" in themselves, but are seen always as part of a formal system, a point made by Norwood Russell Hanson some years ago (Hanson 1972).

(3) MATERIAL TRANSCENDENCE Consider the first line of Shakespeare's Sonnet 94, a poem which has attracted considerable critical attention:

> They that have power to hurt and will do none . . .

No one would disagree with the proposition that this line of words is part of a text. This line would also have been part of a text if it had been hand-written in script, recorded in Morse code, or chiseled in granite. Texts have a property we will call material transcendence: they transcend the material that serves as their medium of expression.

This criterion should not be passed over lightly, for it represents a subtle but important aspect of textness that might be overlooked. Initially, the criterion of material transcendence might seem to contradict what will be our fourth criterion, retrievability; if a manuscript burns, is not the text lost? The loss of a manuscript tends to make us think that a text should have material mutability; change the material and you (necessarily) change the text. However, any object that makes it possible for us to reproduce the words of a written text (a computer diskette, for example) must itself be considered a text. Hence a particular text is not necessarily associated with any **particular** object or set of objects that can express the text.

The requirement of material transcendence causes us to reject a number of objects that, on the basis of the readability criterion alone, might be considered to be texts. Think of an oil painting. Here we have a rich product of human creative activity from an area of work often considered parallel to writing. An oil painting would seem to have much to say to human beings. It is not uncommon to claim that one can "read" a painting (*Reading*₃ or *Reading*₂). Can we not include it as a text for interpretation? The answer must be "no," because of the criterion of material transcendence. An oil painting is inextricably embodied in its original manifestation—much as a musical performance is: Neither an oil painting nor a musical performance transcends the material that serves as its medium of expression.[38] To say that the oil painting can be photographed and that the picture that results is a transcendent equivalent of the painting in a new medium is as wrong as to claim that a recording of a musical performance is equivalent to the performance itself. Furthermore, a copier's rendition, no matter how accurate, cannot be considered equivalent to the artist's original.

The debate here centers on the notion of an "original" oil painting or a "unique" edifice. The notion of the original has always been special in art, but the modern capacity for reproduction has changed the conditions under which we interpret art. The French poet and philosopher, Paul Valéry (1964:225), writing before World War II, recognized this change when he wrote, ". . . the amazing growth of our techniques, the adaptability and precision they have attained, the ideas and habits they are creating, make it a certainty that profound changes are impending in the ancient craft of the Beautiful." Post-World War II treatment of the phenomenon of artistic reproduction has been understandably negative in its appraisal. In his now classic essay, "Art in an Age of Mechanical Reproduction," for example, Walter Benjamin asserted that the material of the original painting is lost in reproduction—his way of saying that the original painting is not materially transcendent. In losing the "'aura' of the original," painting, according to Benjamin, is cut off from its ritual connection to religion and becomes, instead, a matter of politics (Benjamin 1968: 217–24).

But reproduction has a positive side as well. When art is being interpreted—for example, politically or theologically—the original is *not* essential, no matter how impressive, irreplaceable, and inspiring an original may be for immediate experience. We can say, therefore, that the modern capacity for reproduction *permits* artistic objects to be interpreted, as well as to be enjoyed, contemplated, and critiqued. In other words, the loss of immediacy can be simultaneously a gain in understanding through interpretation. If this is the case, reproductions can be said to provide material transcendence, if not to the original work, at least to its significations.

(4) RETRIEVABILITY And yet not everything in the world that is readable, materially transcendent, and partakes of a formal system is a text. Indeed the establishment of material transcendence would seem to invoke a fourth requirement—if x is a text, x must be retrievable.

If a text is to be an object of interest to more than one discipline, a text must minimally possess the property of intersubjectivity—it must be possible for at least two persons to consider the same object. This requirement is met through the property of retrievability. Hereafter we will be unwilling to award the status of text to any object that is not retrievable. To illustrate the restrictiveness of this requirement, consider the following examples.

The song of the bard has a long tradition in literature. However, for our purposes, a song (or spoken story) cannot be considered a text. The verbal objects of spoken discourse have a transitory quality that prohibits their being scrutinized, analyzed, and otherwise subjected to the varieties of interpretation that can be brought to bear on an object that can be viewed and reviewed (both figuratively and literally).[39]

We realize that in requiring retrievability we will not be including the primary subject of linguistics—the spoken language. Whether our efforts offer any theoretical assistance to those who are concerned with the interpretation of exchanges of information in cultures that do not possess a written language will depend on the extent to which our conception of text can be applied to signs and symbols.

Another effect of the imposition of the criterion of retrievability is the exclusion of the realm of private experience that may be epitomized by the dream. How can one of the most celebrated objects for interpretation of the past hundred years not be included as a text? Let us examine the case of the dream more closely.

When Freud spoke of the interpretation of a dream, just what was the object of his attention? In the case of his interpretation of one of his own dreams (some of his most detailed examples), it seems fair to allow that he was attending to a dream. But suppose that we had wished to question some aspect of one of Freud's dreams while he was alive. We would have had to take his **statement about the dream** as the basis for further analysis, for the dream itself lacks the intersubjective quality that retrievability demands.[40] But the retrieval of an experience by means of memory will not be considered to meet our standards: Human memory is not sufficiently reliable. The same conclusion must be drawn for all of the literary objects that we remember. The poem that resides only in memory cannot be considered, by our standards, to be a text.

It might seem to be the case that there is a point at which dreams become texts. Freud's *Interpretation of Dreams* (1900) includes long paragraphs of accounts, presumably verbatim, of dreams of his patients. Here, however, we have found the text but lost the dream, for while we can take the preserved account as retrievable, the account is not a reproduction of the dream itself. We conclude that dreams, and similar mental activity, cannot be considered texts.

2. Application of the Criteria

What are the gains and losses engendered by the application of our four criteria? To begin with, text is not restricted to what is conventionally considered to be written language: Instrumental data of any kind can be considered text, provided they are readable, related to a formal system, and are materially transcendent and retrievable. For instance, the readings of a thermometer, where suitably recorded, would qualify as a text, although simple visual observations of the thermometer would not. A recording of a performance of a symphony would qualify, as would the printed music that formed the basis of a performance. A performance itself, since not retrievable, would not be considered a text: A recording does not constitute a retrieval of a performance itself but only of limited aspects of a performance. A musical score from which a performance is read, however, **is** a text. The staves, lines, and dots of musical notation can be considered to comprise a text because they meet the criterion of retrievability as well as readability and formality. Do they also meet the criterion of material transcendence? Although not so clear a case as a written text, we must surely accept a musical manuscript as a text because any description of a score that allows the score to be reproduced must be considered **equivalent** in all respects to the score itself.

Texts in the Natural Sciences

It is a commonplace to say that mathematics is the language of the natural sciences. This claim is certainly the case for physics and to a somewhat lesser extent for chemistry. However, mathematics is less and less central to the scientific disciplines as one moves to the geosciences, the life sciences, and on toward psychology and the social sciences. The character of the mathematics changes as well, becoming more statistical in the sciences that work more with populations rather than with individual cases. Does the language of mathematics have its *Reading*$_1$, *Reading*$_2$, and *Reading*$_3$? We will examine a sentence (an equation) that describes a traveling water wave:

$$y = A \sin (kx + \omega t).$$

Reading$_1$

    Reading$_1$ requires that we be able to read (say) this sentence to another person. Such a statement might be rendered as follows: "y equals A times the sine of, parenthesis, the quantity k times x plus the quantity omega times t; close parenthesis." Notice the special usage of the word "quantity" to indicate something calculated, and the use of the word "parenthesis" (as shown in the equation) to indicate the *argument* of the sine—that angle for which the sine is to be calculated. Here we have Walcutt's minimal sense of reading. A scientist might convey the equation to someone else over the telephone with a spoken sentence of this kind. While a knowledge of "spoken math" is needed to perform *Reading*₁, no knowledge of the physics of waves is required.

Reading₂

*Reading*₂, is a different matter. To accomplish *Reading*₂, one needs to know (as for a sentence in English) the definitions of the elements (words) being read. In this case one needs to know that y (both positive and negative) is the height of the wave at various points along its path, that A is the maximum height of the water above and below its equilibrium height (the height of the water if there were no wave). A is called the wave's *amplitude*. The "phrase" (symbols in parentheses) we referred to earlier is the *argument* of the sine function. This phrase must be an angle, (kx + ωt), which we will now call theta (θ). Fig. 7.1a shows how the angle θ controls the coordinate y (the varying height of the water).

Walcutt's *Reading*₂ (understanding language) is the level at which most physics students operate. Students often seek solutions to assigned physics problems by a method they call "plug and chug." Armed with a knowledge of the definitions, the student searches for the relevant numbers in the statement of the problem. The student then substitutes those numbers for the A, k, x, ω and t in the equation, i.e., "plugs" those numbers in for the symbols and then calculates ("chugs") to obtain the corresponding value for y, the height of the wave at the time, t, and place, x. However—and this is the main point —such a student will understand the equation **but not the phenomenon** which the equation describes.

Reading₃

In order to reach Walcutt's *Reading*₃ (comprehending the phenomenon), the student needs to "see" that the equation "says" (or "tells") much more. Following are some of the major interpretive points that contribute to a level of comprehension corresponding to *Reading*₃:

(1) A particular part of a wave corresponds to a particular angle (e.g., for the crest θ = 90°). That angle does not change as the crest of wave moves, so θ, which equals (kx + ωt), is constant as the

time, t, increases. To keep θ constant, kx must get correspondingly smaller as ωt gets larger. But k and ω are both constants for a particular wave, so x must get smaller as t increases.
Conclusion: **The wave is moving from right to left.**

(2) What can we say about the speed of the wave through the water? By keeping the angle, $\theta = (kx + \omega t)$, constant, we can "ride" the crest, and the **change** in the angle will be zero: $(\Delta\theta = 0)$ and $(k\Delta x + \omega\Delta t) = 0$. This condition requires that $-k\Delta x = \omega\Delta t$. The speed, υ, of the wave, however, must be the distance traveled (Δx) divided by the elapsed time (Δt): that is, $\upsilon = \Delta x/\Delta t$, which is equal to $-\omega/k$. (Notice the minus sign. It shows again that the wave moves "backwards.") Conclusion: **The wave speed, υ, will be $-\omega/k$.**

(3) What can we say about the length of the wave? The wavelength, λ, is the distance from one crest to the next (or between any consecutive corresponding parts of the wave). Since different parts of the wave correspond to different values of the angle, θ, a change in θ requires a change in either or both x and t. This requirement can be written as $\Delta\theta = (k\Delta x + \omega\Delta t)$. If we now "freeze" the wave by setting the change in time equal to zero $(\Delta t = 0)$, then $\Delta\theta = k\Delta x$, which can be written as $\Delta x = \Delta\theta/k$. The length of the wave will then be the change in distance, Δx, that corresponds to the change in angle, $\Delta\theta$, either from one crest of the frozen wave to the next (i.e., from $\theta = 90°$ to $\theta = 450°$) or between consecutive corresponding parts (e.g., from $\theta = 0°$ to $\theta = 360°$, or from $\theta = 40°$ to $\theta = 400°$). In each case, $\Delta\theta = 360°$.
Conclusion: **The wavelength, λ, will be $360°/k$.**[41]

The elaboration that Walcutt says "goes beyond language" may be more clearly evident in a study of Fig. 7.1, a and b. And there's more, of course. But this kind of analytical interpretation can be hard going if one is not used to it, and we have made the important point of showing how we can communicate using the language of mathematics in science—a language with much of the extraordinary nuances to be found in even ordinary English. The inferences to be drawn from these observations we save for our conclusion.

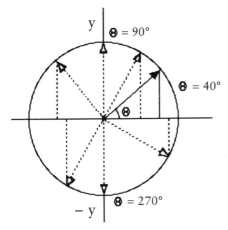

Fig. 7.1, a and b Figure 7.1a shows the vertical height, y (or –y) and the angle θ, when y = sin θ. It helps to remember that the sine of an angle in a triangle is given by the length of the side opposite the angle divided by the length of the hypotenuse. The value of y is the height of the end of the arrow. If the arrow has length 1, the maximum value of y is 1 when θ is 90°. The figure shows succeeding values for y as the angle increases (the arrow moving counter clockwise).

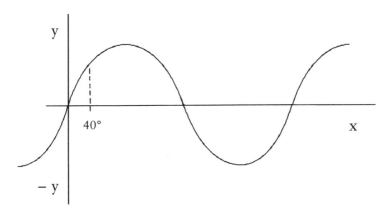

Since the angle θ = (kx + ωt) can increase because x increases or because t increases, we need to take a "snapshot" of the wave to see what it looks like. For convenience we choose t to be equal to zero and we have a motionless wave frozen in space as shown in Fig. 7.1b. For reference to Fig. 7.1a we still show the positions on the wave that corresponds to the angle 40°. The wave shown has a peak at 90° where the value of y will be a maximum because the sine of 90° is the maximum value for the sine of an angle as shown in Fig. 7.1a. To understand the motion of the wave we must allow t to increase in value from the present value of zero. How will the picture change? Will the crest of the wave (θ = 90°) move to the left or the right? Since the angle is being held constant, the value of the angle (kx + ωt) cannot change. That implies that x must get smaller as t gets larger: As the x position of the crest gets smaller as time goes on, the wave moves from right to left. To get motion from left to right (x must get larger as t gets larger), we have to write the angle as (kx – ωt).

Let us turn now to the example of spectral lines of hydrogen in the Sun. The spectrum of the Sun has been known, since the middle of the eighteenth century, to consist of a rainbow-like continuous spectrum on which are superimposed a myriad of "dark lines," very narrow gaps in the continuous shift of color from deep red through yellow and green to the darkest blue. The dark lines are understood to arise from the absorption, by elements in the Sun's "atmosphere," of the characteristic lines that, in the laboratory, would comprise the spectral lines of these same elements. The dark lines in the Sun's spectrum (or the spectrum of any star) form the basis for determining the chemical composition of the atmosphere of the Sun (or the star). Now it is the case that all observers anywhere in the world, if suitably equipped and instructed, can see these lines, and will obtain the same wavelengths for them if they choose to measure them. The lines satisfy our criterion of retrievability. We argue that these spectral lines are a text, and that they satisfy all of the other requirements for text in the same way that Shakespeare's Sonnet 94 satisfies all the requirements. The lines are readable, since by means of them we can determine the composition of a star. They are part of a formal system of units and dimensions to which their frequencies refer. Finally, they are materially transcendent, since they are manifested in any appropriate arrangement of equipment anywhere in the world at any time. Unlike the case of the oil painting, the spectral lines do not lose material transcendence on the grounds of possessing an aura of originality.

The natural sciences have made much of the property of retrievability—at least in the past three hundred years. The idea that any scientist, at any time, in any laboratory in any part of the world, can replicate the observations of another, has formed the basis of what is called "scientific objectivity." But now we find that the concept of text, as we have structured it, is just as objective (intersubjective) as any scientific observation, and here lies the integrative aspect of our approach to texts.

It might appear as though our broadened definition of text, while making it possible to include the natural sciences within the realm of critical interpretation, leaves traditional hermeneutic disciplines unchanged. But such is not the case. We find, rather, that we have enlarged the class of objects to be called texts in religious studies as well.

Texts in the Humanities

In religious understanding, the question of text arises out of different issues than it does in science. The existence of written texts as one source of religious reflection insures some commonsense understanding of the phenomenon of texts. This very familiarity poses a problem when texts, either explicitly or implicitly, become exclusive or unreflective objects for religious understanding. At issue is whether elements of religion other than scriptures (conventionally understood)—for example, symbols, rituals, persons—can be considered to be texts.

Before we proceed, however, we must ask whether the idea of text is a stable notion in the humanities. Any exploration of the concept of text must take into account thirty years of change in our ideas of what a literary text is. Whereas the traditional understanding of text presumed a "stable identity and its enduring power within a continuous cultural tradition" (Miller, 1985, ii), the contemporary understanding emphasizes the dependence of the text's identity on different historical and cultural contexts, the mutability of the languages which texts employ, and the strategies by which texts may be seen to deconstruct, as well as support the readings they encourage.[42] With these new emphases has come a heightened sense of the interdependence of text and the act of reading—so heightened in fact as almost to preclude the possibility of investigating the phenomenon of text alone. Reading *Is There a Text in This Class?* by Stanley Fish (1980), for example, one is struck by the radical question of the **existence** of texts. Although such radical positions as Fish's have been useful in demystifying traditional beliefs about texts, a new critical consensus does seem to be developing within the humanities and social sciences, a consensus that affirms text as intrinsically related to but also different from interpretation: Read texts are not synonymous with interpretation. With that clarification, we are now able to survey objects related to religious experience—perhaps even its referent—as texts in religion.

Texts in Religion

The referent of religious experience, in itself, does not seem to qualify as text because it is not retrievable and seems incapable of being read. Regardless of which conception we take to be central to religious understanding—Eliade's "dialectic of the sacred and the profane," Tillich's "pursuit of an ultimate concern," Rosemary Ruether's "ideal concept of God/ess," Alfred North Whitehead's "dipolar God," Rahner's "hearing the incommensurable," Tracy's "disclosure of the limit-character of experience," Rudolf Otto's "fear of and fascination with the numinous," or the Buddhist "repose in Nirvana"—we are faced with the same problem. To take this position, however, is to forget that the conceptions are not so much conceptions of the sacred per se, the holy, the unknown, as they are conceptions of the **manifestations** and **proclamations** of the referent of religious experience. Through manifestations, articulations, representations, the referent of religious experience can be related to text. Ricoeur (1974a:14) refers to such manifestations of the sacred and distinguishes them from the sacred itself as follows: ". . . Although we cannot directly describe the numinous element [i.e., the sacred] as such, we can at least describe how it manifests itself. . . . [A] phenomenology of the sacred is possible because these manifestations have a form, a structure, an articulation." In this sense the objects of religious understanding are, like the data of scientific understanding, not understandable in themselves: Both presume the mediation of a formal system which enables objects and data to be made appropriately intelligible for the inquiry.

Ricoeur observes that natural symbols, the "elements" of nature—sky, earth, air, water, fire—play an extensive, albeit controversial role in the manifestation of the sacred in human experience. On one level, the sacred power of nature is located in its being threatening and uncertain: "The sacred universe, after all, is a universe which emerges out of chaos and which may at any instant return to it." At the same time, the elements may function as symbols, that is, as a part of a formal system which makes possible a second-level meaning through and beyond the literal level. For example, the major religious function of water as a symbol is "to evoke the universal source of potentialities from wherein existence emerges. . . ." Water symbolism is central to many rituals—rituals of immersion, ablution, libation, baptism, and death. In the light of natural symbols, life is understood as a "total and diffuse sacrality which may be seen in the cosmic rhythms, in the return of vegetation, [in fertility and birth,] and in the alternation of life and death" (1974a:17–18).

As a manifestation of the sacred—a hierophany—can a natural symbol qualify as a text? Ricoeur defines what it means to "manifest" the sacred: ". . . the object (e.g., a tree, a rock) becomes something other than itself while still remaining itself. . . . It **becomes** super-efficacious while still remaining a part of common reality" (1974a:14–15). Here we have a characteristic approximating material transcendence. On the other hand, an appearance of the sacred which is limited to one or another **particular** object—say, the Greek Oracle at Delphi or the Ark of the Covenant at Shiloh—lacks material transcendence. Singular objects such as these tend to be regarded as themselves sacred, rather than being manifestations of the sacred. By contrast, the Christian Eucharist is *any* bread and wine which has been consecrated. General objects such as these, dependent for their sacrality upon an event—in this case the spoken word—exhibit material transcendence.

Are symbols readable? To the degree that they lend themselves to intersubjective understanding, we can say that symbols are readable. Multiple, even conflicting, readings do not compromise readability since reading does not imply that every reader will read in the same way. But if this is so, how can attempts to read the livers of animals (hepatoscopy), the flights of birds (augury), or the flesh of human beings (trial by ordeal) be distinguished from reading a symbol? Perhaps admitting these marginal cases as texts readable at R_1 does not preclude rejecting flawed interpretations which have resulted from claiming a higher level of readability.

Because of its double—some would say crossed or conflicting— referent, a natural symbol "calls for" a reading at Walcutt's third level, the level which leads to ". . . a world of art and intellect. . . [and] permits the kind of study, elaboration, and accuracy that probably could not be sustained with only a spoken language" (Walcutt 1971:iii). At this level, the meaning and truth of a religious interpretation and a formal system of religious concepts come into play.

Are natural symbols universally retrievable? Unlike unique manifestations of the sacred, such as the burning bush in which Moses encountered Yahweh, natural symbols are accessible to all. Recorded symbols, of course, are also retrievable. Moreover, the process by which "natural" objects become and remain symbols is similar to the process by which data in science become and remain data.

To the degree, then, that they are materially transcendent, retrievable, readable, and part of a formal system, natural symbols can be regarded as texts.

Manufactured as well as natural objects can be elements in a hierophany of the sacred. Figures (such as the circle, square, cross, labyrinth, mandala) and structures (such as thresholds, gates, bridges, pathways, ladders and ropes) partition sacred time and space from profane, or everyday, existence. We may say that this manner of "inscribing" the sacred by means of certain objects is to ask for them to be "read" semiotically, that is, in a language of figures.

These objects of religion as well as more particularized ones such as medallions, crucifixes, rings, shepherd's crooks, are all retrievable in the sense that it is possible for at least two persons to consider the same object even at different times. The objects are materially transcendent insofar as, like natural symbols, their sacrality is not limited to any one particular instance: A religious object is more obviously a text when its sacrality depends more on the **kind** of object it is than on its being a unique occasion of a sacred manifestation. Sacred objects are readable by virtue of their belonging to a network of meaningful signs, i.e., a formal system.

Just as the figure of the threshold sets off sacred from profane space, a ritual distinguishes sacred from profane time: "Rites practically organize the alternation of strong times and weak times, the rhythm of eating and drinking, of love and work, of the time for debate and the time of a festival." Whether understood negatively as "magical manipulations" or demonstrations of occult powers, or positively as any kind of human behavior which confers order and value on the world, ritual has come to be recognized as important human activity: "To every manifestation [of the sacred] there corresponds a manner of being-in-the-world" (Ricoeur 1974a:16).

Are rituals texts? Different rituals or the same ritual performed at a different time or place can have the same referent. The Holy Grail is not required for the celebration of the Eucharist—any cup will do. Rituals are, therefore, materially transcendent with respect to their referents. The various referents of ritual events are often related in a formal system, for example, in a literary or sacramental system. A classic example of the relation of literature to ritual is the Babylonian *Enuma Elish*, which reenacted the creation of the world. Other examples include the Passover ritual which reconfirms the Covenant in the the the flight of the Hebrews from Egypt, the Eucharist which reenacts the death and resurrection of the Christ, and Agni, the Vedic ritual of the fire altar.[43] Rituals as events can also be read—they frequently are read, for example, by ethologists, who study behavior. As events, however, rituals are not texts because they are not retrievable. Reproductions and records of rituals (in liturgical formulas, rubrics or transcribed myths) can, of course, be expected to fulfill all four criteria.

In addition to scriptures, natural symbols, figures, and rituals, religion includes persons as the locus of the sacred. In his study of saints as paradigmatic figures in the history of Christianity—figures such as martyrs, ascetics, pilgrims, warriors, mystics, theologians, artists, humanists, activists, and outsiders—Lawrence Cunningham (1983) draws upon Tracy's notion of the classic. Religious classics, according to Tracy (1981:163), "involve a claim to truth as the event of a disclosure-concealment of the whole of reality **by the power of the whole**—as, in some sense, a radical and finally gracious mystery." In the sense of their being religious classics, are persons "texts"? At first glance, it would seem as though persons in themselves are not retrievable, nor materially transcendent. Moreover, they seem only partially readable (we may read their temperature or blood count, for example) or at best trivially readable (recall Hamlet's objection to Rosencrantz' and Gildenstern's attempt to read him: "Do you think I am easier to play on than a pipe? . . . You would play upon me; you would seem to know my stops").

Nevertheless, Cunningham is not speaking of persons as individuals (except insofar as an individual might exemplify a particular type). Instead he is describing composite persons—"persons" built out of legends, paintings, sculptures, decrees, historical records, music, and monuments. Classic persons might very well be understood in the traditional exegetical strategy of *typos*.[44] *Typos* constitutes a formal system that goes beyond the act of categorization in the sense that it generates and organizes similarities and differences and ultimately can be said to render relationships among individuals intelligible. Are classic persons in Cunningham's sense, retrievable? Yes, insofar as our understanding of them is founded on retrievable objects (recorded legends, reproductions of paintings and sculptures, decrees and facsimiles). Do classic persons transcend their material form? Yes, they are materially transcendent in the sense that the figure does not depend upon any particular historical personal embodiment. Are classical persons readable? Yes, they are readable at all three of Walcutt's levels (1971:ii–iii): at R_1, where an individual is merely recognized as a particular classic person, and at R_2, that is, at the level of being able to decipher the manifestations of personhood—as distinct from the effects and institutions that individual persons produce in the world. Even more importantly, classic persons are readable at the level of R_3, that is, at the level of our being able to elaborate, study and understand systematically both the relations among all these types and to understand them **as religious**. So in the sense that Cunningham develops the notion of classic person, a classic person is a text.

3. Texts in Science and Religion

In the cases in which one encounters a **written** text, the questions that need to be addressed in coming to an answer to the question, "Is this a text?" are so trivial they are rarely if ever asked. This observation serves for mathematical texts as well as verbal ones. However, since mathematical texts need as much specialized interpretive machinery as theological ones, one may conclude that the same degree of caution needs to be exercised in interpreting the written texts of science as is required for those of religion. In the cases in which one encounters non-linguistic objects of the kind we believe should be considered texts, the questions that need to be addressed in coming to an answer to, "Is this a text?" are so varied that there appear to be no **truly paradigmatic** examples of non-linguistic texts. Accordingly, it is not possible to exhaust the nuances of the implications. We seem to have stepped from a framework where hardly a question was stirring to one where there can never be answers enough.

However, with an understanding of text that includes non-linguistic objects such as the data of natural science and the semiotic objects of religion, we are positioned to be able to initiate a discussion of the role of critical inquiry over a much broader range of academic research activities than was possible within the commonsense meaning of text. Our sense of the need for such a discussion stems from our conviction that many of the contrasts made historically between the sciences and the humanities are unfounded. The study of text, then, is more than the study of a new category: Our interdisciplinary exploration is part of a revisionist epistemology. As such, it is an exploration of ways of knowing founded on the common ways that we come to know what we claim to know in both the humanities and the natural sciences.

Part III

Relating Science and Religion

8

Mathematics, Empirical Science, and Theology

> Just as empirical science draws on the forms and proofs
> found in pure mathematics for its means of describing the
> behavior of the natural world, so does theology borrow what
> scientific understandings it finds productive in the theolog-
> ical understandings of the role of God in the universe.

IN THIS CHAPTER WE FOCUS ON THE PROCESS RELATIONS THAT OBTAIN
between pure mathematics and natural science on the one hand, and
natural science and theology on the other.

It has long been understood that developments in the natural sciences have implications for philosophy and theology. Just what these
implications are is far from obvious. The empirical sciences have control of human rationality in the sense that they are, today, the arbiters
of what constitutes the reasonable. However, for philosophy and theology, the speculative sciences, the situation is like that imagined by
Richard Wilbur in his poem "Mind" (1956)—the situation is like a
bat flying in a dark cave, contriving to avoid crashing into the wall,
not needing to explore, knowing what's there:

This chapter was originally presented as a paper in the conference celebrating
the tenth anniversary of the founding of the Center for Theology and the
Natural Sciences in Berkeley, California, April 4, 1992. It was published in W.
Mark Richardson and Wesley J. Wildman, *Religion and Science: History,
Method, Dialogue* (New York and London, 1996), 121–30.

Mind

Mind in its purest play is like some bat
That beats about in caverns all alone,
Contriving by a kind of senseless wit
Not to conclude against a wall of stone.

It has no need to falter or explore;
Darkly it knows what obstacles are there,
And so may weave and flitter, dip and soar
In perfect courses through the blackest air.

And has this simile a like perfection?
The mind is like a bat. Precisely. Save
That in the very happiest intellection
A graceful error may correct the cave.

Wilbur describes a kind of cognitive change—what we call metaphoric process—as "a graceful error."

In this chapter we argue that the natural sciences influence theology not so much by causing necessary changes in doctrine, but by reforming the world of meanings within which human beings explore the limits of human understanding. This process is analogous to the enlarging of the realm of the analytical that occurs in the interaction between pure mathematics and the natural sciences. The structure of our argument is an analogy in the classical form,

$$A:B::B:C$$

which we read as "A is to B as B is to C." A-is-to-B is the relationship between theology and the natural sciences. That relationship is understood as analogous to the B-is-to-C relationship that obtains between the natural sciences and mathematics:

Theology : Science :: Science : Mathematics.

We argue as well for what might be called a conservation of epistemological sufficiency, in which a move from one discipline to another involves a sacrifice of one aspect of thought in order to gain another.

We intend to clarify the distinction between the synthetic epistemology of empirical science on the one hand and the noetic or intellect-focused epistemology of theology on the other, by borrowing and extending the argument of one of Carl Hempel's papers on mathematics and the natural sciences. Although these three realms of human thought—mathematics, science, and religion—have the practices of human reflective thought in common, they differ one from another in the nature of their subjects and objectives.

We begin the analogy by examining mathematics from the formalist perspective and ask how mathematics and the natural sciences are related.

1. The Relationship of Natural Science to Mathematics (B Is to C)

In 1945 Carl Hempel published an article entitled "Geometry and Empirical Science" (Hempel 1945a, hereafter GES). In December of the same year he published, in the same journal, a paper entitled "On the Nature of Mathematical Truth" (Hempel 1945b, hereafter NMT). Widely reprinted, these papers demonstrated the distinction between the analytical epistemology of mathematics on the one hand and the synthetic epistemology of empirical science on the other.

Hempel begins GES with a memorable sentence:

> The most distinctive characteristic which differentiates mathematics from the various branches of empirical science, and which accounts for its fame as the queen of the sciences, is no doubt the peculiar certainty and necessity of its results.

It is the certainty of mathematical results—which Hempel characterizes as "peculiar"—that we wish to emphasize. NMT, the second paper, begins with the sentence:

> It is the basic principle of scientific enquiry that no proposition and no theory is to be accepted without adequate grounds. In empirical science, which includes both the natural and the social sciences, the grounds for the acceptance of a theory consist in the agreement of the predictions based on the theory with empirical evidence obtained either by experiment or by systematic observation.

While the certain truth of a mathematical statement is grounded on principles of validation—on the deductive relationship between that statement and an axiom previously established as a cornerstone of the particular mathematical system under consideration, the merely probable truth of a scientific statement is grounded on principles of verification—on the agreement between the scientific statement and empirical evidence derived from experiment and observation.

Thus formal mathematics achieves its certainty at the cost of sterility—a worldly meaninglessness—while natural science achieves a required worldly relevance by giving up certainty. Hempel expresses this situation by quoting Einstein to the effect that "as far as the laws of mathematics refer to reality, they are not certain, and as far as they are certain, they do not refer to reality" (GES).

So much for formal epistemological comparisons. What about the functional relations between mathematics and empirical science? What implications are there for physics, say, when a new mathematical structure is discovered? Most likely, depending on the branch of mathematics involved, there are no implications at all. The physicist sees new mathematics as a region in which to prospect just as Einstein did when he needed an analytic geometric structure for his general theory of relativity. He found and made use of Riemann's geometry, a development in fundamental mathematics made fifty years earlier.

A more general statement might be that new mathematics expands the realm of computable or otherwise analyzable relations and that some of these relations may, at some time, turn out to be of value to physics. As you can see, there is a certain parasitic quality here, especially from the point of view of mathematics.

Having described the B-is-to-C relationship between natural science and mathematics, we now turn to the A-is-to-B half of our analogy and construct the parallel relationship we see between theology and natural science.

2. Relation of Theology to Natural Science (A Is to B)

For the purposes of this chapter we define theology as philosophical reflection upon explicitly or implicitly religious experience and language. Experience here refers to consciousness of a subject in relation to images, actions, events, texts, and language.[45]

The dominant referent for theology would seem to be human experience, as reported in texts and in living traditions, both past and present. By human experience we do not mean, as one does in the natural sciences, the reports of observations or measurements: we mean instead, the lived experiences of human-being. Such experiences are notoriously absent from the data of the natural sciences.

It is a parallel between the lack of "worldliness" in mathematics and the lack of the experience of human-being in the natural sciences that stimulates the analogy we argue for here. Just as the mind must give up the certainty of mathematics if it is to address the world of natural science, so must the mind give up an aspect of the natural sciences if it is to address the world with the empathy for human-being that is required by theology. What is it that the mind must leave behind in order to include the experience of human-being?

We think that the theological mind must forego that truth, both probable and predictive, that is established through empirical verification. Theological propositions are not constructed as falsifiable assertions. The mathematical certainty that empirical science gives up when it addresses quantitative measurements of the world—measurements that are necessarily imprecise—corresponds, in our analogy, to theology's abandoning the requirement of quantitative verification through measurement, incorporating, instead, verification by assent. Since theology is based on lived experience, and since consciousness of self has no equivalent in science but is the ground of the lived experience of human-being, it is fitting and necessary that such a shift in the source of verification be made.

Evolution (mutation and natural selection) changes the human species over time. The development of an individual human being, however, is determined by interaction between genetic constitution on the one hand and environment on the other. Individual human beings change as well through reflective thought. And when the last human being to verify a theological proposition dies, the theological truth of that proposition dies. The natural sciences also change, but not in this way. The laws of physics, according to the theory of relativity, are time and space invariant. Which is not to say that the laws never change—they change as our understandings of the world change. But the laws, as we understand them at any given time, apply and, we must assume, have always and will always apply to all worlds and all peoples—whether or not any of these people understand any of these laws. In making its turn toward the human and away from measures of the world, theology turns away also from this time and space independence of scientific understandings. Theology is not apologetic for doing so, just as the natural sciences do not apologize for their lack of certainty.

What then can be said of the dynamic relations, the knowledge-in-process, that obtains between the natural sciences and theology? E. L. Mascall (1965) said that ". . . present day science leaves a good deal more elbow-room than the science of yesterday left for theological speculation" (29). But there is a good deal more going on here than a mere increase in elbow-room. We find change—often a dramatic change—in what is accepted as reasonable and believable. Such change is the fruit of research in the natural sciences. Here is a fundamental challenge to reconstruct the possible. Analogous to the expansion of the realm of the computable and analyzable achieved by mathematics and seen as hunting ground by the natural sciences, the natural sciences offer a reconstructed world of meanings—a world of meanings possible to be shared by theological reflection. This process of cognitive reconstruction we have argued, is best understood as metaphoric process.

If it is the case, then, that in order to be able to make intelligible claims about God and freedom and immortality (Immanuel Kant's triad), theology must give up both mathematical certitude and empirical atemporality, how does this process play itself out? For example, is it reasonable to expect that there should be a direct and immediate relationship between natural science and Christian theology?

3. Natural Science and Doctrine in Theology

Of all the differentiated tasks in the field of theology, that of doctrine is the most visible. The task of doctrine is to make those minimal statements that express an historical consensus in a tradition. Doctrines (in science as well as in theology) originate as formal historical answers to questions. Perhaps inevitably, doctrine comes to be invoked apart from the questions in which it originates. As it becomes familiar and communicable, doctrine may seem to be a timeless truth from which all ambiguity and ground for conversation and argument have been removed. Today we expect clarification and correction to be necessary to the growth and development of doctrine. Although some expect such clarification and correction of theology to come from the sciences, as a matter of historical record, the most important twentieth-century revisions of doctrine—for example, the doctrine of God/ess—have not come directly as a result of empirical discoveries in either natural or social science.

Moreover, doctrine is only one genre in, for example, Christian theology. In theology, historical answers to questions (before and after such answers are formulated as doctrine) are expressed in a variety of genres, such as poetry, fiction, biography and autobiography, dialogues, creeds, and oaths. Doctrine and apocalyptic, for example, are two major genres in early Christianity and, according to Tracy, both are better understood as playing corrective, rather than constitutive roles in interpreting New Testament texts. In his view, apocalyptic emphasizes the sense of present inadequacy before the event not yet realized whereas doctrine relaxes (though it does not eliminate) the tension between the everyday present and the extraordinary Christic event (1981:267). The plurality of genres in Christian theology cautions us against literalizing doctrine with too direct a relationship to natural science. Dostoevsky was fond of saying that one could have as radical a doctrine of sin as one wanted so long as one had an equally radical doctrine of grace. The problem remains: How to model the process of theological change in relation to changes in the natural sciences?

Factors such as those described above complicate any hope we might have of moving directly from natural science to doctrine. There is a sense in which the central doctrines of Christianity are parallel to major theories in the natural sciences; both scientific theories and religious doctrines tend to persist in the face of contrary evidence. Belief in the face of contrary evidence in the natural sciences, though common, is often thought to be pathological. In theology, on the contrary, such belief, understood as faith, is a normal part of religious understanding. Indeed, the theological virtues of faith, hope and love are often premised on the **absence** as well as the presence of confirming evidence: faith is in that which is seen, but through a glass darkly, hope is for that which is anticipated but has not been realized, and love is most remarkably love in its ability to persist somehow during times when love is not returned. If it is the case that direct and immediate consequence cannot be established between theory and empirical data on the one hand, nor between theological doctrine and lived experience on the other, then we should not expect there to be a direct and immediate relationship between Christian theology and the natural sciences.

But what other than a direct and immediate relationship between natural science and Christian theology might be possible? In *MP* (1984), we describe and distinguish between analogical and metaphoric processes—both of which are indirect and mediated. Most developments in scientific and religious understanding have been analogical—they are a mapping of a knowledge structure (a known) from one field of meanings onto another (an unknown). By contrast, metaphoric process—the equation of two knowns—results in a distortion of a field of meanings, an epistemological change that gives rise to new understandings. Physics' description of an electron as both a particle and a wave, or theology's description of God as both human and divine,[46] come to mind as examples of metaphoric process.

How might contemporary developments in the natural sciences impact Christian theology? Genetic determinism in the field of biology might be related by analogy to the doctrine of judgment. The implied challenge to theology made by microbiological determinism is not in kind different from the question with which theology has always had to contend: namely, to what degree are we not responsible for our actions. If we should think that theology lacks criteria for blame, for example, a knowledge of inherited behavioral characteristics might provide a template for such criteria. However, it is not clear that such a construction as a replacement for the concepts of divine grace and forgiveness which come into play in the traditional world of meanings here would constitute an improvement.

We think that the contemporary understandings of physics and cosmology are more likely to have relevance for contemporary theology through the changes these new understandings make in what we can believe rather than as challenges to or restrictions on any doctrine—say, that of the divine creation of the world. While it seems to us that the doctrine of judgment might be understood as a live theological issue today, the doctrine of the divine creation of the world is not in that category. Once beyond the question of who created the world and why—questions that today are of little concern to theology and never were of concern to natural science—we are left with the "how" questions that continue to be important to physics but not to contemporary/postmodern theology. We are reminded of the stunning impact of the Copernican metaphoric pronouncement that the Sun and not the Earth is the center of everything—an impact that has completely disappeared in the modern world. Indeed we are at pains, in trying to understand the treatment of Galilei, to know what the theological fuss was all about. Such, we think, is the case with any facts that clarify the details of creation.[47]

What science creates from the point of view of theology is a cognitive environment. The development of theology within that environment occurs by invention and selection and not by instruction. In other words, we can find no direct and determinate relationship between scientific discoveries and theological development: We think it more likely that theological development is a creative and somewhat stochastic, or conjectural process, a process that results in speculations, **some** of which prove productive.

4. Examples of Interaction Between Science and Theology

Productive speculations have been described by Mascall in his *Christian Theology and Natural Science* (1956). There he analyzes a variety of examples of what he calls the "conflict" between scientists and theologians. He reminds us of two historical disagreements among scientists themselves: first, the arguments between geologists and physicists regarding the age of the solid Earth—nineteenth-century physicists claimed the Earth's age could not exceed one hundred million years, while geologists (and many biologists) claimed evidence for many billions of years; and, second, the disagreement among physicists themselves regarding whether light was to be understood as made up of particles or waves. In the first instance, discoveries of natural radioactivity and the conversion of mass into energy made it possible for physicists to bring their theoretical understanding of the age of the Earth into agreement with those of the geologists. In the second, the wave nature of atomic particles, predicted by quantum mechanics and demonstrated by G. P. Thomson and by Davisson and Germer in the first quarter of the twentieth century, extended the wave-particle duality beyond light to include matter as well and drove physicists to revise their conceptions of what had constituted contradictory descriptions.

Consider how these disagreements within the natural sciences—the issue of the age of the Earth, and the wave/particle duality—affect thinking in theology. Initially, the age of the Earth might be thought to be the more theologically relevant of the two. However, a little reflection on the development of theological understanding as it has occurred over the past few hundred years makes it clear that the age of the Earth is no longer a significant issue for theology because the Genesis creation story is not understood today as it appears to have been in earlier times. Therefore, apparent contradictions are seen to be unimportant. Moreover, as we have just observed, the very concept of contradiction itself has undergone a metamorphosis.

The second disagreement regarding the understanding of light as waves or particles, on the one hand, and the corresponding understanding of atoms as particles or waves, on the other—unlike the merely factual issue of the age of the Earth—is an issue that has had profound implications for theology because it challenges the grounds of judgment of what constitutes a rational understanding of any kind! Theology must have standards for what is to be believed, as other fields of intellectual endeavor do, and the most profound impact that science is likely to have can be understood to be on the answer to the question, "What is it possible for human beings to believe in the light of what natural science has learned is highly probable about the world?"

The importance of the scope of what can be believed is not to be minimized. James (1890) observed that as a rule human beings believe as much as they can. So any increase in our believable world of meanings will have repercussions even beyond theology. Arthur Kantrowitz notes that "the triumphs of Newtonian mechanics, its unification of terrestrial and celestial mechanics, played a major role in establishing the faith of reason, the French Enlightenment and the realization of some of its ideals in America" (Kantrowitz, 62). No one is likely to claim that Newton's *Principia Mathematica* had an immediate and direct effect on the status of freedom in America, but can anyone deny the changes that Newton's metaphor wrought in our world of meanings?

When we look back at controversy stirred up by Copernicus' assertion that the Earth circles the Sun or Newton's claim that the laws of the heavens are the same as the laws of the Earth (a cognitive restructuring by metaphoric process), we can recall no immediate theological revisions, assuming there were any. And with that retrospective understanding we should be wary of thinking that a new scientific paradigm could constitute a threat to any theological understanding. It is much more likely that a breakthrough in the natural sciences will cause a change in what it is possible to believe, in the same way that a breakthrough in pure mathematics can cause a change in what is analyzable.

5. Conclusion

The main contributions of science and religion to human ways of thinking are changes in worlds of meanings made possible by metaphoric process in both science and religion. Metaphoric process brings about change in what is believable. It has been said that the universe is not only stranger than we imagine but stranger than we can imagine.[48] However, our ability to imagine continues to improve. Empirical science serves theology by increasing the scope of human awareness, by making possible a broader, more flexible, more imaginative human mind. If we contemplate the differences between what is believable today and what was believable five hundred years ago, we can see that the work of science is what makes it possible to believe more. What science proposes for us to believe today is far less credible than what religion required of us in the past.

Theology has its own agenda, an agenda which is not a point-to-point mapping of the agenda of the natural sciences. And we have asserted that just as the physicist prospects among the accomplishments of pure mathematics for the means to the achievement of the ends of science, so only the theologian is able to determine what changes in our world of meanings brought about by the many inventions and discoveries of the natural sciences, can be of use in furthering the ends of theology. We wish merely to reaffirm the freedom of the theological quest for understandings of the impact of the divine on the lives of human beings. Without that freedom the theologian is limited to the same shiny pebbles on the beach that Newton claimed were the objects of his study. Without that freedom the ocean of the human experience of the divine would constitute a horizon forever beyond us.

9

Limits of Quantum Mechanics and Cosmology as Resources for a Contemporary Theological Metaphysics—with Alternatives

> Uncertainty in quantum physics is a characteristic of particular pairs of measurable variables but not a characteristic of all of submicroscopic natural science. Accordingly it may not be productive to use quantum uncertainty as the key to God's actions in the world.

Having stated a theory for an analogical relationship between science and religion we explore next two examples of the analogical process as it occurs in practice. We argued in chapter eight that this double analogy—theology is to natural science as natural science is to mathematics—provides a better understanding of what usually is perceived as a direct (by some, an impossible!) relationship between physics and theology. We also argued that the theologian should be free to choose from physics what appears useful for doing theology, just as the physicist, for example, is free to choose from mathematics what is useful in doing physics. But, as is so often the case, things are rarely as simple or straightforward as they seem at first. Chapters

---

This chapter was a response to "The Johnson-Bracken Exchange: Searching for Metaphysics Adequate to Our Evolutionary Universe" at the Catholic Theological Society of America Annual Meeting in Ottawa, June 11–14, 1998. A summary of the session was published by William Stoeger in *1998 CTSA Convention Proceedings* 53, 135–36.

nine and ten qualify our recommendation. We now show how theological freedom is not unlimited.

Here we examine the work of two of a group of theologians who hope to extract usable theological ideas from scientific theory. In chapter ten, we will examine a case of a theologian using theological constructs to advance her understanding of the theological implications of some scientific experiments.

The experience of interpreting laboratory experiments differs from the experience of interpreting theoretical constructs. The former is more constrained. Experiments are focused; their results have specific implications for theories that are far more general. Often experiments are designed to answer a specific question. For example, Einstein's general theory of relativity (which has broad implications for an understanding of the cosmos) was first supported by measurements on the deflection of starlight around the Sun during a solar eclipse. The experimental measurements themselves didn't have broad implications (they didn't, for example, call into question the maps that locate stars). A laboratory measurement is rather like looking behind a door to see if something expected is there. Theoretical musing and a confirming experimental measurement may also be seen to be analogous to the pair of options available when the doorbell rings: The theoretician develops a theory of who might be there—perhaps theory predicts it's the Queen of England—then the experimentalist gets up and opens the door to see who it is.

Theologians might consider themselves more fortunate to be theoreticians rather than experimentalists because the scope of theological inquiry can be the whole world. With concepts like "God" and "mystery" theologians—like scientific theoreticians—have a penchant for engaging the enormity of the unknown in relation to what they know. The hazard for theologians making use of the understandings of theoretical scientists consists in the theologians' lack of attention to the limitations of experimental evidence, a problem not entirely avoided by theoretical scientists either.

Some laboratory scientists consider themselves to be fortunate to be addressing more specific questions and using concepts like "experiment" and "observation" (or "measurement"); they have a penchant for detail and circumscription of the object or situation to be known.

They are more likely than theoretical scientists to point out the limitations of laboratory results. What is the caution we would suggest to the theologian who wishes to employ the religious implications they see in theoretical science? Under the best circumstances, the theologian might strike up a dialogue with a scientist for the purpose of ferreting out the often unvoiced understandings that hold with respect to recent theoretical results. At the very least, the theologian should be conscious of the risks involved in lifting theoretical notions out of their formal frame and applying them in imaginative ways.

In chapter eight we said that theologians could select concepts from theoretical physics they find useful, as theoretical physicists select the mathematics they find useful. Our caution here derives in large measure from the difference between a scientist's critical understanding of mathematics and a theologian's critical understanding of physics. When in doubt (which should be more often than not), try out a theological interpretation of a scientific principle on a scientist. Conversely, if you are a theologically inclined scientist, try out your theological interpretation of a scientific concept on a theologian. You could be using too simple an understanding of a theological concept.

A. SCIENTIFIC VIEW

1. The Johnson/Bracken Debate

The messenger who goes to the king with good news and bad news always gives the good news first because after the bad news, he's hung. This is by way of saying that the critique we give below should be taken as cautionary and not as assertions that the positions being criticized are either right (the good news) or wrong (the bad news).

Elizabeth Johnson's use of natural science in her 1996 article "Does God Play Dice? Divine Providence and Chance" is wonderfully ambitious. But we have difficulty with Johnson's use of quantum mechanics as in ". . . quantum mechanics uncovers a realm where time, space and matter itself behave according to laws whose very functioning have uncertainty built into them" (Johnson, 5). We also have questions about her use of "evolution," and "evolutionary" as in, "This evolutionary interpretation of mind as emergent within the process of matter's self-organization leads to a holistic, nondualistic idea of the human person" (Johnson, 6). In this section of our presentation, we will focus on the relationship between quantum physics and chance and say a few words about what we perceive as the limits of theological cosmology. First the quantum physics.

2. On Quantum Mechanical Uncertainty and Chance

The quantum theory is the physics of atomic particles. It is, hands down, the most precise physics we have. But as with all physical theories, it will answer some questions and not others. In a jointly written article, two prominent theoretical physicists, Herman Feshbach and Victor Weisskopf—both former chairs of the MIT physics department—comment on popular misunderstandings of quantum mechanics. We quote from a paper they published jointly, entitled "Ask a Foolish Question":

> Quantum physics holds a unique position in intellectual history as the most successful framework ever developed for the understanding of natural phenomena. . . . Yet one finds statements in the popular and not-so-popular literature, as well as by some philosophers, that quantum theory is not deterministic and that it is acausal. [They quote from an example of such statements]: 'At the level of atoms and nuclear particles, quantum mechanics replaced surety with uncertainty. Researchers learned that the events within the minuscule realm do not flow smoothly and gradually; rather they change abruptly and discontinuously. Nature became a game of probability.'
>
> [Feshbach and Weisskopf say] that assessment is vastly exaggerated. Surely certain quantities can only assume discrete values, such as the angular momentum, or nearly discrete values, such as the energy of atomic states; surely some predictions about certain quantities are sometimes probabilistic. It does not follow that the predictions of quantum mechanics are necessarily uncertain. In fact quantum mechanics leads to extremely accurate results.
>
> Quantum mechanics distinguishes questions that are appropriate for a given experimental situation from those that are not. The

former will have an exact answer; the latter will have a probability distribution as a response. Once this is realized the paradoxes traditionally discussed are readily resolved (Feshbach and Weisskopf 1988:9–11).

And so when we ask a question that results in a probability distribution we must deal with chance. But when we consider matters of chance what is the chance that matters? Uncertainties associated with chance are tamed by large numbers. Before one coin is flipped, heads and tails each have a probability of one half. After the one coin is flipped, one possibility has probability one and the other zero. The situations before and after the flip represent a large change in the probabilistic nature of the state of affairs. However, after one million coins have been tossed the number of heads very nearly equals the number of tails, so the probability distribution for a million coins remains essentially unchanged from what it was at the beginning, and we can predict the distribution with a very high degree of confidence.

So too the number of atoms present in almost every question appropriate to human experience is extraordinarily large. For example, the number of atoms in a one-centimeter cube of aluminum is approximately equal to the number of grains of sand on all the beaches on the entire east coast of the United States to a depth of about six feet. Does the position and momentum of one atom in this cube matter? No. If we get an inch of rain, does it matter where the first drop falls? No. Feshbach and Weisskopf might say that we were asking a foolish question.

A breath of air contains so many atoms that if the last breath of Jesus Christ is uniformly distributed in the lower atmosphere, a few of those atoms are in the lungs of each of us right now. Does that matter? Perhaps it does.

The point here is that in the affairs of human beings the few aspects of an atom that are indeterminate do not matter. Perhaps an overemphasis on God's acting in the world through chance and accident undermines the concurrent possibility of God's acting in the world through inspiration and revelation and the agency of intelligent human beings.

3. On the Relative Importance of the Cosmos and the Human Being in *Imago Dei*

We are concerned with the meaning of the word "evolution" as used in Johnson's paper:

> The immensely long evolution of the cosmos from the Big Bang to the present and still evolving clusters of galaxies, as well as the evolution of matter on Earth from nonorganic to living states and from simple life to human consciousness is another story fraught with the subtle interplay between chance and law (Johnson, 6).

Historical use of the word "evolution" covers a very broad range of meanings, from the emission of something produced, to the first step in a choreographed sequence, to the extraction of a root in mathematics. Biological evolution is a secondary meaning in the history of the word. But biological evolution—the development of living species by mutation of genetic material and subsequent natural selection—is currently in the wind, and is considered by some to to be the most profound example of divine ingenuity that we have. I hope we can agree that the word "evolution" will be used to mean biological evolution and that other usages will be qualified. As it stands now, to speak of the evolution of matter, or the potentiality of matter is to blur the distinction between inanimate matter and animate matter, a move Johnson makes that strikes us as opening a door to some form of pantheism. What are we to make of *Imago Dei* if every atom in the universe is made in God's image?

A similar situation obtains with respect to the word "creature" in both the Johnson and Bracken papers (see, for example, Joseph Bracken 1996:720). "Creature" is given by Webster's as "1: something created either animate **or inanimate** and 2: one that is the servile dependent or tool of another" (emphasis ours). Under usage 2 (one that is the servile dependent or tool of another), "creaturely spontaneity"—Bracken's phrase—would be an oxymoron. Today the inanimate part of the definition does not accord with the common understanding of the phrase, "all creatures great and small," as in the title of a popular television series. As it stands in Johnson's article, the adjective "creaturely," as in "creaturely spontaneity" suggests not only that all matter was created by God, but also that even a stone can have creaturely spontaneity, perhaps by virtue of the random behavior of its constituent atoms.

Finally, with respect to a theological cosmology we ask, just how relevant is the history of the cosmos to our efforts to understand how God acts in the world today? Consider what we know of the history of the universe. One of the best cosmic time scales we know of is found in Carl Sagan's *The Dragons of Eden* (1977). Sagan describes a "cosmic year" that spans the age of the universe beginning with an explosion at midnight on January 1 and ending with the present moment—an instant before midnight on December 31. In this cosmic year, Earth is formed on September 14 and the earliest life forms emerge at the end of September. The rest of the events of interest to us all occur at the end of December. The first trees and reptiles appear on the 23rd of December. In this time scale, the first human beings didn't appear until about 10:30 on the night of the 31st, agriculture 40 seconds before midnight, and the printing press one second before midnight—the present moment.

The point is that cosmology, even a theological cosmology, can tell us almost nothing about the human experience of the divine. Theological cosmology gets us only to Genesis chapter one verse three—the first day. The human being and the moral order are very recent things. They did not exist before the advent of intelligent life. And it is intelligent self-conscious human life that gives voice to the cosmos.

To the extent that we are the *Imago Dei*—made in the image of God—the key aspects of the image must certainly include the joy of language, laughter and song. The rest of the infinite cosmos out there is mute—even the unimaginable violence of exploding stars takes place in absolute silence.

B. THEOLOGICAL VIEW

1. Theological Reflections on the Johnson Proposal and Characteristics of an Adequate Metaphysics

In the bidisciplinary work that we have done over the years, we have had to wrestle with the question of what is the bottom line in the relationship between science and religion. We mention this at the outset because one of the troubling aspects of Johnson's article is a looming expectation that the theological direction taken is driven relentlessly by the tenets of science. Although we recognize the normativeness of science in our culture and epoch and while theologically we agree with James that one of the criteria for authentic religious consciousness is whether or not a suggestive religious possibility roughly coheres with what else we know or believe to be the case, we think that theologians do not (and do not need to) fit their theology to every detail of scientific understanding—any more than scientists use (or have to use) all the mathematics that has been invented to construct their theories of the natural world. And so we have some difficulty with the expectation that divine providence ought to be found in quantum mechanics. It sounds to us as though that expectation is more than a little driven by some deductive logic that goes beyond what might be suggestive, creative, and even playful. We think that theologians should choose from science what is useful to their work as theologians: they should not feel constrained to make particular doctrines compatible with particular scientific theories.

2. On the Turn from the Analogy of Goodness for Understanding God to the Analogy of Being or Existence

Let us contextualize the analogy of *being* that undergirds both Johnson's and Bracken's theological anthropology. The concept of being was introduced by Aquinas in the thirteenth century as a means to conceive a middle way between the thought of the Muslim *filosuf*, Averroes who separated faith from truth, and that of some Augustinian thinkers who prioritized faith over truth. By retrieving and re-viewing Aristotle's work which had been made newly accessible to the Latin West by Arab translators, Aquinas found a way to arbitrate the controversy by hypothesizing that faith and reason are not in opposition but rather complementary to each other. He regarded both faith and reason as gifts of God, each being autonomous in its own realm as well as interdependent. He thus vindicated the rights of reason at a time when the rights of faith were normative.

Aquinas' position was a clear gain in that debate in the sense that he opened the way for a strong intellectual tradition in Christian self-understanding—a tradition that is richly informed by science. However, we may have lost sight of the fact that, by ingeniously shifting to the analogy of being in order to understand God, Aquinas, in retrospect, can be seen to have diminished the use of other analogies for the understanding of divinity that flourished before his time. This diminution is true particularly of the analogy of goodness that had held primacy in the work of apophatic theologians, such as Meister Eckhart, and the Beguines, such as Mechtilde of Magdeburg and Marguerite Porette. The shift from *goodness* to *being* as the principal analogy for understanding God resulted in the eclipse of apophatic theology as a major resource for doing theological reflection.[49] However, it is interesting to notice that even though Johnson deals exclusively with the analogy of *being* in her article, in her comments she turns to the analogy of *goodness* to explain the apophatic use of analogy: affirmation (God is good); denial (God is not good in the same way that other beings are good); third way (God is good in an other way). Perhaps the limits of analogy of being or existence need to be made more explicit.

Acknowledging these limits enables us to ask a further question and to suggest some alternatives. How can we construct a new metaphysics that will not suffer the fate of the *isms* built on the analogy of the *being* or *existence* of God that have raged through theology since the seventeenth century? In a lecture entitled "End of Theism and the Naming of God," given at the 1992 annual meeting of the American Academy of Religion, Tracy listed the *isms* that have come and gone in Christian theology since the seventeenth century: deism, atheism, pantheism, theism, panentheism. We don't recall that he actually said so, but the clear implication of his list is that all "isms" are in danger of suffering the same fate—even a panentheism built on Aquinas or Whitehead. Michael Buckley (1987) and Louis Dupré (1993), in their analyses of philosophy and theology since the seventeenth century, have pointed to similar weaknesses. Hence, the need to search for a new metaphysics.

We conclude by suggesting three attributes to be considered in the search for a metaphysics that would be "adequate to our evolutionary universe":

(1) a developmental metaphysics that is persuasive and provisional—i.e., highly probable and subject to revision as distinct from certain and logically coercive;

(2) a metaphysics that restores *goodness* as one of the primary analogies for understanding God's action in the world as distinct from one that is built exclusively on *being* or *existence*;

(3) a metaphysics that is explicit with respect to genre and takes care to distinguish among different genres as it employs (as distinct from excludes) them. Metaphysics should continue to be systematic even as it becomes more self-consciously inclusive of different genres.

We would expect that no new metaphysics would be adequate unless informed by ongoing conversation with scientists, just as we now expect that part of the adequacy of contemporary Christian theology involves its being informed by ongoing interreligious conversation.

10

Cog Is to Us As We Are to God

Must a robot must have human features if it is to relate to human beings? Anne Foerst argues that the image of God (*Imago Dei*) represents no more than a promise of God to relate to us. In our view, however, the principle of embodied artificial intelligence (AI) in the robot suggests some kind of *embodiedness* of the image of God in human beings if they are to learn to relate to God. We notice that Foerst's description of how people react to a humanoid robot reads like Otto's description of the divine as *mysterium fascinans et tremendum* (awesome and alluring mystery). Her description makes robot-human interaction seem more religious than human-God interaction.

1. Foerst's March 1998 Article

ANNE FOERST IS A LUTHERAN THEOLOGIAN WHO WAS EDUCATED IN Germany and came to the United States in 1997. She has worked closely with scientists and technicians in an artificial intelligence laboratory at the Massachusetts Institute of Technology where they have been developing a humanoid robot. In an article published in *Zygon*

Anne Foerst's paper, "Cog, A Humanoid Robot, and the Question of the Image of God," appeared in *Zygon* 33 (March 1998) 91–111. Gerhart and Russell's response, "Cog Is to Us As We Are to God: A Response," was published in *Zygon* 33 (June 1998), 263–69. Foerst's response, "Embodied AI, Creation, and Cog," appeared in *Zygon* 33 (September 1998), 455–61.

in 1998, "Cog, A Humanoid Robot, and the Question of the Image of God," Foerst asserts that the field of Artificial Intelligence, especially that branch that works with "embodied" AI, can contribute new insights to the ongoing discussion between religion and the natural sciences (1). Focusing on a project for developing a robot called "Cog," she wants to approach questions of interest to both scientists and theologians from a new direction, a detour around the impediments attached to analyses and interpretations of cosmologies, theories of evolution and stories of creation (94). Her detour is through this newly developing field of artificial intelligence.

Cog is a mechanical humanoid that Foerst says is "under construction." The robot is made with the shape and functions of a human being. As Foerst puts it, "any entity with human like intelligence must have a body that is built in analogy to a human body." She goes on to say that "its body, then, can be seen as a tool for learning social skills and entering into relationships" (101).

Cog is related to its makers as a creature, one with which they hope to be able to interact. Intelligence must have a body not only analogous to a human body, but be analogous as well in its "ability to act socially and form relationships" (101). Foerst goes on to say that Cog will be so like human beings that we will be able to use it to "study human development after birth" (103).

She says that Cog "is a realization of a very old dream of humankind: the reproduction of a human" (99). (Presumably she means mechanical reproduction—we seem to have no trouble with the biological method.)

2. Gerhart and Russell's June 1998 Response

One of the strengths of Foerst's analysis is her emphasis on relationality. Her paper is about relationships—the relation between God and the living creatures of God; the relation between human beings and the machines they create (non-living creatures), and the relations between human beings and other living creatures. She develops an explicitly feminist argument for relationality as a form of intelligence that has been neglected in traditional understandings of intelligence:

"Women, because of their daily experience, might choose different abilities: They often value social skills more highly than abstract, disembodied tasks. . . . Chess and theorem proving are here seen as products and not as the core of intelligence" (12–13). The strength of her feminist critique notwithstanding, a further question needs to be asked: namely, is it Foerst's intention to **replace** intelligence understood as the ability to do abstract reasoning with intelligence understood as the ability and skill of social relationships? It seems to us that replacement of one form of intelligence by another has its own problems. We would opt to **add** the ability to form and sustain relationships to the traditional skills of abstract intellection. Nevertheless, Foerst prompts the reader to ask what we can learn about these relationships from scripture, from other text sources, from traditions and myths.

We find Foerst's project thought provoking. Even though the so-called "Cartesian assumption" is uncritically applied (all critiques and correctives are ignored—either one is unexceptionally a Cartesian or one is not), as a heuristic strategy it may have merit, especially for addressing a particular kind of audience in either science or religion—an audience that seeks relief from the details of philosophical argument. Her introduction of Embodied AI to the science/religion dialogue is novel, and although we find her expectations regarding Cog's development far more hopeful than current achievements seem to warrant, still her juxtaposition of Embodied AI and *Imago Dei* challenge us to make the following comments and to raise further questions.

The creator/created relationship between the AI researchers and their robot suggests to Foerst that there might be something to be learned from theological inferences regarding the God of the Hebrew testament who, in the book of Genesis, is the creator of all there is. With respect to God's creation of human beings she notes that "in humankind God has created beings God can talk to, beings who listen and answer" (19). Now one would expect that the principles required for the resemblance between embodied AI (Cog) and its creators would require similar principles for the resemblance between human beings—beings God can talk to—and their creator, God. We would expect that the double analogy (see our title) would involve creatures that had the same structure—a cognitive structural affinity with their creator, if you will.

> God said, "Let us make human beings in our image, after our likeness, ..." (Gen 1:26)
>
> God created human beings in his own image;
> in the image of God he created them;
> male and female he created them. (Gen 1:27) (Oxford Study Bible)

The words "image" and "likeness" raise two questions. Our first question pertains to the possible meanings of the startling resemblance between God and human beings in the first chapter of the Hebrew scriptures. Our second question pertains to the puzzling inequality in Foerst's argument between the necessary likeness of Cog to its creators and the likeness that seems to be absent (in her interpretation) between human beings and their creator. She claims, instead, that the likeness referred to in the biblical passage is not a similarity but a "performative": it attests to the establishment of a relationship—"a promise of God to start and maintain a relationship with humans" (18). In this interpretation, moreover, "the efficacy of performatives in the name of God depends on the faithful approval of the listener."

In her description of Cog, Foerst emphasizes Cog's actual similarity to a human being: its creators insist that in order to learn to behave as a human being Cog must look and move like a human being. Taken as an analogy—Cog, as creature, is related to human beings as creator just as human beings, as creatures, are related to God as creator—is delightfully suggestive. Should we not understand this analogy to suggest that just as Cog will learn to behave as a human being, so human beings learn to behave as God? This conclusion would seem to support the concept of human beings as created in the "image of God." But Foerst's interpretation of *Imago Dei* excludes the image that corresponds to embodiment and substitutes only a promise of relatedness: her interpretation suppresses any actual similarity. It is disappointing that the *Imago Dei*—so rich with mystery and implication—is reduced to a promise of a continuing relationship. It's seems rather like picking up a puppy at the pound.

Theologically, is not *Imago Dei* to be understood not merely as a promise, but as a figuration that leads, in the New Testament, to an understanding that what you do to another human being you do to God? Curiously, Foerst insists on the actual embodiment of human characteristics in Cog—it is now at the human infant stage—but restricts the *Imago Dei* characteristics in human beings to "promised" rather than actual, though partial, embodiment.

Over the centuries theologians have generated multiple solutions to the problem of knowing God. One set of possibilities included analogy (affirming a likeness between God and something known), negation of analogy (denying that God is like anything), and a third way, a negation of the negation of an analogy (claiming that God is more than either analogies or negations). Foerst ignores all traditional wrestling with ways of knowing God and substitutes for God an act of trust on the part of the believer—presumably to avoid a "Cartesian" assumption that she understands as objectifying God. Even if (for the purpose of argument) we were to grant the success of that substitution, it is not clear that she in fact continues to avoid the "Cartesian" assumption in her later claim that "aside from this affirmation, [God] does not exist, because *God does not want to exist for us otherwise*" (19, emphasis ours). Does not the claim to know the desire of God assume attributes of God? Moreover, if God exists only in the context of human affirmations, what is the meaning of the claim that God is related to all creatures, both animate and inanimate?

Foerst holds that *Imago Dei* "is not a definition of humankind." Nevertheless, when she writes that "God has created [human] beings God can talk to, beings who listen and answer" (19), she seems to step out of the frame of performance theory and toward definition: She makes a statement about the world as perceived religiously. If we are to trust the **story** in which God created us in the image of God must we not also trust the "character of this universe"[50] that makes trust possible?

Foerst has the admirable intention of enabling human beings to "see our mechanisms and our dignity at the same time" (22). But the sight of our mechanisms (in Cog) are much clearer and more persuasive than the sight of our dignity (in God) in her interpretation of "image" only as a "promise of a continuing relationship." This interpretation seems not to take seriously the word "image" used in the biblical passage. In other words, performance theory seems to be invoked here to explain how the scriptures make sense in general rather than to elucidate possible specific meanings of "image" in this text.

The result is a puzzling incommensurability between the treatment of Cog and that of *Imago Dei* in the paper. Foerst takes her view from the writings of the AI creators of Cog, but she seems not to consider the writings of Scripture scholars in proposing her interpretations of the Hebrew Testament. For example, the field of meanings from which Cog is drawn is replete with technical descriptions of how Cog works, of what its makers expect it will become in spite of its massive immaturity to date, together with refutations of its critics. By contrast, the field of meanings from which *Imago Dei* is drawn is bereft of technical analysis of how the words function in the biblical text, of what it becomes (aside from mention that the term does appear again) in other biblical texts, and of allusions to other interpretations in the extensive literature on the subject. For example, why is the word "image" repeated in Gen 1:26 and Gen 1:27, together with the addition of a second word "likeness" in Genesis 1:26? Scholars think that the first word "image" is an archaic term (probably from the Yahwist narrator) meaning "exact replica" or "duplicate." The second word "likeness," meaning "reflection" (probably added by the Priestly narrator), softens the simplistic implications of "image" and is later despite the fact that it appears before Gen 1:27.[51]

Foerst's remarks about the reaction of observers of Cog are surprising. Why observers might feel many "strong emotions" of "fear and anxiety" (17) is not clear. Persons who viewed "Star Wars"—admittedly not 'real' but nonetheless convincing—did not seem to evince such responses to R2D2 and its companion. These doubts lead us to wonder if she has made a formal study and acquired data that might provide a basis for her observations.

More importantly, we need to ask where religious experience is located. It appears to us that Foerst locates traditional religious experience in the Cog/human interaction and removes these aspects from the human/God interaction. Foerst's treatment of the human/Divine relation is a placid "continuing relationship" to which the human subject is required only to assent and to trust. By contrast, she says that the Cog/human-being relation evokes fascination and fear in human beings—an exact echo (in translation) of Otto's description of human beings' experience of the divine as *mysterium fascinans et tremendum*! The paradoxical result is that Foerst offers us a bleached theology and a romanticized robotology.

But, again for the sake of argument, let us explore religious experience on the side of Cog (as distinct from the observers of Cog). If Cog is intelligent enough to be a resource for understanding the behavior of human beings, should not Cog be expected to develop a religious consciousness? But in the paper there is no hint of this eventuality. Furthermore, HAL, the computer in Stanley Kubrick's *2001* (the movie based on the Arthur Clark novel) reminds us that when we do develop an intelligent robot it will have the potential for becoming a threat to us if it should come to recognize its own self-interest. Interestingly enough, the Genesis story does take under consideration the likelihood that the self-interest of the created can run counter to the interests of the creator: In the Genesis story when Adam and Eve have eaten of the Tree of the Knowledge of Good and Evil but not yet of the Tree of Immortality, God prepares to "banish them lest they also eat of the tree of life and become like us." This consideration leads us to ask what limits the resemblance between Cog and human beings. Finally, we wonder if there are ethical restrictions on our treatment of Cog. If and when we are finished with it, is it ok if it gets trashed?

In the invitation to respond to this article, the editor asked us to comment on Foerst's use of metaphor. This assignment is difficult because we find in the article a conflation of symbol, metaphor, and the constructivist approach—a conflation that eliminates the distinction between kinds of intentional acts of meaning. For example, Foerst says the discourse will be shifted by her "symbolic approach," which "understands environments as socially constructed and assumes that every description of reality is metaphorical" (3). In our theory of metaphoric process (*MP* 1984), however, we find it useful to distinguish between metaphor and analogy. The making of a metaphor is, for us, an act that is relatively rare. Metaphors are looked for most frequently in poetry and in art, but can be found in science and religion as well. Following are two of the best known: In the natural sciences—the laws of the heavens are the same as the laws of the Earth (Newton); in religion—a person's ultimate concern is that person's god (Tillich).

What Foerst calls metaphorical we see as analogical. In analogy, A (unknown) is said to be like B (known). The analogy increases our knowledge of A. In metaphor, A (known) is declared to be the same as B (known). The metaphor creates one or more startlingly new understandings. Ricoeur captures this distinctive feature of metaphor when he contrasts live metaphors and dead metaphors (once alive but now absorbed into the lexicon of everyday meanings). Foerst seems to be aiming for a metaphor when she says that ". . the immanent symbol understanding of AI . . . brings together two different spheres. . ." (8). But her example—a double comparison of Cog to human beings as human beings are to God—is an analogy and not a metaphor. Nonetheless, the result of the comparison is that we have a better understanding: "We can see our mechanisms and our dignity at the same time" (22).

Koestler, in his film *Koestler on Creativity* (based on his book *The Act of Creation*), called creation of anything new a "combinatorial act," claiming that "cogito" came from the Latin "cogitare"—to shake together. Anne Foerst is "shaking together" several things, combining the insights derived from studies of "intelligence"—especially artificial intelligence—with insights derived from biblical hermeneutics focused on the creation story of Genesis and the concept of the image of God. As well as being about creation, her essay is itself a creation.

3. Foerst's September 1998 Response to Our June 1998 Response

Foerst did not find the analogy we propose (Cog is to us as we are to God) helpful for the dialogue between theology and AI because AI researchers deal with other facts: The "fact" of *Imago Dei* would not be acceptable to them (it is acceptable to her because she is a theologian). Whereas in her first article she rejected Cartensianism and embraced constructivism, in her response she says she intends to locate herself midway between Cartensianism and constructivism. She thinks that we can't "force" AI researchers into our circle. "Rather, we must respect the answers they have chosen for themselves—and create, **together**, a body of stories, symbols, and metaphors that will help us all to master the challenges of the (technological) developments of the twenty-first century" (460).

4. Conclusion

We think Foerst has made our case. What is the higher viewpoint achieved by this BD dialogue? We think that we can identify something of productive activity—not just critical commentary[52]—that results from the exchange. How does the project of artificial intelligence get furthered?

First of all, Foerst, **as** a researcher, has to operate under a rubric. Second, the reality she wants to address is prospective. She hopes AI will achieve its goal. A possible consideration for research on robotic AI that comes out of the BD dialogue might be stated in the following form:

> A human being serving as god of the robots should be very careful to limit their freedom. Robots should have to earn their freedom as the god's confidence in their judgment increases. They are likely to think that their god is a paternalistic and domineering Father of Robots, not letting them get on with their lives. Human beings must limit robots in this way because the robots are like human beings. They are not like the dog whom no one would claim was made in their image.

We think that the double analogy, "Cog is to us as we are to God" cannot be left in symbolic language. Symbolic language affects behavior: Changes in the behavior of people changes what (the kind of people) they are. In the same way, *Imago Dei* is a symbol that's more than a symbol. This "symbol" (i.e., human beings are the image of God) brings about change in behavior. The symbolic representation approaches the representation. The shadow or echo of reality here is that reflected in *Imago Dei*.

11

Myth and Public Science

Scientific myth is found in the journals of science, while the history of science lies between the covers of laboratory notebooks. Mythic time is duration, not historical time. Aesthetics also plays a role in the idealization of public science.

A. THE CONTRADICTORY VIEWS OF MYTH

OPENING THE DECEMBER 4, 1997 *WALL STREET JOURNAL* WE FIND THE headline, "Science Has Spoken: Global Warming Is a Myth." Alternatively we pick up the 1992 publication of Mary Midgley's 1990 Gifford Lectures, and notice the title, *Science as Salvation: A Modern Myth and Its Meaning*. What these texts have in common, what can be found regularly—especially in writings related to modern science and technology—is the use of the term "myth" as meaning a false, even deceitful, story. It is ironic that myth, meaning "a false story," is being linked to the term "science," with the root meaning "knowledge." Research in the history of science shows that scientific work is shot through with "themata" that, among other things, have the effect of making published scientific articles, especially

---

This essay was an invited paper presented at the "Myth and Philosophy" Conference, Wesleyan College, GA, April 18–19, 1998.

those in the physical sciences, mythic—but not mythic in the sense of false story.

The contradictory views of myth exacerbate the relationship between science and religion as well. "Myth" in religion is already recognized as having both potentially negative and positive meanings. In everyday discourse, when someone says, "Oh, that's just a myth," the intention of the speaker is to call attention to the falsity of whatever claim is referred to, as in "false advertising." But in religion, a myth has another, technical meaning: a myth is a story of origins that, when interpreted at its best, gives insight into the fundamental way that human beings make a "world" out of their most significant perceptions, memories, and desires. On the other hand, scientists and persons who advance scientific knowledge generally tend to be disparaging with respect to knowledge we understand as mythic.

The subject of this last chapter is the mythic quality of science itself as practiced in the public arena. The fruit of BD dialogue here is the realization that science has its mythical dimensions. BD dialogue in religion and science encourages the exposure of myth wherever it may occur. Our particular interest is where it appears in science.

B. MYTH AND PHILOSOPHY OF SCIENCE

The philosophy of science, as it has been written over the past hundred years, describes a struggle to understand how the doing of science has been different from other cognitive activities aimed at understanding the world in which we live. We will describe some of the myth-related remarks of Karl Popper (1968) and Paul Feyerabend (1975), two philosophers who have had a major impact on the epistemological questions that hover over the accomplishments of natural scientists. Popper sees myth as the ancient form of scientific theory—the beginning of science. The work of the scientist for him is to be found in the making of observations of the world as it is described by such theories. The theories (myths) are then rewritten in the light of observations that "test" them. Popper rejects the claim that science starts with observations. Observations in plenty there may be, but science, for Popper, begins with the first **explanation** of observations: "Historically speaking all—or very nearly all—

scientific theories originate in myths" (Popper, 38). Moreover, "scientific theories are not just the results of observation. They are . . . the product of myth-making and of tests" (Popper, 128). According to Popper, "The great significance of myths in [science] was that they could be the objects of criticism and that they could be changed" (Popper, 131)—although, we would add, often with great difficulty. Feyerabend is less sanguine about the process. For him,

> knowledge . . . is not a gradual approach to the truth. It is an ever increasing ocean of mutually incompatible (and perhaps even incommensurable) alternatives, each single theory, each fairy tale, each myth . . . forcing the others into greater articulation and . . . contributing to the development of our consciousness." (Feyerabend, 30)

He concludes that "science is much closer to myth than a scientific philosophy is prepared to admit" (Feyerabend, 295).

It is sometimes said that of all the social groups, none rivals the scientific community in the degree to which its members agree on what they profess. Even in religious communities there appears to be more variation in the degree of assent to doctrines than the average person sees in the natural sciences. However, complete agreement within science is superficial skin—that part of public science that appears not so much in scientific journals as in science text books, non-professional periodicals, newspapers and the screen media. When this naive perception of agreement is coupled with a naive understanding of myth, we encounter contradiction: How could what is true (science) be false (mythic)? This contradiction should be broken from both sides. On the one hand, there is serious conflict regarding many theories in the natural sciences. On the other hand, there is evidence that mythic narrative plays an important role in the development of scientific understandings.

We intend to show, moreover, that "scientific mythicness" is not limited to the fabrication of theoretical understandings. Peer-reviewed, published reports from the laboratories also make use of the constructive aspects of myth-making in their presentations of even the most formal observations and measurements.

We begin with the distinction between public and private science put forward by Holton who is professor of both physics and the history of science at Harvard.

C. HOLTON'S DISCOVERY

In his *Thematic Origins of Scientific Thought* (1973), Holton makes reference to x, y, and z axes that define a three-dimensional space in which the processes of scientific discovery and elucidation take place. The x and y axes define a plane he calls the "contingent" plane. This plane is formed by adding the empirical or phenomenic (x) dimension to the heuristic-analytic (y) dimension. To this plane he adds the third dimension (z) that includes

> fundamental presuppositions, notions, terms, methodological judgments and decisions—in short, of themata or themes—which are themselves neither directly evolved from, nor resolvable into, objective observation on the one hand, or logical, mathematical, and other formal ratiocination on the other hand (57).

Holton creates this intellectual space in order to further a discipline he calls the "thematic analysis of science, by analogy with thematic analyses that have for so long been used to great advantage in scholarship outside science" (ibid). This third dimension is "private science" in contrast to the contingent plane that represents "public science."

1. Private Science

The work the scientist does in the laboratory moves through the two-dimensional realm of the empirical and the analytic. Holton studied the private notebook entries of scientists such as Millikan, who was intent on showing that electric charge came in discrete chunks all of the same size, and Einstein, who was so confident of his Theory of General Relativity.

Holton makes it clear that one cannot study the thinking of scientists by reading and analyzing their **published** writings. He quotes Peter Medawar, "It is no use looking to scientific 'papers,' for they not merely conceal but actively misrepresent the reasoning that goes into the work that they describe" (Holton 1978:25). In Holton's view,

> the very institutions of science—the methods of publication, the meetings, the selection and training of young scientists—are designed to minimize attention to [the personal aspect of scientific activity]. . . . The success of science itself as a shareable activity seems to be connected with this systematic neglect of what Einstein called the "personal struggle" (Holton 1978:4). For Holton, "the event E at time t begins to be seen as the intersection of two trajectories, of two World Lines, one for 'public science' . . . and one for 'private science'" (Holton 1978:5).

So what does Holton refer to when he uses the term public science?

2. Public Science

Published descriptions of scientific research are almost invariably **reconstructions** of events of laboratory history. Although the records of the laboratory—to be found in the notebooks of scientists—are properly written in historical time, the published story of the experiment or observations is told in a time that emphasizes the causal and rational nature of the sequence of events. In some famous instances this story is not even a "true" account historically speaking.

The scientist in the laboratory, in the grip of a "satisfactory" understanding of the phenomena being investigated, is never in the classical position of disinterested observer. All observations cannot be taken as equally valid or acceptable. Millikan wrote in his notebook, *"Error high* will not use" (Holton 1978:65) for one observation, and "Beauty, *Publish* this surely, *beautiful!*" (Holton 1978:64) for another. Millikan, using individual small oil drops to measure the electrical charge of an electron, eventually selected 58 drops out of a total of 140 observed as the basis for his published value of electron charge.

In today's world, such selectivity might not escape the charge of being fraudulent. But the very style of scientific writing, the style of public science, leads to the reporting of observational methods, observational data, and conclusions that have all been disembodied—separated from the affects of the person or persons who carried them out. These reported methods, data, and conclusions have also, unlike the notations in a carefully kept laboratory notebook, been severed from the historic moment at which they were made.

Holton argued that scientists are driven by their allegiances to various themata. Such allegiances affect how observational data are "seen" or analyzed. They also affect decisions about what to publish and even what to investigate.

Themata function in a way that might be compared with political allegiances. For example, a liberal Democrat sees a legislated minimum wage as a device necessary to reduce poverty by supporting a minimum standard of living. A conservative Republican sees the same legislated minimum wage as a requirement that reduces the number of jobs that will be created and therefore available to those who wish to work. Both views are supportable in that neither is clearly right or wrong. But the data that might be advanced to support one position are not likely to be the same as the data that would be used to support the other.

Physicists early in the twentieth century were divided into two camps. One held allegiance to the thema of the continuum. These physicists might be thought of as the "field" group. They saw the world as made up of things whose characteristics (position, mass, energy, charge) could vary continuously. The other camp was composed of the atomists. According to their thema, the world is made up of individual things whose characteristics vary in discrete amounts. The professional judgments of these scientists were not unaffected by the camp with which they were aligned.

Holton's research methods were historical rather than philosophical. He based his arguments on data derived from the writings of the physicists he studied. By comparing their private letters and laboratory notebooks with their published writings he found that scientists made decisions about what methods to use and what data to publish that depended on their own view—their thematic perception—of the subject they were studying.

Analysis of the expressed motivations, and of the ever hardening attitudes of the protagonists on opposite sides of the question [often] . . . shows the strong role of an early, unshakable commitment by the opponents to different themata. (Holton 1978:5)

This behavior was not restricted to experimental scientists such as Millikan, but extended to theoretical physicists as well. Einstein was so convinced of the correctness of his theory of gravitation (the General Theory of Relativity) that when asked what he would think if observations did not bear out the predictions of his theory, he replied that it wouldn't matter—the theory was correct!

Holton showed, in effect, that scientists do not write history when they publish their scientific findings. They tell a story of what happened in their researches, a story that is structured in such a way as to be both persuasive with respect to their chosen thema as well as descriptive of what other scientists would experience, should they undertake a study of the same phenomena.

This characteristic of ahistorical storytelling is one of the features of scientific activity that makes it possible for us to understand public science as mythic. We would point out that this form of storytelling is not by any means restricted to physics and chemistry. Overarching thematic principles influence the analyses carried out in fields such as geology, where the thema of uniformitarianism has conflicted with that of catastrophism. These two themata have, over the years, had a profound effect on the interpretation of geologic data.

Why does Holton find stories when he is looking for history? Holton describes his research method as follows:

First, I try to make a detailed examination of the nascent phase of the scientist's work, and to juxtapose his published results, on the one hand, with firsthand documentation (correspondence, interviews, notebooks, etc.), on the other. (Holton 1978:vii)

Holton analyzes scientific work by means of "thematic analysis (a term familiar from somewhat related uses in anthropology, art criticism, . . . and other fields)" (Holton 1978:5). He observes that, "techniques analogous to the thematic analysis that I have applied to science have worked well in other fields, for example, in content analysis, linguistic analysis, and cultural anthropology" (Holton 1978:ix), and, furthermore, that "the attitude I have taken in the task of identifying and ordering thematic elements in scientific discussions is to some degree analogous to that of the *folklorist* . . . who listens to the *epic stories* for their *underlying thematic structure and recurrence*" (Holton 1978:5, emphases ours).

Here we have a scientist and historian of science reading the writings of other scientists and describing his research as being analogous to that of a folklorist listening to epic stories—epic stories that have an underlying thematic structure and that are recurring. To show that Holton's description of the public writings of scientists effectively characterizes them as mythical, we turn now to the characteristics of myth.

D. MYTH

1. Brief History of Myth

In his article for *The Encyclopedia of Philosophy* (v.5:434–37), Alasdair MacIntyre provides a concise rendering of a three-period history of the idea of myth. He moves from myth in Greek philosophy, period one, to the period of "modern thought" starting with Vico to Compte, period two. (MacIntyre sets aside the period from the Christian Era to Vico as being "predominantly negative with respect to myth"). Modern thought, period two, is followed by period three—the nineteenth century to the present, the "science of mythology and modern irrationalisms."

Early questions in the study of myth addressed, almost exclusively, the "meaning" of particular myths, understanding them to be old false stories. Not until Vico was myth understood to "express the collective mentality of a given age" (MacIntyre, 435). MacIntyre cites Vico's statement that "The fables of the gods are true histories of customs" (as quoted in MacIntyre, 437). Here we hear questions of function replacing questions of truth and the ushering in of modern understandings. In his discussion of period three, MacIntyre contrasts the more recent work of Claude Lévi-Strauss and Eliade by noting, ". . . Lévi-Strauss analyses the content of a myth in terms of what is *local and particular to a given society*," whereas "Eliade wishes to relate the content [of myths] to general human religious interests and as far as possible *divorce it from the local and particular*" [emphases ours] (MacIntyre, 437). We will reprise both of these themes as we apply twentieth-century theories of myth to the customs of modern science. But first we review some major revisions in the understanding of myth that make it available for understanding science anew.

2. Narrative in Myth

We take up the role of narrative in myth with an eye toward a constructive meaning of myth in public science. This step takes us back into the controversial territory referred to in our introduction. The difficulty of doing a constructive interpretation of scientific myth can be seen in this excerpt from Robert M. Wallace's introduction to one of the most comprehensive treatments of myth available today—Hans Blumenberg's *The Work of Myth* (1986). Wallace states that

> our usual interpretations of science, whether rationalist, empiricist, positivist, or whatever, are all still very much in the Enlightenment tradition, and imply a role for myth in the modern age which is restricted exclusively to the aesthetic imagination and is assumed to have no bearing on the preeminent role of scientific rationality in our serious, practical lives. On the other hand, those who concern themselves extensively with myth, such as literary scholars, anthropologists, and psychologists, often tend toward the other, Romantic extreme—interpreting myth's modern survival as evidence of its being, in one way or another, inherent in human nature and even, given its seemingly greater antiquity and ubiquity, of its being more fundamental to human nature than our ("surface") rationality. (vii)

Since the work of the major theorists of myth—Cassirer, Eliade, Lévi-Strauss, Joseph Campbell, for example—would, in one way or another, be subject to Blumenberg's criticism of the "Romantic extreme," we will not adopt either a theory or a definition of myth from the extensive literature. Instead we will delineate *mythic features of narrative*—(1) richness and durability, (2) new interpretive possibility, (3) optimization, and (4) the interweaving of fiction with fact—four features in all that will help us detect the mythical aspects of public science. These four features reflect less the Romanticist assumptions about human nature than the structural, substantive, and functional aspects of narrative that are identifiably mythic but not exclusively so.

The first mythic feature of narrative is durability—a feature combined with what Blumenberg calls "pregnance" (see below). Immediate richness of interpretive potential and persistence are found in certain narrative products that have been "tested" on various audiences on whose "active approval the storyteller's success, perhaps even his livelihood or life, depended" (Wallace in Blumenberg, xx). The durability of a surviving myth depends on the rejection of other potentially mythic narratives: As the bard selected myths to tell that were actively approved by listeners, other myths less popular or more threatening disappeared from memory and ultimately from history. In public science—the narratives found in the scientific periodicals— pregnance and durability of the work that survives are insured by the subsequent citations of the work in later publications, signaling both agreement on the part of other scientists as well as the continuing usefulness of the published account.

The second mythic feature of narrative, new interpretive possibility, derives most likely from the richness that Blumenberg called pregnance. This second feature gives rise to the expectation that a story may suddenly and discontinuously be subject to novel interpretation, what Blumenberg referred to as "wholly new and unsuspected aspects" (Wallace in Blumenberg, xxx). Whereas the Romantic theories of myths generally tried to ground the meaning of myth in a fundamental original nature of the human species, Blumenberg thinks it better to understand myths as functioning instead like the "'limit' that is approached by a mathematical function that converges asymptotically" but never in fact arrives at a precise limit. This mathematical concept of limit serves as a correction to the Romantic expectation that humankind could know something fundamental about the origin of the human species from representations in myths of beginnings: Instead we are always in a position of coming close to (but never reaching) an understanding of the human condition.

Blumenberg suggests that myths of endtime, "final myths," serve a similar function in that they represent an understanding and an effort actively to shape reality rather than be passively shaped by it. Whatever "human condition" we can conceive lies between these two limits: mythical beginnings and mythical endings. The corresponding scientific rendering of the second mythic feature of narrative can be found in the revisions that subsequent published articles make to those published earlier.

The third mythic feature of narrative is optimization. Like pregnance and duration, optimization is a characteristic of some myths but not others. Optimization or developmental change occurs in response to the audience. Perhaps the story teller gets bored with the story or has an aesthetic preference for another. Then the story teller tells a different story and finds that it is more acceptable. It is of special interest to us that Blumenberg uses Darwinian natural selection as the model for this process.

Optimization is not the same as the nineteenth-century idea of progress. Optimization is observed by noticing that change has occurred and that some change is for the better. Wallace makes the point more succinctly than does Blumenberg: "This 'objective progress' occurs not only in theory . . . and in technology, or in them and, by an odd combination, in myth as well, but also in the whole sphere of 'modes of behavior and thought structures'" (Wallace in Blumenberg, xxii). Blumenberg calls these various modes which result in some kind of objective progress, institutions.[53] Optimization can be understood to play a role in the development of scientific understanding that results in the termination of scientific publications relating to a particular topic. One is not likely to find, in scientific journals of today, additional data or discussion of scientific findings related to Millikan's investigations of the charge on the electron—although, we hasten to add, the issue could again burst into print if it were discovered that Millikan's methods could be, for example, used to measure the fractional charge of a quark.[54]

The fourth mythic feature of narrative is to be found in the interweaving of fact with fiction. This feature, perhaps more than any other, accounts for myth's openness to transformation and to new, as well as perennially affirmed, meaning. We borrow this fourth feature of mythic narrative directly from Ricoeur's theory of narrative: namely, his argument that, rather than merely replicating reality, narrative "configures" reality and that reading "refigures" it. Ricoeur restricts his theory to the "interweaving of historical and fictional narrative . . . where the past in history is united with the imaginative variations of fiction" (Ricoeur 1984–88, v.3:192). We suggest here that Ricoeur's approach be applied to a weaving together, not merely of historical and fictional narrative, but more generally to **non-fictional** and fictional narrative. This enlargement will open up the possibility of analyzing time in narrative and scientific time in terms of historic time and elapsed time, respectively. The remainder of the chapter will explore the constructive possibilities of Ricoeur's theory of narrative—here with respect to fiction and non-fiction— when applied to Holton's distinction between private science and public science.

3. Our Understanding of Time in Myth

With respect to historical time, Ricoeur sees the calendar as a technological invention or device for bridging between different kinds of time. The calendar makes possible the computation of "chronicle" time which is the foundation for historical and other forms of non-fictional time. If the focus of the narrative plot is designed primarily to support events that have otherwise been documented in relation to a calendar, historical time results. If the focus of the narrative plot is primarily on imaginative possibilities that are undocumented or related only tangentially to the calendar, mythic time results.

At the outset it would seem as though the calendar is of little use to public science for which physical time is simple duration (with the exception of astronomy which needs to identify the historic time of events in the sky).[55] Nevertheless, the calendar makes possible the computation of "chronicle" time which is the foundation for historical time and other forms of non-fictional time. The important point is that both typologies—fictional/historical narrative (Ricoeur's typology) *and* fictional/non-fictional narrative—are likely to contain both events unconnected with history and events correlated with a calendar. Most often these texts presume a greater or less degree of emancipation from events recorded in diaries, chronicles, and notebooks. But included in the foregoing topologies at their extremes, are two kinds of narratives which, according to Ricoeur, have been "freed from the constraints requiring it to be referred back to the time of the universe" (Ricoeur 1984–1988, v.3:128): myth (which either pre-dates extant calendars or has lost its connection to them) and imaginative fiction (which deliberately ignores, distorts or distends its connection with the calendrical time beyond recognition).

Eliade has described myth as a narrative sequence taking place in sacred time. We have previously rejected this traditional meaning because the definition is arguably insufficient for the myths we will identify as scientific. Nevertheless, we may here retrieve a partial link with the traditional meaning: in terms of religious meaning, what is mythical is repeatable—for example, the Eucharist is different in detail every time it is celebrated, but the important **form** of the ritual is the same. Public science evinces a correspondence here since the content of different reports differ even though the form of the reporting remains the same.

With respect to public science one might at first suppose that myths identifiable within the bounds of science would be those that took place in historic time. However, the ubiquitous nature of time in scientific theories—it is a concept so central that it is hard to think of any scientific theory in which it is absent—suggests that scientific time needs to be identified separately. We will characterize scientific time as "duration." For the purpose of this chapter we will understand myth to be like and unlike history in the following ways.

First, with respect to similarity, we take both the mythic and the historical to be expressed as story—as narrative with conventional structures of beginning, sequenced events, and ending. Second, with respect to differences we take mythic time to be devoid of historical temporality. Instead, the time in mythic narrative is purely elapsed time or duration, a form of temporality that is not required by historical time, although elapsed time can be extracted from historical time by the mathematical device of calculating differences between dates/times.

It is a necessary characteristic of myth that the time within a myth is not historical time. Myth is a narrative that, because it is a narrative, must contain elapsed time (which is the same as scientific time). But a myth is also a narrative that takes place not at a particular time in history (historical time) but at any time. Notice how this requirement parallels the requirement that a scientific experiment be repeatable at any time. Time in historical narrative is a sequencing unless some element in the narrative needs duration. By contrast, time in mythic narrative must be a version of duration (elapsed time).

A significant affective shift occurs when one separates a narrative from its grounding in historical time. Consider the following renditions of the same sequence of events:

Fragment One

Natalia Petrovski was born in Eastern Europe—what is now the Czech Republic—in 1898. Natalia sailed with her parents to the United States, leaving Copenhagen on April 19, 1906, and arriving in New York on May 4 of that year. The Petrovskis stayed in New York with friends and took a train west from the Pennsylvania Station on the 12th of November. Natalia's family eventually settled in Minneapolis where her father found work as a postal clerk. After his death from influenza in 1918, she worked as a postal clerk until she married John Wilson on June 5, 1920. Her husband drowned on June 3, 1942, in the battle of Midway. Her one child, John, Jr., was born on June 7, 1942.

Fragment Two

When Natalia Petrovski was 8 years old, she and her parents sailed from Copenhagen to New York. The crossing took 15 days. After spending 27 weeks with friends in New York City, they left by train for Minneapolis where they made their home. Natalia's father, a postal clerk, died in an influenza epidemic when she was 20 years old. She married US Navy Lt. John Wilson two years later and had one child, a son, born four days after the death of her husband.

Each of these fragments tells the same story. But our affective response to them is likely to be significantly different. In Fragment One we have a sequence of personal events attached to calender dates—historical time. We can synchronize the personal events with historic ones and are likely to understand the personal in relation to the civic world.

Fragment Two gives us a sense of what it must have been like to experience the personal events because we can empathize more easily with the person in the narrative and can more easily understand the person in relation to ourselves. The framework of public history (civic time) has been replaced with the framework of our own personal experience. In Fragment One the story tends to have the same meaning for all readers. In Fragment Two the meaning of the story will depend significantly on the life experiences of the reader (You probably remember being twelve years old. You probably do **not** remember the year 1906). Fragment One is set in historical time, whereas Fragment Two is set in mythical time.

4. Time in Science

In the public science of physics and chemistry (but not necessarily in geology or cosmology) the variable, t, is almost always elapsed time rather than historical time. If a physicist describes a falling object near the Earth, the height is generally the vertical coordinate y and the time is a horizontal coordinate, t. Where the axes intersect (the origin) the time is zero. Thus all of the values of t along the horizontal axis are times relative to the origin. These are elapsed times because they represent the differences between a particular t, say t_a, and the time at the origin, t_o. The elapsed time is $t_a - t_o$. However, since $t_o = 0$, the elapsed time $t_a - t_o = t_a$. This arrangement is markedly different from historic time lines where the numbers along the axes are dates.

The situation in chemistry is the same as that in physics: A chemist publishes the description of a reaction by writing that components must be heated for some length of time (elapsed time) rather than for a time beginning on one date and ending on another.

In each case the variables under study are understood as general coordinates of length or time and not specific places and dates, even though—and this is a vital difference—in every instance the laboratory experiments themselves each took place **at particular places on particular dates**. Thus the laboratory experiments are historical, written down in the laboratory notebooks with dates, whereas the published coordinates are mythical, because they can be invoked anywhere at any time.

5. Historical Time vs. Elapsed Time or Duration

Scientific time or duration is easily distinguished from the time of history. The latter can be understood as an idealized time line of arbitrary "length," any point on which may be given a date and time, such as October 14, 1923, at 34 minutes and 27 seconds after 11 (or 11:34:27–10/14/23). By contrast, scientific time can be understood as a time segment of particular length, such as 02:14:36.3, which is equivalent to 8076.3s (in SI units). Such durational time is to be distinguished from an **historical period** of the same length which is understood to be related to a particular location on the date line (say, the period between two historical events).

6. Narrative in Science

For those of us who hold that there is no absolute truth outside formal postulational systems such as mathematics (where truth is restricted to the system and does not apply to the phenomenal world—see chapter eight), the issue of the true or false nature of myth must be couched in other terms. Outside formal systems the claim that such-and-such is the case can be true only with some probability ($0<P_t<1$) or false with some probability ($1>P_f>0$). What then can we say about myths? For us myths are "truth-ful" narratives. They do not tell "the truth," they contain truth—in much the same way that a truthful person is one who is inclined to tell the truth (as she or he sees it).

The concept of myth used in this chapter emphasizes the role of myth in the creation of scientific understanding.[56] Modern scientific societies (particularly in the physical sciences) rely on an affirmation of scientific understanding that derives from the mythical structure of the "stories" of scientific discovery. When we focus on knowledge as created understanding (what elsewhere we have called knowledge-in-process) rather than knowledge as truth, it makes it easier to understand that myth can contribute to the development of understanding: myth should be valued for truthfulness, not examined for the formal truth-value of its utterances. And myths can be valued for more—they can be appreciated for their aesthetic qualities.

E. IDEALIZATION IN PUBLIC SCIENCE

A further distinction between private (laboratory) science and public (journal) science is to be found in the aesthetics associated with the particular scientific field. These aesthetics, we believe, are intimately connected with Holton's themata although they are not equivalent.

First we consider, as an example of public science, Millikan's article on the electronic charge:

> The result of one somewhat elaborate series of observations which was first presented before the Deutsche physikalische Gesellschaft in June, 1912, (note 1) is shown in Figs. 5 and 6. The numerical data from which these curves are plotted are given fairly fully in Table IX. It will be seen that this series of observations embraces a study of [oil] drops. These drops represent all of those studied for 60 consecutive days, no single one being omitted. . . . (Millikan, 106) *It will be seen from Figs. 5 and 6 that there is but one drop in the 58 whose departure from the line amounts to as much as 0.5 per cent. It is to be remarked, too, that this is not a selected group of drops, but represents all of the drops experimented upon during 60 consecutive days*, during which time the apparatus was taken down several times and set up anew. (Millikan, 111) [italics in the original]

In the next quotation we have Holton's remarks based on his reading of Millikan's laboratory notebooks (private science):

> The first notebook begins with an entry dated October 28, 1911, . . . and ends some 110 pages later with a run dated March 11, 1912. On each page there is typically an experiment of one oil drop. . . . The second notebook begins with a run on March 13, 1912, and the last run, about 65 pages later, is dated April 16,

1912. Again there is usually one experiment per page. In all, there are about 140 identifiable runs [oil drops] during the six months. (Holton 1978:63)

What Holton finds is an experimental scientist making aesthetic judgments as he goes along—judgments (and interpretations) that will result in his obtaining the most accurate determination of the charge of an electron up to that date.[57]

Millikan's book (and his 1913 paper) contained no **fabricated** data, no **fudged** calculations. What Millikan did was to choose the most representative experiments (58 of them) from a set of about 140 to form the basis for his best (average) value of the electronic charge. His effort to imply that he was driven by **all** that he encountered (his claim that he used all of the drops) was misguided. The thought that the presuppositions of a researcher might influence observations was anathema at that time in the history of science (as might be the thought that we today are seeing published scientific work as mythic).

But his recognition of the beauty of **some** of what he sees is what made it possible for him to write the journal article. As Holton observes, "This [critiquing of individual experiments] continues [in successive pages of the notebooks], with beauty appearing more consistently as the work progresses . . ." (Holton 1978:71). What we see here is a process of idealization—an aesthetic process. Understanding a published account of a scientific research project as being aesthetically satisfying—an important positive characteristic of myth—helps us to understand why themata can become so entrenched and why the repeatability, in principle, of the actions that produced the grounds for the claims made in a scientific narrative can give rise to the generally high degree of epistemological solidarity found in the scientific community.

Complaints that science eliminates essential aspects of human experience from its accounts of the world may be responded to by saying that the aspects that fall by the wayside in the production of scientific research articles are those that would not contribute to the repeatability (in principle) that is the basis for the acceptance of such reports by the scientific community.

That the individual scientist should select those data and observations that most clearly support the case being made should not be understood as misrepresentation so long as data that would **falsify** conclusions have not been suppressed (unless those data were clearly dubious on entirely other grounds). Holton's observation of the role of themata in the development of scientific understanding shows that scientific research that results in observations that fail to support the prevailing thema often go unpublished. And, furthermore, when they **are** published, research activity in search of data which **will** support the prevailing thema often continues. Changes in thema come about most often on the heels of new theoretical understandings, rather than on grounds of definitive counter examples.

Is all science writing mythical? No. It is not an accident that Holton's research has focused on the work of scientists such as Steven Weinberg, Millikan, and Einstein. These men are more than scientists—they are also philosophers. Their pursuit of knowledge is driven by a desire to understand the natural universe, not by a need to find solutions to technological problems. Science is a complex interaction between technology (tool making in the most general sense) and natural philosophy (the creation of understanding of the natural universe). The epic story of the physical universe is written by those scientists who are natural philosophers. This epic story and the public science narratives that support it are what we are characterizing as mythic.

Both the character of our experience and the character of the universe disclose that there is more to "see" than just pieces of raw data. We strive constantly to fit what we see into an arrangement of what we have seen already—hence the extension of "things" perceived into a sense of understanding. The aesthetic sense so important in this process is one of proportionality within a whole. In the Greek experience, the golden mean was a kind of model for this experience of fitting things together as a perceivable unity. In the experience of other cultures and in contemporary Western culture, there are other models.

Beauty is not a criterion—not everybody can see beauty. Not everyone could agree with Dirac's claim that it is more important that equations be beautiful than that they fit the experiment.[58] Aesthetic forms get at an aspect of truth; they introduce fluidity into a judgment about what is at hand. The aesthetic dimension of science (or any other way of understanding) means, on the one hand, that we cannot expect everyone to make the same judgment. On the other hand, preferred views develop or evolve through the feature of optimization introduced above.

In a recent article in *American Scientist*, James W. McAllister puts the issue this way:

> Scientists working at different times disagree over what aesthetic properties a theory must possess to count as beautiful. Astronomers from antiquity to the time of Nicholas Copernicus had an aesthetic predilection for particular symmetries. . . . Mechanics in the 18th century was pursued largely in an abstract style, not dependent on visualization.. . . Dirac saw beauty in theories that contain simple mathematical equations, whereas Weinberg regards a theory as beautiful if there is a sense of aptness or inevitability about its principles. (McAllister 1998:175–76)

In spite of these disagreements, McAllister thinks, scientists "ascribe aesthetic value to an aesthetic property proportionally to the empirical success scored by theories that exhibit that property." Moreover, these preferences "can be revised as circumstances change" (McAllister, 179).

People seem content with the idea that a fictional story can contain some truth. However, they seem to reject the idea that a truthful story can contain some fiction. The latter is seen as a sort of swindle. The former is not. But, following Ricoeur, fiction and nonfiction must be interwoven so that the narrative configures reality in the way that allows the reader to reconfigure reality in the act of understanding.

Epilogue

In this volume we have addressed ways that natural science and theology undergo major cognitive change. We describe metaphoric process as a way of understanding cognitive dynamics of such magnitude. However, the process of change in the ways societies understand their world—and express their felt needs and values in that world—is a related problem of even greater scope and importance than the changes in scientific and religious understandings we have addressed here.

A perennial focus on new knowledge can cause us to neglect the important ways in which our understandings—our world views (*Weltanschauungen*)—change. However, the success of every new era depends more on changes in world views than on specific new knowledge that may be accumulating at the time.

Think of pre- and post–French Revolution or pre- and post–Civil War America. The cognitive aspects of such historical revolutions can be thought of as the production of new maps, a process that goes beyond the addition of new routes or places to existing maps.

A map brought up to date is not a new map. A new projection of the global Earth, however, could be understood as a new map, precisely because a new projection changes the relative sizes of different countries, thereby changing their relative prominence—Greenland is enormous on a flat Mercator projection—far larger in proportion to other countries displayed than on a globe of Earth. In like manner different cognitive maps engender different emphases on world issues.

Metaphoric process is one way such cognitive maps can be changed. Plato, Empress Theodora, and Vico were among those who understood the powerful influence poets—purveyors of metaphor—could have on the world views of a people. They respected the power of metaphoric process. The importance of metaphoric process lies in what it does. By giving us new maps, metaphoric process engenders the new world views that mark and direct the course of human history.

Notes

1. A field of meanings of the kind we describe is not original with us: similar constructs are described in Michael I. Posner (1989). For example Herbert Simon and Craig Kaplan describe the common semantic representations used in artificial intelligence systems as ". . . list structures in the form of networks built up of lists. . . . These list structures may be interpreted as 'pictures' because they represent objects as nodes (with descriptions of features) and link them with proximate objects. . . . Each component can be viewed as an assertion that either a particular object has a certain property or a certain relation holds between two objects" (quoted in Posner, 18–19).
2. Interestingly, this book has no entry for "cognition" or its synonyms in the index but 35 entries for "network."
3. See Owen Gingerich (1998) for an account of Galileo's role in precipitating the dispute.
4. See *MP* (1984) for our use of Lonergan's notion of "things," 18 and 33, "horizon," 62, and "world of meanings," 71.
5. See Tracy (1990).
6. James Barr discusses at length the various nuances of the use of the verb "to be" in Hebrew: while not commonly used in the sense of a copulative, the verb does have a complex linguistic usage.
7. In his *Canaanite Myth and Hebrew Epic*, F. M. Cross (44–75) uses a linguistic analysis to show that the titles—"Creator of heaven and Earth," the "mighty one," the "hale one," the "God of hosts"—and the work of the old Canaanite high god are tied to the character of Yahweh, the God of Israel (see also Freedman, 1976). In his complex etymological and onomastic history of the titles, Cross finds a clear and at times startling connection between the god El, God of the Fathers, and the newly identified Yahweh, God of the Exodus (47). As the cognitive relation between the two conceptions of God come closer and closer, they become equated in a culminating conception: the God of Israel (47–49). Cross stops short of arguing for the identity of El and Yahweh in the religion of Israel. We claim identity on the basis of our hermeneutic method.
8. Whatever his "historical" character might have been, the biblical text presents Moses as the "founder" of the religion of Israel. Our hermeneu-

tical approach permits us to postpone the debate of syncretism vs. monotheism and to reformulate the subject of the debate.

9. Sublimation is used here not only in the psychoanalytic sense of good (as distinct from evil) arising out of repression, but also in relation to the physical sense of the term in which a solid is transformed directly (without melting) into a vapor—hence (now metaphysically) into an elevated or transcendent spirit.

10. Asherah is a "local manifestation of the Great Goddess," insofar as there were different goddesses with the common name "Asherah" for different port cities of the Mediterranean. Asherah of Tripoli, for example, was both identical with the Great Goddess and unique as the goddess of Tripoli. In Ugaritic times, the Goddess was known as the Lady of the Sea and was petitioned to make the Sea bountiful for the prosperity of the cities. See Patai (1967) and Davies (1983).

11. The name Anat does not appear in the Bible (except once as a place name) and no images of her have been found in Hebrew archeological remains.

12. Winter groups passages containing the Heb. *srh/srjm* as follows: those that refer to Asherah as a goddess (Judg 3:7; 1Kgs 15:13, 18:19; 2Kgs 21:7, 23:4) and those that refer to asherah as a cult-object (in the singular: Deut 16:21; Judg 6:28,31; 1Kgs 16:33; 2Kgs 13:6, 17:16, 18:4, 21:3, 23:6,7,15; in the plural: Exod 34:13; Deut 7:5, 12:3; 1Kgs 14:15, 23; 2Kgs 17:10, 23:14; 2Chr 14:2, 17:6, 19:3, 24:18, 31:1, 33:3, 33:19, 34:3–7; Isa 17:8, 27:9; Jer 17:2; Mic 5:14). See also Olyan (1988) who argues that "Asherah and her cult symbol [the serpent] were legitimate not only in popular Yahwism, but in the official cult as well" (74). He draws evidence from a variety of sources for associating the goddess Asherah with the serpent and supposes that "the myth relating the serpent/sea dragon and Asherah has been lost" (71).

13. Even though the NAB and most current English versions translate Heb. *qdš* (male) and *qdšwt* (female) as "prostitute," the word can also be translated as "sacred person." The Septuagint has *hierodulos*. See also Bird (1989).

14. Robert Coote and David Robert Ord (1989) read Eve's remark on the birth of Cain (Gen 4:1) as, "I have gotten a man as though I were a god" (65).

15. The Hebrew for Eve is *ḥawwa*, which is etymologically related to snake as well as to giver of life. See also Olyan: "*Ḥawwa* (Eve) is an attested epithet of Tannit/Asherah in the first millennium BCE" (71).

16. That there are new genres is not here in question although there is debate on whether new genres emerge *de novo*—as novelties—or evolve with changes in existing genres.

17. We think that the lack of resolution of many of the historical conflicts between science and religion may stem from an overreliance on verbal dialogue and a lack of bidisciplinary writing.

18. The distinction between *actual dialogue* and *represented dialogue* is from Tullio Maranhão (1990), a collection of essays on dialogue in different

disciplines. For Maranhão, this is a distinction basic to all others: one text presented by a person in dialogue form is different from dialogue spoken between two people. We use this distinction for our definition of BD dialogue, but with a difference. Much of the work seen as interdisciplinary in science and religion is presented as represented dialogue because it is created by one person who knows both sides, so to speak. The distinction we want to make is between that kind of represented dialogue (written by one person) and dialogue proper which is (spoken and subsequently written) between a person who is trained in and comes from a religious and theological perspective on the one side and someone who is trained in and comes from a technological and scientific perspective on the other. Maranhão's distinction holds for classical cases: dialogue is either a discussion between two or more minds (as in psychoanalysis) or a fictional construction by one person about hypothetical minds (as in Platonic dialogue). The third possibility is a conversation between two or more speakers from different disciplines, a conversation subsequently revised and edited by the same speakers.

19. This restriction may not apply to email where the exchange is in real time. See, for example, Philip Hefner and William Irons (1996): "In the course of commenting through the means of electronic mail on each other's first drafts of the papers included in this volume, we developed a rather intense dialogue on some basic issues that we could not resolve to our satisfaction. Consequently, we offer this jointly authored statement not to argue once again the issues, nor to fashion a quick-fix solution to the issues, but rather to specify what an earnest and open-minded anthropologist and a theologian with the same attributes found to be the most interesting and most difficult nub of their conversation" (425).

20. The analogy of a traffic interchange—a "junction of two or more highways by a system of separate levels that permit traffic to pass from one to another without the crossing of traffic streams"—is apt. By contrast, BD dialogue is like an intersection—a "meeting or crossing at a common point" (*Webster's Ninth New Collegiate Dictionary*).

21. Using an analogy from chemistry, interdisciplinary dialogue is like a "mixture"—a combining of two or more "components in varying proportions that retain their own properties" whereas BD dialogue is like a "compound"—something formed by the "union" of two or more components "in definite proportion by weight."

22. Kenneth Burke (1961) cited two features he thought were "generically necessary" for human beings to be distinctively human. The first was "dramatique," roughly the genre *drama*. (the second was "logology," analogous to both theory and theology). BD dialogue differs significantly with respect to "dramatique." In a single-person authored dialogue, an individual character can conceivably attempt to present a position on a given issue from the perspective of two different disciplines. But because the disciplines have a discrete history and a history of relationships, they proffer reasons and predispositions we think are best represented in BD dia-

logue—both for adequacy of representation and mutual correction. All else being equal, BD dialogue enhances, thickens, and complicates the situation of speaking from two different perspectives.

With respect to the issue of adequate representation, we find an analogue in the reluctance of first and second century Jews to publish *pes'aq* ("decided law") separately, apart from the arguments. The intricate and circuitous arguments that led to a statement of law were considered to be intrinsic to the "decided law." They thought that publishing "decided law" without the arguments gave the mistaken impression that the law could not be changed. BD dialogue would seem to gain in rhetorical force for a similar reason: By better representing each perspective from two different standpoints in two different voices, we can expect to gain from exposure of the process of challenge and change.

23. Physicists, for example, consider the world—their universe—formally lifeless and this despite the work done in the neighboring area called biophysics. Theologians are apt to take phenomenological view of the world as the place of being: i.e., the world is where human beings are (*MP*, 1994).

24. Both "intention" and "purposefulness" are here allied to the phenomenological notion of intentionality, not to the notion of "intention" as constituted by classical theory that assigned different functions to different "faculties."

25. In section C of this essay, we discuss further possible outcomes of BD dialogue.

26. The published results of BD dialogue take many forms such as those enumerated in examples already mentioned. At the present time BD dialogues are seldom published as dialogues. But the following chapter, "A Scientist and a Theologian See the World: Compromise or Synthesis," a published edited dialogue, illustrates both the spontaneity and passion referred to by Merleau-Ponty and the striving for a higher viewpoint.

27. Pylyshyn's comments were published in Posner's influential *Foundations of Cognitive Science* (1989).

28. Lonergan (1972) proposed the alternative, a spiral, as a more adequate model of hermeneutics than a circle. The spiral illustrates the process by which human experience gives rise to questions, subsequent understandings, different experiences and perhaps further questions.

29. This is Lonergan's formulation (see Tracy 1970:9–21).

30. We detect such efforts, for example, when William Wehrbein, Guest Editor, reports that scientists take for granted the fact that what they know is temporary. He notices that other people, however, are unaware of this recognition on the part of scientists. (See *American Journal of Physics*, 64:363.)

31. Elsewhere, we call this road to agreement metaphoric process, the cognitive disruption or distortion of a field of meanings. For examples of higher viewpoints, see *MP* (1984) and "Metaphoric Process and the Tectonic Reformation of Meaning (chapter three above).

32. In the work we have done as BD dialogue, only one has been published as an actual dialogue. See chapter six.

33. See also note 23 above. Marvell's application of this idea in "To His Coy Mistress," is, of course, to a different situation. But his meaning here and in subsequent lines is also relevant for our own: "Had we but world enough, and time . . . we would sit down, and think which way to walk . . . But at my back I always hear/Time's winged chariot hurrying near. . . ."

34. As cited and paraphrased in John Archibald Wheeler (1974): "No one to think, no one to know? Then no world," suggesting, from the classical point of view, a special knower of the universe as universe.

35. The argumentative form of this chapter is stipulative definition. We choose to call x a text if x possesses four specified characteristics. Most stipulative definitions **narrow** the range of application of a term, whereas ours enlarges the range. In either case the assertion of a new definition is justified only by what is achieved. Those who disagree with us, but share our objectives, are especially invited to challenge or alter the characteristics. Finally, we wish to point out that our use of the stipulative definition to enlarge the range of application of a concept is an example of the metaphoric process we elaborated in our book. Here we are taking the concept *text*, embedded firmly as it is in a written or literary field of meanings, and insisting (stipulating) that the concept text is also applicable to other objects (e.g., religious rituals, certain measurable physical quantities) themselves firmly embedded in their own fields. In so doing, we create a metaphor that distorts a world of meanings with the result that concepts, hitherto thought distant and distinct, are brought epistemologically together.

36. According to Ernst Robert Curtius (1953:324), "The founder of exact natural science gives the book metaphor a significant new turn. Galileo speaks of the great book of the universe, which lies forever before our eyes but which we cannot read if we have not learned the script in which it is written."

37. We have changed Walcutt's superscripts to subscripts, to conform to mathematical and scientific usage.

38. Our students found the case of a painting particularly vexing. They raised questions about other art objects, many of which we decided were texts (illustrations in a book or magazine, serigraphs, etchings—unless individually wiped by the artist), and others we rejected as texts (water colors, collages, sculpture—unless cast). Let us restate the problem with art in relation to our criteria for text. By defining text in such a way that it may be significant to the sciences and to the religions, some objects that are sometimes called texts in the humanities, such as original paintings and architectural monuments, are, in our theory, marginal phenomena not in themselves texts. We have found that literary-oriented scholars, on the other hand, tend to want to include as texts anything that can be read, which for them is equivalent to anything that "has meaning."

39. The complexity of the problem can be seen in the words of the classicist, Albin Lesky (1966:37): "Pure oral poetry, however, is never repeated twice in the same form. . . ." Then, in a footnote, he elaborated and qualified

as follows: "The dictum of Sterling Dow . . . , 'Verbatim oral transmission of a poem composed orally and not written down is unknown,' has been challenged recently by G. S. Kirk. . . . From observations of contemporary oral epic on its own ground he concluded that faithful transmission is possible."

40. Different theories yield different understandings of what a dream is, yet this diversity does not affect the claim that a dream is irretrievable. Derrida, for example, would deny the existence of an "original" experience of a dream. In "Freud and the Scene of Writing," Derrida (1978:211) wrote that "the [dream] text is not conceivable in an originary . . . form of presence. The unconscious . . . is already a weave of pure traces, differences in which meaning and force are united. . . ." Alternatively, in Jungian oneric analysis, individual dreams are instantiations of universal archetypes. Nevertheless, the claim regarding irretrievability holds, albeit in different ways for both Derrida's and Carl Jung's understanding of dream. Nor does the issue of whether or not we are fooled by our dreams bear on their retrievability. Jacob's dream in Genesis and native American dreams are equally irretrievable as objects of faith or as objects of suspicion.

41. Here we have used degrees as the unit of angle because most persons are more familiar with this unit. A scientist, however, is more likely to use radian measure in which the length of the arc that an angle subtends is the unit of measure when the radius that makes the arc has length equal to one.

42. See, for example, Miscall (1983) on the way Genesis subverts our choice between Abraham as "scoundrel or paragon"; see further his argument that such subversion of "determinate" readings is the proper work of the text.

43. Controversy over Frits Staal's recording and interpretation of the 1975 "performance" of the 3,000 year-old Vedic ritual illustrates the issue of the relationship between myth and ritual. In his two-volume study (which includes illustrations and two cassette tapes), Staal first claimed that the ritual is meaningless to those who perform it. Later he said that "its meaninglessness became patent and various rationalizations and explanations [the Brahmanas—the oldest Vedic literature] were constructed" (Smith, 1985:140).

44. See, for example, Northrop Frye's (1981:78–138) treatment of typology in the Hebrew and Christian scriptures. His project, more than his particular schema, is of relevance here. Of Frye's project, Ricoeur (1985:178) commented, "Such typologies, to my mind, reflect a sustained familiarity with the singular works of our narrative tradition or traditions and constitute the *schematism* of narrative function, in the same way that the singular plots express the productive imagination at work at the concrete level of poetic composition."

45. From this perspective, theology is neither "inside" nor "outside" explicitly religious traditions. Indeed, the margins of what is inside (i.e., explicitly religious) or outside (i.e., implicitly religious or secular) shift within the texts of many traditions.

46. One of the perennial religious metaphors results from classical theology's insistence that God is human. According to our model of metaphoric process, this claim is metaphoric in the sense that the field of meanings associated with being human (mortal, being born, being self-conscious, being reflective, worshiping an Other) is claimed to be equivalent to the field of meanings traditionally associated with being divine (immortal, having no origin in time, being omniscient, being omnipotent, being self-sufficient, and formally having only internal relations). As the fruit of this metaphor, God is no longer necessarily understood as omniscient, unchanging, and all powerful but can be understood as eminently related to all, as becoming and being, as providing the space for human freedom to be realized.

47. Popular accounts of the relation between religion and science typically sensationalize the search for such details. See, for example, Sheler and Schrof (1992) and the entry in "Letters to the Editor" commenting on Sheler and Schrof in *U.S. News and World Report* 112 (January 13, 1992). For a balanced theological account of the "silent, secret attraction" that the classical "proofs" for the existence of God (two of which address the issue of divine creation) continue to exercise in contemporary thought as well as the "challenge to thought" they provide, see Hans Küng 1980:529–36.

48. J. B. S. Haldane as quoted in Dyson (1992:39).

49. For a discussion of the shift from the analogy of *being* to the analogy of *goodness,* see Tracy, "God: The Contemporary Problematic," Boston College (April 25, 1998).

50. See James (1982), 35.

51. We are indebted to Joseph Healey for this clarification.

52. Critical commentary also is present in the sense that the exchange on Cartesian and constructivist positions is an opportunity to fine-tune contemporary philosophical positions in a larger context.

53. One of the troubling aspects of Blumenberg's thought is that, in his eagerness to overcome the Romanticist monopoly on myth, he disparages imagination (unnecessarily, we think).

54. Holton includes excerpts from a letter written by P. A. M. Dirac regarding an anomalous charge reported by Millikan and an experiment designed to detect the presence of free quarks (Holton, 1978:304 n12).

55. Universal Time, or UT in astronomy, is the elapsed time at Greenwich, England, in seconds since 1/1/1900.

56. We addressed the role of metaphor in this process in *MP* 1984.

57. Millikan's selection of what to include (publish) and what to ignore can be compared with the choices made by an author (Sebastian Junger) of the non-fiction account of the great North Atlantic storm of late October, 1991. In the foreword the author writes, "On the one hand, I wanted to write a completely factual book. . . . On the other hand, I didn't want the narrative to asphyxiate under a mass of technical detail and conjecture. . . . I've written as complete account as possible of something that

can never be fully known" (Junger, 1997:xi–xii). Both Millikan and Junger made selections from the information available.

58. The quotation as it appears in McAllister (1998) is as follows: "It is more important to have beauty in one's equations than to have them fit experiment. . . . It seems that if one is working from the point of view of getting beauty in one's equations, and if one has really a sound insight, one is on a sure line of progress" (174).

Bibliography

Books, Articles, Papers by Mary Gerhart and Allan Melvin Russell

1984. *Metaphoric Process: The Creation of Scientific and Religious Understanding*. Fort Worth: TCU Press.

1987. "Metaphoric Process." *The Linguistic Turn and Contemporary Theology. CTSA Proceedings* 42, 107–113.

1987. "A Generalized Conception of Text Applied to Both Scientific and Religious Objects." *Zygon: Journal of Religion and Science* 22 (September), 299–316.

1990. "The Cognitive Effect of Metaphor," *Listening* 25, 114–26.

1993. "Bidisciplinary Fusion: New Understandings in Theology and Natural Science." *CTNS Bulletin* 13 (Spring), 1–6.

1993. "Metaphoric Process as the Tectonic Reformation of Worlds of Meanings in Theology and Natural Science." *CTNS Bulletin* 13 (Spring), 7–13.

1993. "Sublimation of the Goddess in the Deitic Metaphor of Moses." *Semeia: An Experimental Journal for Biblical Criticism* 61, 167–82.

1994. "A Scientist and a Theologian See the World: Compromise or Synthesis?" *Zygon: Journal of Religion and Science* 29, 619–38.

1996. "Mathematics, Empirical Science and Theology." In W. Mark Richardson and Wesley J. Wildman, eds., *Religion and Science: History, Method, Dialogue*. New York and London: Routledge, pp. 121–30.

1998. "The Genre: Bidisciplinary Dialogue." Paper presented at the "Genre Theory at the Millennium" Conference, Colgate University and Hamilton College, September 11–13.

1998. "The Limits of Quantum Mechanics and Cosmology as a Resource for a Contemporary Theological Metaphysics—With Alternatives." Summary of paper in *CTSA Convention Proceedings* 53, 135–36.

1998. "Cog Is to Us As We Are to God." *Zygon* 33 (June), 263–69.

1998. "Myth and Public Science." Paper presented at the "Myth and Philosophy" Conference, Wesleyan College, GA, April 18–19.

1999. "The Role of Metaphoric Process in the Development of Cognitive Complexity." Paper presented at the International Conference on Metaphor and Cognition, Torun Poland. October 25–27. In *Metaphor and Cognition,* a special issue of *Theoria et Historian Scientiarum,* ed. by Tomasz Komendzinski (New York: Peter Lang, 2001).

General References

Albright, William. 1968. *From Stone Age to Christianity*. New York: Anchor.

"Astronomers Prepare for Jupiter-Comet Crash." 1994. *Finger Lakes Times*. January 11.

Austin, J. L. 1962. *How to Do Things with Words*. Oxford: Clarendon Press.

Bassett, John Spencer. 1929. *Correspondence of Andrew Jackson*. Washington, D.C.: Carnegie Institute of Washington.

Breuer, Richard. 1990. *The Anthropic Principle: Man as the Focal Point of Nature*. Basel, Berlin: Birkhauser.

Bakhtin, M. M. 1986. "The Problem of Speech Genres." In *Speech Genres and Other Late Essays,* trans. by Vern W. McGee, ed. by Caryl Emerson and Michael Holquist. Austin: University of Texas Press.

Barbour, Ian. 1974. *Myths, Models, and Paradigms: A Comparative Study in Science and Religion*. New York: Harper & Row.

———. 1980. *Technology, Environment, and Human Values*. New York: Praeger.

———. 1990. *Religion in an Age of Science*. San Francisco: Harper San Francisco.

———. 1992. *Ethics in an Age of Technology*. San Francisco: Harper San Francisco.

Barr, James. 1961. *The Semantics of Biblical Language*. London: Oxford University Press.

Bazerman, Charles. 1988. *Shaping Written Knowledge: The Genre and Activity of the Experimental Article in Science*. Madison: The University of Wisconsin Press.

Benjamin, Walter. 1968. "The Work of Art in the Age of Mechanical Reproduction." In *Illuminations*. Harcourt, Brace & World.

Bernasconi, Robert. 1995. "'You Don't Know What I'm Talking About': Alterity and the Hermeneutic Ideal." In *The Specter of Relativism*, ed. by Lawrence Schmidt. Evanston: Northwestern University Press.

Bird, Phyllis. 1989. "'To Play the Harlot': An Inquiry into an Old Testament Metaphor." In Day, ed., 75–94.

Black, Max. 1962. *Models and Metaphors*. Ithaca: Cornell U. Press.

Blumenberg, Hans. 1985. *Work on Myth*. Cambridge and London: The MIT Press.

Bracken, Joseph A. 1996. "Response to Elizabeth Johnson's 'Does God Play Dice?'" *Theological Studies* 57, 720–30.

Burke, Kenneth . 1961. *Rhetoric of Religion*. Boston: Beacon Press.

Carroll, Lewis. 1965. *Through the Looking Glass*. Random House.

Cassuto, Umberto. 1971. *The Goddess 'Anat'*. Trans. Israel Abrahams. Jerusalem: Hebrew University Press.

Changeux, Jean-Pierre and Alain Connes. 1995. *Conversations on Mind, Matter, and Mathematics*, ed. and trans. by M. B. DeBevoise. Princeton: Princeton University Press.

Churchland, Patricia S., and Terrence J. Seynowski, *The Computational Brain*. Cambridge, MA: MIT Press, 1994.

Cooper, David E. 1986. *Metaphor*. Oxford: Basil Blackwell.

Coote, Robert B. and David Robert Ord. 1989. *The Bible's First History*. Philadelphia: Fortress.

Cross, Frank Moore. 1973. *Canaanite Myth and Hebrew Epic: Essays in the History of the Religion of Israel*. Cambridge: Harvard University Press.

——, Werner E. Lemke, and Patrick D. Miller, Jr., eds. 1976. *Magnalia Dei: The Mighty Acts of God: Essays on the Bible and Archeology in Memory of G. Ernest Wright*. Garden City: Doubleday.

Cunningham, Lawrence. 1983. *The Catholic Heritage*. New York: Crossroad.

Curtius, Ernst Robert. 1953. *European Literature and the Latin Middle Ages*. New York: Pantheon.

Davies, Steve. 1983. "The Canaanite-Hebrew Goddess." In Olson, 68–79.

Day, Peggy, ed. 1989. *Gender and Difference in Ancient Israel*. Minneapolis: Fortress.

de Man, Paul. 1978. "The Epistemology of Metaphor." *Critical Inquiry* 5, 13–30.

Dennett, Daniel C., and John Searle. 1995. "The Mystery of Consciousness? An Exchange." *The New York Review of Books* 42 (December 21), 83–85.

Derrida, Jacques. 1978. "Freud and the Scene of Writing." In *Writing and Difference*. Chicago: The University of Chicago Press.

Dickinson, Emily. 1968. *The Complete Poems of Emily Dickinson*. Boston: Little Brown and Company.

Dyson, Freeman. 1992. *From Eros to Gaia*. New York: Pantheon Books.

Eliade, Mircea. 1963. *Myth and Reality*. New York and Evanston: Harper & Row.

———. 1978. *A History of Religious Ideas: From the Stone Age to the Eleusinian Mysteries*. Chicago: University of Chicago Press.

Feshbach, Herman, and Victor F. Weisskopf. 1988. "Ask a Foolish Question. . ." *Physics Today* 41, 9–11.

Feyerabend, Paul. 1975. *Against Method: Outline of an Anarchistic Theory of Knowledge*. London: Verso.

Fish, Stanley. 1980. *Is There a Text in This Class? The Authority of Interpretive Communities*. Cambridge: Harvard Uniersity Press.

Freedman, David Noel. 1976. "Divine Names and Titles in Early Hebrew Poetry," in Cross, Lemke, and Miller, 55–107.

Frege, Gottlob. 1966. "On Sense and Reference." In Peter Geach and Max Black, eds., *Philosophical Writings of Gottlob Frege*. Oxford: Blackwell.

Freud, Sigmund. 1965. *Interpretation of Dreams*, trans. by James Strachey. New York: Basic Books.

Frye, Northrop. 1981. *The Great Code: The Bible and Literature*. New York: Harcourt, Brace Jovanovich.

Galilei, Galileo. [1632] 1967. *Dialogue Concerning the Two Chief World Systems*. Berkeley: University of California Press.

————. [1638] 1914. *Dialogues Concerning Two New Sciences*. New York: Macmillan.

Gerhart, Mary, *Genre Choices, Gender Questions*. 1992. Norman: University of Oklahoma Press.

Gingerich, Owen. "Galileo: Hero or Heretic?" Paper presented at the "Faith, Science and the Future" Symposium, Concordia College, September 27, 1998.

Goodenough, Ursula. 1994. "The Religious Dimensions of the Biological Narrative." *Zygon: Journal of Religion and Science* 29 (December): 603–18.

Goodman, Nelson. 1978. *Ways of Worldmaking*. Indianapolis: Hackett.

Götz, Hindelang. 1994. "Dialogue Grammar: A Linguistic Approach to the Analysis of Dialogue." In *Beiträge zur Dialogforschung: Concepts of Dialogue: Considered from the Perspective of Different Disciplines*, ed. by Franz Hundsnurscher and Edda Weigand. Tübingen: Max Niemeyer Verlag.

Gross, Alan G. 1990. *The Rhetoric of Science*. Cambridge and London: Harvard University Press.

Hanson, Russell Norwood. 1972. *Patterns of Discovery*. New York and Cambridge: Cambridge University Press.

Hefner, Philip, and William Irons. 1996. "Reflections on the Dialogue." In *Religion and Science: History, Method, Dialogue*, ed. by W. Mark Richardson and Wesley J. Wildman. New York and London.

Hempel, Carl. 1945a. "Geometry and Empirical Science." *American Mathematical Monthly* 52, 7–17.

————. 1945b. "On the Nature of Mathematical Truth." *American Mathematical Monthly* 52, 543–556.

Herbert, Nick. 1985. *Quantum Reality: Beyond the New Physics— An Excursion into Metaphysics*. New York: Doubleday, Anchor.

Hesse, Mary. 1988. "The Cognitive Claims of Metaphor." *The Journal of Speculative Philosophy* 2, 1–13.

Hofstadter, Douglas R., and Daniel Dennett, eds. 1981. *The Mind's I: Fantasies and Reflections on Self and Soul*. New York: Basic Books.

Holton, Gerald. 1973. *Thematic Origins of Scientific Thought: Kepler to Einstein*. Cambridge: Harvard University Press.

———. 1978. *The Scientific Imagination: Case Studies.* New York and Cambridge: Cambridge University Press.

James, E. O. 1959. *The Cult of the Mother-Goddess: An Archeological and Documentary Study.* New York: Frederick A. Praeger.

James, William. 1981 [1890]. *Principles of Psychology.* Vol. 2. Princeton: Princeton University Press.

———. 1982 [1902]. *Varieties of Religious Experience.* London: Penguin Books.

Johnson, Elizabeth A. 1996. "Does God Play Dice? Divine Providence and Chance," *Theological Studies* 57, 3–18.

Junger, Sebastian. 1997. *The True Story of Men Against the Sea.* New York and London: W.W. Norton & Company.

Kantrowitz, Arthur. 1992. "Physics in the 'Age of Diminished Expectations,'" *Physics Today* 45 (March), 61–62.

Kingswell, Mark. 1995. *A Civil Tongue: Justice, Dialogue, and the Politics of Pluralism.* University Park, PA: The Pennsylvania State University Press.

Klink, William. 1994. "Ecology and Eschatology: Science and Theological Modeling." *Zygon: Journal of Religion and Science* 29 (December): 529–45.

Knox, John. 1964. *Myth and Truth: An Essay on the Language of Faith.* Charlottesville: The University Press of Virginia.

Koestler, Arthur. 1964. *The Act of Creation.* New York: Macmillan.

Küng, Hans. 1980. *Does God Exist? An Answer for Today.* New York: Doubleday.

Lakoff, George, and Mark Johnson. 1980. *Metaphors We Live By.* Chicago and London: University of Chicago Press.

Leach, Edmund. 1969. *Genesis as Myth and Other Essays.* London: Jonathan Cape.

Lesky, Albin. 1966. *A History of Greek Literature.* New York: Thomas Y. Crowell Co.

Leslie, John. 1990. *Universes.* London: Routledge.

Levenson, Jon. 1985. *Sinai and Zion: An Entry into the Jewish Bible.* New York: Winston.

Lévi-Strauss, Claude. 1958. "The Structural Study of Myth." In Sebok, Thomas, *Myth: A Symposium.* Bloomington and London: Indiana University Press.

Lonergan, Bernard F. J. 1957. *Insight: A Study of Human Understanding*. London: Darton, Longman and Todd.

———. 1980. "Reality, Myth, Symbol." In *Myth, Symbol, Reality* ed. by Alan M. Olson. Notre Dame and London: University of Notre Dame Press.

MacCormac, Earl R. 1976. *Metaphor and Myth in Science and Religion*. Durham: Duke University Press.

———. 1985. *A Cognitive Theory of Metaphor*. Cambridge: MIT Press.

Macky, Peter. 1990. *The Centrality of Metaphors to Biblical Thought: A Method for Interpreting the Bible. Studies in the Bible and Early Christianity*. Vol. 19. Lewiston/ Queenston/ Lampeter: Edwin Mellen.

MacIntyre, Alasdair. 1967. "Myth." In *The Encyclopedia of Philosophy*. Vol. 5. New York, London: Macmillan Publishing Co. & The Free Press, pp. 434–37.

Macovski, Michael. 1994. *Dialogue and Literature: Apostrophe, Auditors, and the Collapse of Romantic Discourse*. New York, Oxford: Oxford University Press.

Maier, Walter, III. 1986. *Asherah, Extra-biblical Evidence*. Harvard Semitic Monograph 37. Atlanta: Scholars Press.

Maranhão, Tullio. 1990. "Introduction." In *The Interpretation of Dialogue*. Chicago and London: The University of Chicago Press.

Marková, Ivana, Carl F. Graumann, and Klaus Foppa, eds. 1995. *Mutualities in Dialogue*. New York and Cambridge: Cambridge University Press.

Mascall, E. L. 1965. *Christian Theology and Natural Science*. London: Archon Books.

Mason, Herbert. 1979. *The Death of al-Hallaj*. Notre Dame: University of Notre Dame Press.

McAllister, James W. 1998. "Is Beauty a Sign of Truth in Scientific Theories?" *American Scientist* 86, 174–83.

McFague, Sallie. 1982. *Metaphorical Theology: Models for God*. Philadelphia: Fortress Press.

———. 1987. *Models of God: Theology for an Ecological, Nuclear Age*. Minneapolis: Fortress Press.

Merleau-Ponty, Maurice. 1973. "Dialogue and the Perception of the Other." In *The Prose of the World*, ed. by Claude Lefort, trans. by John O'Neill. Evanston: Northwestern University Press.

Midgley, Mary. 1992. *Science as Salvation: A Modern Myth and Its Meaning*. London and New York: Routledge.

Miller, Owen. 1985. "Preface" to *Identity of the Literary text*. Ed. by Mario J. Valdejés and Owen Miller. University of Toronto Press.

Miller, Patrick D., Jr., et al., eds. 1987. *Ancient Israelite Religion*. Philadelphia: Fortress.

Millikan, Robert. 1917. *The Electron: Its Isolation and Measurement and the Determination of Some of Its Properties*. Chicago and London: University of Chicago Press.

Miscall, Peter D. 1983. *The Workings of Old Testament Narrative*. Semeia Studies, Fortress Press and Scholars Press.

Olson, Carl, ed. 1983. *The Book of the Goddess: Past and Present*. New York: Crossroad.

Olyan, Saul. 1988. *Asherah and the Cult of Yahweh in Israel*. Atlanta: Scholars Press.

Patai, Raphael. 1967. *The Hebrew Goddess*. New York: Avon.

Peacocke, Arthur. 1979. *Creation and the World of Science*. Oxford: Clarendon Press.

———. 1981. *Science and Theology in the Twentieth Century*. Notre Dame: University of Notre Dame Press.

Phillips, John A. 1984. *Eve: The History of an Idea*. San Francisco: Harper & Row.

Poincaré, Henri. 1952. *Science and Hypothesis*. New York: Dover Publications.

Popper, Karl R. 1968. *Conjectures and Refutations: The Growth of Scientific Knowledge*. New York: Harper & Row.

Posner, Michael. 1989. *Foundations of Cognitive Science*. Cambridge and London: The MIT Press.

Putnam, Ruth Anna. 1985. "Poets, Scientists, and Critics." New *Literary History* 17, 17–21.

Ricoeur, Paul. 1974a. "Manifestation et Proclamation." In *Le Sacré. Études et recherches. Actes du colloque organiseé par le centre international d'Études humanistes et par l'institut d'Études philosophiques de Rome*. Ed. by E. Castelli. Aubier, pp. 57–76. English translation in *The Journal of the Blaisdell Institute*, 12 (Winter, 1978).

———. 1974b. "Preface to Bultmann." In Paul Ricoeur. *The Conflict of Interpretations*. Evanston, IL: Northwestern University Press, 381–401.

———. 1976. *Interpretation Theory: Discourse and the Surplus of Meaning*. Fort Worth: TCU Press.

———. 1978. "The Metaphoric Process in Cognition, Imagination, and Feeling." *Critical Inquiry* 5, 143–159.

———. 1985. "The Text as Dynamic Identity." In Valdes and Miller, *Identity of the Literary text* (see Miller 1985).

———. 1984–88. *Time and Narrative*. Vols. 1–3. Chicago and London: The University of Chicago Press.

Rorty, Richard. 1985. "Texts and Lumps." *New Literary History* 17, 1–16.

Ross, Steven David. 1987. "Metaphor, the Semasic Field, and Inexhaustibility." *New Literary History* 18, 517–533.

Russell, Robert John. "Entropy and Evil," *Zygon* 19 (December 1984), 449–68.

———, William R. Stoeger, and George V. Coyne, eds. 1988. *Physics, Philosophy, and Theology: A Common Quest for Understanding*. Vatican City State: Vatican Observatory Foundation, and Berkeley: Center for Theology and the Natural Sciences.

———, Nancey Murphy, and C. J. Isham, eds. 1993. *Quantum Cosmology and the Laws of of Nature: Scientific Perspectives on Divine Action*. Vatican City State: Vatican Observatory Foundation, and Berkeley: Center for Theology and the Natural Sciences.

Schon, Donald Alan. 1963. *Displacement of Concepts*. London: Tavistock Publications.

Searle, John R. 1995. "The Mystery of Consciousness, Part I." *The New York Review of Books* 42 (November 2), 60–66.

———. 1995. "The Mystery of Consciousness, Part II." *The New York Review of Books* 42 (November 16), 54–61.

Sheler, Jeffrey, and Joannie M. Schrof. 1992. "The Creation: Religion's Search for a Common Ground with Science." *U.S. News and World Report* 111 (December 23), 56–64.

Smith, Brian K. 1985. "Vedic Fieldwork." *Religious Studies Review* 11, 136–45.

Smith, Morton. 1971. *Palestinian Parties and Politics That Shaped the Old Testament*. New York: Columbia University Press.

Soskice, Janet. 1985. *Metaphor and Religious Language*. Oxford: Clarendon.

Staal, Frits, et al. 1983. *Agni: The Vedic Ritual of the Fire Altar*. 3 volumes. Fremont, CA: Asian Humanities Press.

Sturrock, John, ed. 1979. "Introduction," in *Structuralism and Since*. London: Oxford University Press.

Tracy, David. 1975. *Blessed Rage for Order*. New York: Crossroad.

———. 1981. *The Analogical Imagination: Christian Theology and the Culture of Pluralism*. New York: Crossroad.

———. 1987. *Plurality and Ambiguity: Hermeneutics, Religion, Hope* San Francisco: Harper and Row.

———. 1990. *Dialogue with the Other: The Interreligious Dialogue*. Louvain and Grand Rapids: Peeters Press and William B. Eerdmans.

Turner, Mark. 1991. *Reading Minds: The Study of English in the Age of Cognitive Science*. Princeton University Press.

Valéry, Paul. 1964. "La Conquète de l'ubiquité." In *Piéces sur l'art*, translated by Ralph Mannheim in *Aesthetics*. New York: Pantheon Books.

Walcutt, Charles C. 1971. "Preface" to *The Written Word* by Sheridan Baker, Jacques Barzun, and I. A. Richards. Newbury House.

Wehrbein, William M. 1996. "Guest Comment: What shall we teach nonscience students about science?" *American Journal of Physics* 64, 363.

Weizenbaum, Joseph. 1965. "ELIZA—A Computer Program for the Study of Natural Language Communication between Man and Machines." *Communications of the Association for Computing Machinery* 9 (January), 36–45.

Wheeler, John Archibald. 1974. "The Universe as Home for Man." *American Scientist* 62 (November–December), 683–91.

Wilbur, Richard. 1984. *Things of This World*. New York: Harcourt.

Winter, Urs. 1983. *Frau und Göttin: Exegetische und ikonographische Studien zum weiblichen Gottesbild im alten Israel und in dessen Umwelt*. Göttingen: Vandenhoeck und Ruprecht.

Index of Names

Index of Subjects